Multicultural Social Studies

Multicultural Social Studies

USING LOCAL HISTORY IN THE CLASSROOM

Anita C. Danker

Teachers College, Columbia University
New York and London

Published by Teachers College Press, 1234 Amsterdam Avenue, New York, NY 10027

Portions of Chapters 1, 2, and 6 are adapted from "Multicultural Social Studies: The Local History Connection," by A. C. Danker, 2003, *The Social Studies*, 94, pp. 111–117. Copyright 2003 by Heldref Publications. Adapted with permission.

Library of Congress Cataloging-in-Publication Data

Danker, Anita C.
    Multicultural social studies : using local history in the classroom / Anita C. Danker.
        p.   cm.
    Includes bibliographical references (p.   ) and index.
    ISBN 0-8077-4586-3 (cloth : alk. paper)—ISBN 0-8077-4585-5 (pbk. : alk. paper)
        1. Social sciences—Study and teaching (Primary)—United States.   2. Social sciences—Study and teaching (Secondary)—United States.   3. Multicultural education—United States.   I. Title.

    H62.5.U5D16 2005
    300'.71'273—dc22

                                                                    2004063660

ISBN 0-8077-4585-5 (paper)
ISBN 0-8077-4586-3 (cloth)

Printed on acid-free paper
Manufactured in the United States of America

12   11   10   09   08   07   06   05   8   7   6   5   4   3   2   1

To my loving husband and best friend,
Frederick Danker,
a gifted scholar and teacher,
who was always there to encourage, inspire,
and listen

Contents

Acknowledgments

THIS BOOK is the result of a long career in teaching, a lifelong interest in local history, and an appreciation of the significance of multicultural perspectives in social studies fostered in numerous courses and workshops in which I was a participant over the past 2 decades. It, therefore, would be impossible for me to recognize all the many individuals to whom I am indebted. However, I would like to thank those directly responsible for the book's development from a series of ideas and interests into a full-length volume. They include my colleagues at Assumption College, who awarded me a professional development grant to help finance some of the travel necessary to conduct on-site research. My mentors at the Boston University School of Education, Charles S. White, Philip Tate, and Jacklyn Blake Clayton, were instrumental in shaping my ideas on social studies, local history, and multicultural education. The staff at the Framingham Historical Society and Museum, particularly researcher Frederic A. Wallace, provided invaluable assistance in the preparation of the material on my hometown. The chapters on Nashville and the Shakers were reviewed by my staunchest supporter, Frederick Danker, Professor Emeritus of American Studies, University of Massachusetts/Boston. Raymond H. Bacon, a Site Manager at the Museum of Work and Culture, assisted in the preparation of the chapter on Woonsocket. Susan Dargan, Director of the Framingham State College Center for Global Education, shared information and inspiration for the material on heritage trails. I am particularly grateful to Brian Ellerbeck and Wendy Schwartz at Teachers College Press for believing in the project and for providing insightful feedback during the revision process. Finally, I would like to thank my students at Assumption College for sharing both their local history lesson plans and their enthusiasm for multicultural social studies.

Introduction

WHEN I BEGAN my career in education as a teacher of 7th- and 8th-grade social studies in the 1960s, the mission was relatively straightforward. Social studies teachers were expected to prepare their students to be good citizens by making them aware of the nation's past, promoting an understanding of the Founding Documents, grounding them in the elements of physical and cultural geography, and keeping them informed about current events. Social studies education, since its beginnings in the early 20th century, had always been an integrated field, comprising history, geography, and citizenship education, rather than a discrete academic discipline. Over time, economics, anthropology, sociology, and other social sciences were added to the mix. The content was fast becoming overloaded in the 1960s, and new initiatives with respect to the skills that social studies teachers should develop in their students also were incorporated into the curriculum. Soon teachers were expected to build research, inquiry, and critical thinking skills in their students as well as help them master the ever more complex content deemed necessary for active, informed citizenship.

Simultaneously with developments in social studies in the post-World War II period, multicultural education, a reform movement with connections to the civil rights movement and the climate of social justice of the 1960s, was born. With its content drawn from history and the social sciences and its mission to prepare students for the duties and responsibilities of active citizenship, social studies was arguably the curriculum field poised to be most dramatically affected by the initiatives called for by the multicultural education reformers. Social studies teachers were prompted to be more inclusive in the teaching of history and to promote the values of diversity, equal opportunity, and social reform, whatever the curriculum topic. One more layer, and a controversial one at that, was added to the charge of social studies educators, already overloaded by being expected to teach content drawn from numerous disciplines, to foster the development of students' social science skills and to promote habits of good citizenship. While embracing for the most part the more conservative celebratory and human relations aspects of multicultural education, many K–12 teachers wondered what impact focusing on differences among cultural groups in the United States would have on the fundamental citizenship mission of social studies.

While grappling with the pros and cons of making social studies education more multicultural, beleaguered classroom teachers were hit with another mandate. For every field of K–12 education, the 1990s became all about setting standards for student achievement and preparing students to achieve on rigorous state-administered examinations. This drive was sparked by the Goals 2000: Educate America Act and has been continued with the more recent passage of the No Child Left Behind legislation. The result in social studies was that professional organizations for each of the principal disciplines contributing to the field—history, geography, economics, and civics and government—as well as the umbrella group for classroom teachers, the National Council for the Social Studies (NCSS), developed separate sets of standards for student achievement. Concurrently, states wrote curriculum guidelines or frameworks to steer school districts into alignment so that students would be well prepared for achievement or exit examinations.

The expectations for teachers with respect to what they will teach and their students will learn in any given school year are often overwhelming. Time will tell whether the various reforms, standards, and tests result in graduates who are better prepared to meet the complexities of life in the 21st century. For the social studies, the question revolves around whether the curriculum changes will result in graduates who are stronger, more committed citizens in a democratic republic whose future rests in the decisions they make.

As they search for ways to present content, build skills, be sensitive to multicultural education, and prepare students to meet learning standards and succeed on standardized tests, teachers necessarily must look for strategies that will assist them in this daunting set of tasks. My suggestion for social studies teachers is that they look no further than their own communities for material that can help students connect to the broad themes and big events of U.S. history and consequently assist them in mastering the content set forth in the standards documents. Local history is people's history, and as such it cannot help but be multicultural, despite efforts, both subconscious and deliberate, by some to interpret it through a monocultural lens. It relies heavily on primary sources that are accessible and familiar, and hence it can foster the social science skills upon which social studies is founded. Finally, because it builds pride and connections to the community, local history can promote the values of good citizenship that are at the heart of the mission of all social studies education.

The book begins with a description of the field of social studies—its origins, traditions, and fundamental mission to prepare students to be active, informed citizens of a democratic republic. Chapter 1, "Social Studies, Multicultural Education, and Local History: An Overview," reviews the development of multicultural education as conceptualized by various researchers and professional organizations. The chapter then goes on to describe a study of social study teachers' beliefs and practices with respect to multicultural education and explains how the goals of social studies and multicultural education can be realized, in part, by incorporating more local history into the curriculum. When local topics are attached to the major events in U.S. history, they also can serve as a powerful mechanism for helping students meet the state and national standards that serve as the basis for standardized tests. Such an approach is in keeping with constructivist learning theory, which emphasizes the role of the learner and the effect of his/her own experiences in interpreting and mastering new curriculum content. The chapter concludes with some thoughts about how to use local institutions and the nearby environment to incorporate multicultural themes and address learning standards in K–12 history/social studies education.

Chapter 2, "Local History from a Multicultural Perspective: A Case Study of Framingham, Massachusetts," takes the history of my own community and reviews it from both traditional and multicultural perspectives that focus on the town's ever present diversity. The principal purpose of the chapter is not simply to celebrate the history of one community but to create a model for teachers who might wish to engage in a similar process of uncovering for students the multicultural heritage of the towns and cities in which their schools are located. The sections are organized chronologically to align with U.S. history content as it usually is covered in K–12 classrooms and to conform to the eras suggested by the *National Standards for History* (National Center for History in the Schools, 1996). Among the multicultural topics addressed in the chapter are the native Nipmuc Indians, the tragedy of King Philip's War, the Salem witch connection, Crispus Attucks and the Boston Massacre, participation of the town's ex-slaves in the War for Independence, women entrepreneurs and the straw bonnet industry, Harmony Grove and the activity of the abolitionists, religious institutions, the work of local women in the suffrage movement, the role of industry in attracting immigrants in the 20th century, the establishment of a Human Relations Commission, and the energy of the new Brazilian community. In telling the story of Framingham, Massachusetts, as a multicultural town, suggestions are presented for learning activities that can help students both master the content for each historical era and be attentive to the town's vibrant diversity. The chapter concludes with two lesson plans that link the town's history to national themes, incorporate diversity, and provide blueprints for educators in any community who wish to promote standards and multicultural social studies using local history.

Chapter 3, "Exploring Race and Class in Nashville," focuses on two aspects of diversity that are often but not necessarily linked, and begins with an overview of what proponents of multicultural education have identified as talking points about this pair of categories. Next the chapter traces the history of the city of Nashville, Tennessee, from a multicultural perspective. Two vastly different aspects of the community's heritage—its role in the civil rights movement of the 1960s and its place as a center of the country music industry—are examined as examples of drives for empowerment by groups historically marginalized by the mainstream, African Americans and poor Whites. This narrative provides an example of how educators can take some well-known events or aspects of a community's heritage and encourage students to both think about them from a different perspective and connect them to larger currents in the nation's history. A model lesson plan for elementary students focuses on civil rights, and a history project for middle or high school students, inspired by Nashville's Country Music Hall of Fame, details how they can create a multicultural hall of fame for their own community.

In Chapter 4, "*La Survivance*: The Struggle to Preserve Ethnic Identity and Language in Woonsocket, Rhode Island," the topic of cultural diversity as it relates to national origins and linguistic expression is explored, with the focus on the French Canadian mill workers who settled in the city during the Industrial Revolution. The chapter opens with a discussion of how ethnicity and language have evolved as aspects of diversity and have triggered discrimination and victimization as well as pride and empowerment. Then the history of the community of Woonsocket is highlighted, with emphasis on how the French Canadian immigrants struggled to maintain their identity while shaping that of their new community and the region. This history has been preserved and showcased by the Museum of Work & Culture in Market Square. The lesson plan and project plan included in the chapter are centered on the theme of change. For elementary students, there is a lesson involving the creation of first-person narratives from the perspectives of immigrant children. The project designed for secondary students focuses on how to conduct a study of social and cultural changes in one's own neighborhood over the course of the last half of the 20th century. Both plans can be used as models for students living in communities that have been shaped by immigration.

Chapter 5, "Religious Beliefs and the Role of Women in American Shaker Communities," discusses religion and gender as aspects of diversity and highlights an unusual sect with connections to the local history of a number of communities in the eastern United States. This utopian group was founded by a woman who defined herself as the female counterpart to Jesus, and the communities organized around her religious teachings provided women with opportunities for spiritual leadership and economic contributions not common in the world outside. The chapter begins with a look at religion and gender as elements of diversity and goes on to present some highlights of Shaker history as it relates to the religious revival that swept the young republic in the late 18th and early 19th centuries. Sections address the role of women in Shaker communities, their attitudes and practices with respect to race, and the plight of the Shakers as pacifists during the Civil War. Because a number of long-lived Shaker communities were established in several states in the eastern region of the country, the lesson plan and project plan for this chapter focus on the group as part of the local scene. The lesson plan provides a model of how to prepare students for a field trip to a local Shaker museum, but can be adapted for classes visiting any historical site. The project plan uses Gardner's multiple intelligences as a framework and suggests a number of activities that are interdisciplinary in nature.

Chapter 6, "Meeting Learning Standards Through Local/Multicultural History," departs from using multicultural themes as starting points, which is the format for Chapters 3–5, and begins instead with content regularly studied in U.S. history courses. The chapter focuses on three major topics that will help students meet learning standards for the colonial, antebellum, and 20th-century periods. A template is presented to illustrate how to begin with the learning standards associated with the study of a historical era and to organize content material that will promote student understandings through local history, multicultural themes, and learning activities. The purpose of this chapter is to pull all the themes developed in the preceding chapters together and to weave local history and multicultural understandings into the study of mandated topics to foster comprehension of social studies concepts and mastery of U.S. history content. The chapter concludes with an outline of a curriculum unit linking a local strike in a small town with the history of the American labor movement.

The final chapter, "Securing the Future of Local/Multicultural History," looks ahead with some suggestions concerning how to promote ongoing involvement in local history by teachers and students. A logical starting point is with those who are preparing to become teachers. Social studies curriculum and methods courses can require preservice candidates to study local topics and design lesson plans and units incorporating community-related content. The projects at the same time should address multicultural themes and issues and be attentive to the overall mission of social studies to promote good citizenship. Similarly, graduate courses, professional development offerings, and workshops with comparable goals for those already teaching will ensure that the future of local history is in good hands. The chapter describes some successful efforts to encourage the use of local/multicultural history by both preservice and experienced teachers. The chapter also revisits the citizenship mission of social studies and underscores the potential of local history to strengthen it through a multicultural approach.

In addition to the specific objectives of the analysis, my purpose was to highlight the unique and diverse histories of a number of communities whose stories, like those of countless other cities and towns throughout the United States, mirror or provide insights to the development of the nation as a whole.

In so doing, my hope is that those who read this book will not only dis-cover useful ways to enhance their practice concerning the teaching of so-cial studies in K–12 classrooms but also gain a deeper understanding of both multicultural education and the history of the United States. Armed with this knowledge and insight, social studies teachers ultimately can help their students become thoughtful and effective citizens. As members of a multicultural society and future decision-makers in a democratic republic, students need to know how communities and nations often are built by individuals and groups from many different backgrounds, who may have conflicting interests and goals. If they can understand the diversity in their own communities as they study local history from a multicultural perspec-tive, they may be able to deal more effectively with the events and issues that will confront them in the future as citizens in a diverse nation and world.

Social Studies, Multicultural Education, and Local History: An Overview

A T FIRST GLANCE, it would appear that much has changed in recent decades in the world of history/social studies education. A visitor dropping in on a class in the autumn of any given school year is likely to observe students and teachers either celebrating the traditions of Native Americans or expressing sadness and anger over their exploitation at the hands of careless and self-serving European intruders. The winter season provides social studies teachers with opportunities to engage students in comparisons of the origins and traditions of Chanukah, Christmas, Kwanzaa, and Ramadan, although sometimes school policy may dictate that curriculum treatment of the special rituals that punctuate the calendars of cultural groups in the United States and other parts of the world be avoided rather than risk offending those who might not be included. In February the contributions and struggles of African Americans are formally recognized, while in March many districts encourage investigations of the role of American women in the nation's past. Throughout the school year, it is common for history/social studies classes to examine content from multiple perspectives and, at the same time, to expose students to the darker side of the nation's story even as they celebrate its triumphs and glory. The cruelty of Columbus and the plunder of the conquistadors, the massacre of Native Americans at Sand Creek, the apartheid of the Jim Crow era, and the internment of Japanese Americans are unsettling topics routinely included now in the secondary history curriculum. Social studies textbooks are generously sprinkled with photos, inserts, quotes, and primary sources highlighting the stories of women, immigrants, and people of color. The National Council for the Social Studies has embraced multicultural education since it first issued a position paper in support of the reform in the 1970s (NCSS Task Force on Ethnic Studies Curriculum Guidelines, 1991). It would appear that the efforts of multicultural reformers have transformed the way American students learn history and social studies content. However, this is not always the case. As the review of social studies education that follows indicates, it is a K–12 curriculum field with a controversial past and a divided present.

DEVELOPMENT OF THE FIELD OF SOCIAL STUDIES

Social studies as a separate and distinct school subject usually is traced to a 1916 report on secondary education issued by the National Education Association (Evans, 2004; Martorella, 1996; Thornton, 1996). Here the term *social studies* was coined, and a scope and sequence document that included community civics and modern problems, which traditionally had not been taught in high schools, was advocated. Shortly thereafter, in 1921, the NCSS was established to act as a clearinghouse and to provide a bridge between social science professionals at the university level and teachers in K–12 classrooms. However, a unified vision of what constitutes social studies has never been clearly formulated.

A Crowded and Confusing History

A number of disciplines traditionally studied at the K–12 level, such as U.S. history, geography, and citizenship education, are clearly under the social studies umbrella. However, when introduced as a K–12 curriculum field, social studies also implied new and progressive approaches to addressing familiar topics. The result in the early years was that school leaders, unsure of what was expected in terms of curriculum reform, went about implementing new guidelines for social studies in a somewhat patchwork fashion.

A Political Agenda. The political and social climate of the ensuing decades did little to clarify the content and method of the social studies curriculum. The introduction of social studies coincided with both the acculturation of the "new immigrants" drawn primarily from southern and eastern Europe and nativist reactions to U.S. involvement in World War I. Promoting unity and stressing the many ways in which all people are alike emerged as an essential component of the social studies curriculum (Jarolimek, 1981), despite tensions between those who supported the melting pot/assimilationist approach and those who advocated respect for cultural pluralism (Schlesinger, 1992).

The twin crises of depression and war in the 1930s and 1940s contributed to a sense of urgency in social studies education. Mainstream educators claimed that faith in a market economic system and the democratic ideals of the U.S. government needed to be strengthened in the nation's classrooms in order to offset real and imagined threats from both within and afar. *Social Education*, the journal of the NCSS for K–12 teachers launched in 1937, published bulletins urging teachers to foster devotion to the ideals of democracy by planning overtly patriotic programs with their students (Field & Burlbaw, 1995). Conflicts raged over textbook adoption, and the pattern of using the social studies classroom to promote political goals was firmly established (Zimmerman, 2002). The Cold War tensions of the post-World War II period only served to underscore the importance of social studies education, while at the same time confusion continued as to what the curriculum should emphasize (Greenawald, 1995).

As a curriculum field during the postwar period, social studies clearly promoted the utilization of the active learning methods espoused by progressive educators (Jarolimek, 1981). Students at all grade levels were encouraged to "do" social studies through participation in field trips, creation of products, artistic expression, and taking action based on conviction. National Science Foundation support in the 1950s strengthened ties between social studies at the K–12 level and the social sciences at the university level by providing funding for curriculum projects in anthropology and sociology (Greenawald, 1995). Such efforts helped usher in the introduction of the New Social Studies, which stressed understanding concepts, critical thinking, and the incorporation of the methodology of the social sciences. By the 1960s, however, leaders in the field of social studies were encouraging teachers to shift their emphasis to current events in order to make class topics explicitly relevant to the lives of students living through the traumas of civil rights, Vietnam, and widespread cultural change (Evans, 2004). Furthermore, the New Social Studies was proving a tough sell due to its sophisticated conceptual base. Social studies as a field continued to attempt to define itself, with a swing toward inquiry-based learning and the process of problem-solving as fresh focal points. This distinctive strand, grounded in social problems of concern to students, was dubbed the "new" New Social Studies (Barth, 1996) or the Newer Social Studies (Evans, 2004), only adding to the confusion that seemed to have plagued the field since its inception.

In more recent decades, the field of social studies has continued to be both reactive and fragmented. The 1980s backlash against the reforms and, in some minds, the excesses of the 1960s and early 1970s in education in general left its mark on social studies (Evans, 2004; Martorella, 1996). Back-to-basics was all the rage, and social studies was criticized by conservative voices for being overly concerned with relevance and making the subject entertaining for students who consequently were poorly versed in the central disciplines of history, geography, and civics. Calls for a return to the teaching of traditional history were followed by a flurry of standards documents published by the professional organizations in the major disciplines that constitute the field of social studies as well as by states issuing framework documents codifying content on which students would be tested, in some cases to determine eligibility for graduation. Some leaders in social studies education protested, while others joined in writing the standards in order for their voices to be included. While these changes had a profound impact on social studies, the scattered and confused nature of the field remained a perplexing constant.

The Three Traditions in Social Studies. Against the backdrop of political and pedagogical change that paralleled the development of social studies as a curriculum field during its first 50 years, three clearly identifiable camps evolved. Published in the 1970s, the seminal works that identify and explain the three traditions in social studies are those of Barth and Shermis (1970) and Barr, Barth, and Shermis (1978). The most pervasive of the three traditions they codified is social studies as citizenship transmission, which is based on the assumption that an identifiable body of content and values must be passed on to the nation's young people in order to promote the values and habits of good citizenship. The most didactic of the strands, social studies as citizenship transmission is based on traditional content and employs teacher-centered methods.

The second of the three traditions, social studies as social science, had been in use since the 1920s when the field was in its infancy and received renewed support with the introduction of the New Social Studies in the late 1950s and 1960s. As advocated by academics from the various social science disciplines, the emphasis was placed on mastery of the concepts and the methodologies of their fields. Whereas the citizenship transmission tradition revolves around content, the social science tradition emphasizes research skills.

The third and most process-oriented of the social studies traditions is the one usually aligned with the new New (or newer) Social Studies, reflective inquiry. Here problem-solving is the key. Students practice the process of making decisions as they identify, research, and reflect on significant social and civic problems. Social studies as reflective inquiry is in keeping with Dewey's argument that education must be a "process of living and not a preparation for future living" (1964/1897, p. 430). Hence, the reflective inquiry tradition has received the support of those in the progressive education camp. It clearly resonates with the education concentrators whom I teach in my social studies curriculum and methods courses. Year after year, they support its question-driven premise and the fact that reflective inquiry values the concerns and interests of young students and the decisions that they make as they engage in class activities. However, when student teachers try to design lessons consistent with the tenets of reflective inquiry, they often have difficulty reconciling the approach with the standards-driven reality of the curriculum they must address in their model classes.

A final caveat from Barr, Barth, and Shermis (1978) is that, whatever the approach, the three traditions in social studies education rest on the assumption that the fundamental mission of the field is the preparation of active, informed citizens. This conclusion is in keeping with the original concept presented in the 1916 National Education Association report that led to the organization of social studies as a curriculum field.

The Citizenship Mission of Social Studies. Social studies education, according to both the literature of the experts and the words of current practitioners, is all about preparing good citizens. This mission has been the bedrock of the field since its earliest years (Morrissett, 1981). If nothing else about social studies is clear, the fundamental charge to promote the habits of good citizenship among students stands alone as one goal that is universally recognized by educators as paramount. However, there are many ways to define good citizenship. Evans (2004) sees the citizenship goal of social studies as set forth by the 1916 founders as one promoting cooperation. Morrissett offers a more neutral twofold explanation, which on the one hand refers to preparing young people to become active, informed future voters and guardians of the republic and on the other seeks to encourage desirable moral values, including respect for the environment, intelligent consumer choices, and following a healthy lifestyle. The NCSS (1994) has underscored the citizenship mission by defining social studies as "the integrated study of the social sciences and humanities to promote civic competence" (p. 3). What constitutes civic competence is arguable, although surely a definition would include the ability to make informed decisions with respect to issues affecting the well-being of society. Martorella (1996), who adds informed social criticism and personal development to the traditions of Barr, Barth, and Shermis, argues for social studies education to promote reflective citizenship whereby individuals will be taught content knowledge as the springboard from which to make decisions, skills to enable them to research and analyze situations and problems, and an awareness of social problems coupled with a nonjudgmental attitude toward difference or diversity.

CONNECTING MULTICULTURAL EDUCATION WITH THE MISSION AND METHODS OF SOCIAL STUDIES

Before taking a closer look at the focus of this book, which is how local history can promote the themes and values of multicultural social studies, we need to clarify what is meant by multicultural education. This is not an easy task given the many variations on the theme that have been evolving during the past 40 or so years that the reform has taken to establish itself.

The Development of Multicultural Education

As a movement, multicultural education is rooted in the liberal reform climate of the 1960s (Banks, 1995), although its origins extend much further back into the nation's diverse origins. It is inextricably linked to such empowering mid-20th-century movements as civil rights and women's rights, and thereby embodies an affirmation of the mainstreaming of groups marginalized in the past over issues of class, disability, ethnicity, gender, race, or religion.

Conflicting Visions of Multicultural Education. Ownership of multicultural education is an unclear proposition, with both centrist liberals and radical social reconstructionists claiming possession. Arguably, the seminal ideological statement of its purpose and process belongs to the late Paulo Freire (1970), whose critical pedagogy approach calls for a redesigning of the student/teacher relationship so as to create a situation of equality and mutual respect where both can learn from one another. Freire decries what he calls a "banking" approach to teaching in which the powerful and all-knowing teacher deposits a body of factual information into the receptive minds of his/her relatively passive students. He proposes a more egalitarian type of education in which both teacher and student enlighten one another. Eventually, society will be reformed through this process so that both the oppressed and their oppressors come to recognize the injustice of a system that perpetuates inequality, and thus they will unite to implement remedial restructuring.

Multicultural authors in the mainstream of the movement acknowledge their debt to Freire both overtly and implicitly in their writings (Banks, 1993; Sleeter & Grant, 1994). The more centrist reformers describe multicultural education as a pervasive approach to learning and teaching that both recognizes and values diversity and promotes democratic ideals such as equal access to educational opportunity and giving voice to all. In revising curriculum, multicultural centrists encourage the inclusion of multiple perspectives and challenge the way academic knowledge is compiled, namely, from a White, male, European point of view. Other liberals such as Ravitch (1995) and Schlesinger (1992) promote a more affirming, consensus-oriented approach to how we view the so-called canon of academic knowledge, and they worry that emphasis on difference and cultural pluralism may lead to fragmentation and divisions in society. Ironically, this is the very state of affairs that Freire and other left-leaning liberals claim has always been the case.

Recent Trends. The problem of clarifying and conceptualizing what is meant by multicultural education and who owns it has been further complicated in recent years by the addition of a number of radical voices from the left (Chavez, 1998; hooks, 2000; McLaren, 1997) who champion an approach to multicultural reform in line with Freire in that they call for radical change in social, economic, political, and class structure in the United States. Their contribution to the discourse lies in their contention that all varieties of liberal multiculturalists ignore to some extent the confrontational nature of diversity. The radicals define diversity and democracy as contentious concepts that are rooted in conflict, a reality that cannot be ignored. The liberals, they argue, are tenacious in clinging to their mainstream consensus-building standards, and as such are guilty of tokenism as they praise the inclusion of women, Blacks, Native Americans, and other cultural groups in textbooks that do not challenge a fundamentally flawed U.S. society. Such arguments, however grounded in reality they might be, do not always strike a responsive chord with the majority of the nation's corps of K–12 social studies teachers.

Uneasiness over Multicultural Education

Classroom teachers, for the most part, are comfortable with multicultural education only if it is compatible with their overarching mission to prepare their students for the duties and responsibilities of citizenship in a democratic republic. While many of them would agree that American society is not perfect and that part of being a responsible citizen involves recognizing when change is needed and how to bring it about, they generally are not ready to attach their teaching to a reform movement that emphasizes conflict and focuses only on the darker side of the nation's past and present. Multicultural reformers who insist on the critical resistance approach in public school classrooms are unrealistic in their goals and, to the extent that they have an audience in the nation's teacher corps, actually may be contributing to the latter's disillusionment with multicultural education. In order for multicultural education to succeed in social studies classrooms, it must be grounded in a definition that is both true to the essence of the reform and aligned with the mission of K–12 teachers. If multiculturalism can be disseminated as an approach to education that recognizes and values diversity, incorporates multiple perspectives, promotes active citizenship, and is grounded in democratic values, it may indeed be around for a very long time.

A STUDY OF SOCIAL STUDIES TEACHERS AND MULTICULTURAL EDUCATION

My conclusions about multicultural education and its implementation in social studies classrooms are based in part on research I conducted between 1997 and 1999 in three school systems with different demographic profiles (Danker, 2001b). In a qualitative interview study, I posed a number of questions concerning how teachers conceptualize their mission as social studies teachers, define the nature of multicultural education, and assess the extent to which they have incorporated multicultural themes and values in their classrooms. My findings indicated that the teachers in the study fell into three distinct categories and that their beliefs and practices had been shaped not so much by their ages or their teaching environments as by the recency of their training to be educators and their personal histories.

The Impact of Multicultural Education on Social Studies Teaching

My review of the literature on social studies teachers and how they had been affected by multicultural reform, conducted prior to interviewing the teachers, revealed that much of the evidence is anecdotal (Bennett, 1999; Garrett, 1994). For example, high school teacher Alice Garrett writes about her efforts, through a seminar approach, to stimulate students to view history through multiple perspectives and to be attentive to the many groups who have influenced the development of the nation. Her reflections on how she structures her classes so that she becomes a learner while her students are teachers seems reminiscent of Freire. Similarly, many of the examples that Bennett (1999) includes in her comprehensive text on multicultural education describe fundamental assumptions and innovative techniques of classroom teachers, many of whom are in the field of social studies, that are in keeping with the tenets of the multiculturalists. These involve exercises to help students develop multiple perspectives on history, to value diverse cultures, to recognize racism and discrimination, and to be aware of the consequences of decisions with respect to their impact on people from varied backgrounds.

Field research indicates mixed results on the question of how the beliefs and practices of social studies teachers have been influenced by multicultural education. In a 1992 survey-based study of the attitudes and practices of social studies teachers concerning multicultural education, Titus found that, while they expressed generally favorable opinions about the need for their curriculum to be more diverse, the majority did not incorporate multicultural tenets and methods in their classes. My findings similarly noted that social studies teachers for the most part say they support multicultural education, but many do not put their beliefs into practice, have a limited vision of what constitutes multicultural education, or worry that it will compromise their efforts to build loyal citizens.

A Pilot Study. Initially I conducted a pilot study in which I interviewed eight social studies teachers, grades 5–12, who taught in a middle-class suburban community. My focus question asked them to explain how they conceptualized multicultural education. Follow-up inquiries explored how they implemented it in their classrooms. Overall, they commented favorably but explained multicultural education in conservative and limited terms. They placed ethnic groups at the center of their definitions and seemed uncomfortable with suggestions that gender, class, or disability might be included under the multicultural umbrella. When asked what they did in their classes that they considered to be multicultural, they mentioned reading folk tales, sampling foods and listening to the music of different cultures, or celebrating heroic figures such as Martin Luther King, Jr., or Rosa Parks. This orientation would fall into the more rudimentary categories developed by Banks (1993) and others with respect to the spectrum of multicultural reform.

When asked about their overall mission as social studies educators, the teachers in the pilot study stressed promoting democracy, unity, and an understanding of Anglo institutions of government. Some expressed concern that multicultural education focuses in social studies on the negative aspects of U.S. history and may promote cynicism, negativity, and anger among students—qualities not conducive to the consensus values they see as paramount to their teaching.

An Expanded Study.   Concerned by the findings of the pilot study, I expanded the research base to include teachers from three additional school districts, all in the same region of the northeast, but with widely divergent characteristics. One district serves students in an economically developed suburb with a diverse population and wide disparities in class and income. Another site is a small city where the majority of residents are White, but with a school population that is racially and ethnically diverse. The third is a regional district, similar in its homogeneity and income levels to the suburban district in the pilot study.

Thirteen certified social studies teachers, four females and nine males, participated in taped individual interviews that were followed up with classroom observation and an additional telephone interview. The subjects discussed were the mission of social studies, the concept of multicultural education, how social studies had been influenced by multicultural education, and the teachers' personal backgrounds with respect to training and experiences that might have shaped their views on the subjects at hand. In terms of teaching experience, their years in the field ranged from more than 20 to less than 1.

The Findings.   The most significant findings concerned the fact that the teachers who participated in the study had similar beliefs about the mission of social studies but had conflicting visions of multicultural education and its impact on their field. The teachers were of one voice about citizenship being the central focus of social studies. They talked about helping students become productive citizens and wise decision-makers, aware of the mechanics and benefits of a democratic government and willing to act responsibly to protect it. In their visions of multicultural education, however, and how it might relate to the citizenship mission of social studies, teachers were divided and seemed to fall into three distinct camps.

One group of teachers, the traditionalists, defined multicultural education in terms of studying "others" or those who are different from the mainstream. They favored multicultural programs to promote positive human relations but were not convinced that the programs would help reduce conflicts among various groups. These teachers were of one mind in their opinion that the social studies curriculum was multicultural enough as it was, and they saw no need for further reform. At the heart of their conviction was the belief that as teachers they are transmitters of the dominant culture.

In contrast to the traditionalists were the multiculturalists, teachers who clearly viewed themselves not as preservers of the status quo, but as agents of change. This group defined multicultural education as revolving around the idea of multiple perspectives and expressed favorable reactions to the idea that education can help reconstruct society. They viewed multicultural education as a vehicle for reducing conflicts among competing groups in society and actively sought ways to make their content and methods more multicultural in orientation.

The largest of the three groups comprised those in the middle, the straddlers, with one foot firmly planted in tradition and the other reaching toward but not into the multicultural camp. These participants gave varying definitions of multicultural education, were comfortable with the contention that it might help reduce tensions among groups, and were open to adding more diversity to the curriculum. Like the traditionalists, the straddlers viewed themselves as transmitters of the dominant culture, but they were open to multicultural changes in so far as those changes might help to improve their effectiveness in the classroom. As a group they recognized that students respond to and are engaged by multicultural materials; however, they worried about the danger of promoting negativity among students toward their government and society.

Reflections on the Findings. In analyzing the factors that might be responsible for such divergent concepts of multicultural education among a group of teachers with very similar views concerning their curriculum field, I noted that pivotal points seemed to revolve around training and personal histories. All but one of those who had received their educational training in the 1990s were strongly multicultural in orientation, and each had shared a bit of personal history in which he/she identified with being an outsider or with members of victimized groups. Many of those who fell into the traditionalist or straddler categories were unclear about the concept of multicultural education because they had not received any formal training in the approach to curriculum reform. Those most solidly in opposition to any extension of multicultural education in their classrooms were those who had attended professional development workshops of short duration and that had left them feeling defensive and angry.

It would seem, based on my research on social studies teachers' beliefs and practices concerning multicultural education, that teacher training programs can be effective in preparing future educators to be comfortable with the concepts involved in, and to engage in methods that promote, multicultural understandings among their students. The multiculturalists in the study had received their credentials most recently and reported taking courses that stressed diversity and addressed multicultural issues. However, there is a critical mass of experienced teachers who have received no such training and who can benefit from full-length courses or professional development engaged in over time that encourages them to see the potential of multicultural education to transform the curriculum in ways that are not only engaging to students but also consistent with the overarching mission of social studies.

Linking Multicultural Education and Democratic Values

Multicultural social studies, whether rooted in local history, as explored in this book, or some broader base, can be successfully integrated into the K–12 curriculum only if common ground between the theoretical proponents and the classroom practitioners is identified and established as a logical starting point. We need to look no further than the familiar concept with which all camps feel comfortable, and that is democracy. When theorists and publicists for multicultural education press their case, they inevitably base their rationale on the argument that in its emphasis on justice, equality, and inclusiveness, it is inherently democratic. They suggest that indeed we cannot claim to be a truly democratic society unless and until we realize that democracy and diversity go hand in hand. Citizenship educator Walter Parker (1997) reminds us that it is in totalitarian societies that the government seeks to bury cultural identities by wiping out old allegiances and replacing them with enforced loyalty to the state. In democratic societies the rights of minorities are respected, and individuals and groups must be free to follow their hearts and celebrate their various identities. It is not their cultural identities but their faith in the civic culture that binds them together as a nation.

When discussing democracy with the teachers in the study, I found that, not surprisingly, most articulated similar definitions of the concept. They echoed Lincoln's familiar reference to a government of, by, and for the people, and stressed participation, equality, and fairness as fundamental to a democratic government. It was when I asked if they saw multicultural education as promoting democratic values that they parted company. Curiously, their answers were not necessarily aligned with their regard for multicultural education as a curriculum reform. Those teachers who were multiculturalist in orientation agreed with the contention that the approach promotes and strengthens our democracy, but some of those who were less than enthusiastic about multicultural reform of the history/social studies curriculum agreed as well. Those who were least receptive to the idea of linking democratic values and multicultural education tended to be those who were most fearful of its fragmenting potential. However, it would appear that there is some common ground upon which to build the argument that democracy and multicultural education go hand in hand. Both stress inclusion, fairness, respect, and participation. The dialogue about multicultural history/social studies education should stress these affirming elements, and then perhaps those who implement the curriculum can embrace it with more faith that it will enhance, not destroy, the citizenship mission that guides their practice. Attention to local history, the theme of this book, can be one important bridge to linking social studies concepts and multicultural themes.

THE RELATIONSHIP AMONG DEMOCRACY, MULTICULTURAL EDUCATION, AND LOCAL HISTORY

The relationship among democracy, multicultural education, and local history may not be obvious to all, but it is clearly rooted in fundamental characteristics all three share. Democracy by its very nature must recognize and value diversity, as must multicultural education. Local history is democratic and multicultural in that it is people's history, made by all those individuals and groups of diverse backgrounds who work, worship, play, learn, and participate in the civic culture of the communities in which they live.

Democratic Ideals

Democracy is a form of government in which the people are sovereign and in which they exercise their power either directly or through representatives whom they have chosen in free elections. Over time, democracy has come to be associated with a society that protects individuals' rights and in which the laws are administered fairly. Justice, equality, and human rights are all terms that are embodied in the ideal of a democratic state.

The Founding Documents are laced with references to the defining elements of such a state. In the Mayflower Compact, the men of Plimoth Plantation pledged to work together in a body politic to enact laws for the general good. Jefferson and the other authors and signatories of the Declaration of Independence pledged their lives, fortunes, and sacred honor in pursuit of equality and protection of unalienable rights. The U.S. Constitution opens with the simple, yet significant, words, "We the people." And one of the goals stated most unambiguously in the Preamble is the creation of a plan of government that will "establish justice."

Democratic Values and Multicultural Education

The familiar and cherished concepts that permeate the Founding Documents also appear regularly in the texts of the multicultural authors as they seek to define the goals and tenets of their approach to teaching, learning, and influencing society. In addition to such phrases as cultural pluralism, affirming diversity, and empowerment, which we have come to associate with multicultural education, its promoters emphasize their faith in democratic values and in social justice, human rights, and equal opportunity for all (Bennett, 1999; Sleeter & Grant, 1994). Perhaps the most eloquent and relevant statement of the mission of multicultural education is expressed by James Banks in his introduction to the NCSS *Curriculum Guidelines for Multicultural Education* (1991), where he writes: "Multicultural education seeks to actualize the idea of *e pluribus unum* within our nation and to create a society that recognizes and respects the cultures of its diverse people, people united within a framework of overarching democratic values" (p. 1). He affirms in the same document the need for students to share pride in their communities and to work within those locales for the common good.

Democracy, Diversity, and the Local Community

It is not much of a reach from the testaments to democratic values found in both the Founding Documents and the writings of multicultural spokespersons to the study of local history and involvement in the community as vehicles for achieving the common goals of democracy and multicultural education. In the first place, let us consider the characteristics of local history. It is the study of the past as played out in individual communities, regions, and states. It is immediate and easy to access. While indeed it may involve "famous" people whose names and deeds are familiar on the national level or events about which the general public has some knowledge, more often than not this is not the case. It is history that records the everyday life and contributions of ordinary people and cultural groups inhabiting a locale at various periods. It is democratic in that it is truly history of, by, and for the people. It is all around—as close at hand as the local library, historical society, town hall, or main street. It can be found in the street signs, public buildings, homes, site markers, and burial grounds that students pass by daily. It is in this sense that it belongs to them and to the residents of their community who came before them. Local history can generate pride in the community and promote active citizenship, as suggested by Banks. At the same time it can help forge connections between students and the larger themes of history by revealing how their community and its residents were influenced or touched in some way by the major events of the nation's chronicle.

These connections between students and their history link back to the themes of multicultural education because they promote a sense of ownership of a common yet diverse heritage and an appreciation of how various cultural groups have built, changed, and provided identity for the communities in which they live. It is history that can be interpreted firsthand by students through artifacts, buildings, photographs, diaries, letters, public records, and a variety of other primary sources. Studying history through the local environment promotes the goal of experiential learning advocated in the NCSS *Curriculum Guidelines for Multicultural Education* because it is so close at hand and immediate. Students can acquire a context for their historical studies by participating in field trips and outings. They can hone their research skills by locating and analyzing nearby resources through which they can creative narratives, photographic essays, biographies, oral histories, virtual museums, and countless other products that can enlarge their understanding of their own communities, U.S. history, and how history is made. Through the process of engaging in the study of local history and in the creation of knowledge, they truly can gain the sense of ownership and empowerment emphasized by the multiculturalists and the pride in place and appreciation of civic culture stressed by social studies educators.

LINKING LOCAL/MULTICULTURAL STUDIES TO NATIONAL STANDARDS

In addition to concerns about what multicultural education entails and its impact on their citizenship mission in the classroom, social studies teachers, like their overtaxed colleagues in all fields, are concerned about the effects any innovation or reform might have on their efforts to both adhere to state and national standards documents and prepare their students for success on standardized tests. Here again, the local history approach can be of assistance.

A Tool for Learning

In the first place, local history is, as outlined earlier, both inherently multicultural and democratic. In addition, it is endorsed by the major standards documents that relate to social studies. In Part I of the *National Standards for History* (1996), the chapter dealing with implementation for grades K–4 has a section devoted entirely to promoting the study of students' home state and region of the United States. Here we are told that students are expected to learn about the indigenous peoples who lived in the area before the arrival of Europeans and Africans and to be able to compare and contrast life long ago for those groups with how they live today. The *Standards* go on to emphasize that students should be taught how to analyze interactions among the indigenous peoples, the explorers, and the settlers from other continents. Further they should be encouraged to trace the various immigrant groups who settled at different times in their local area and to "describe the problems, including prejudice and intolerance, as well as the opportunities that various groups who have lived in their state or region have experienced in housing, the workplace, and the community" (p. 30). The material in the *National Standards for History* with reference to teaching local history to young learners is clearly multicultural in method and perspective. Hence, the document endorses both local history and multicultural approaches and, indeed, links the two, as does this book.

The National Council for the Social Studies framework, *Expectations of Excellence: Curriculum Standards for Social Studies* (1994), also offers many opportunities to build on multicultural/local history to help students meet learning standards. Among the 10 NCSS thematic strands, those addressing culture; time, continuity, and change; people, places, and environments; individuals, groups, and institutions; and civic ideals and practices all lend themselves to local/multicultural approaches. Among the "Standards into Practice" examples are a number showcasing local social studies activities that deal with multicultural themes. Performance Expectations for the theme of culture include learner objectives at early, middle, and high school levels that encourage students to describe, explain, and analyze events from multiple perspectives and to compare ways people from different cultures meet their wants and needs. In the corresponding examples for the early grades is one in which an elementary teacher studies the ethnic composition of her students and then embarks on a project in which her 1st graders analyze how families in their own community meet their wants and needs. They then examine the same theme in the countries from which the students' families originated. Clearly, this teacher is using the local community to address multicultural topics in a way that is tightly woven into the social studies curriculum and effectively meets learning standards identified in the NCSS document. In the section describing how high school students can meet the "People, Places, and Environments" standard, a civics class working on how national issues affect local communities is encouraged by the teacher to attack a problem in their own town and propose solutions. Such activities are aligned with the empowering social action aspect of multicultural education and build on the students' knowledge of their local community's past history and present needs.

A Theoretical Framework for Local History

As the foregoing discussion indicates, local history is inherently multicultural and at the same time explicitly meets a number of the standards proposed in framework documents for history and social studies. As such it can be a valuable tool for helping teachers prepare students to succeed on state-mandated standardized tests. Educational theorists have long underscored the need to build on students' experiences—to attach new material to contexts with which they are familiar—as a way to promote mastery of skills, concept attainment, and genuine understandings in the disciplines. Much of the content of history and social studies courses involves abstract concepts that can be understood better by young learners when they are related to nearby locales and institutions. Democracy, equality, nationalism, freedom, community, culture, change, and countless other ideas that form the heart of history/social studies education can come into clearer focus for students when they are explored through the lens of the familiar.

The Constructivist Argument

I base my contention that local history can foster deeper understanding of the concepts that form the core of the history/social studies curriculum on the work of educational reformers (Brooks & Brooks, 1993) who argue for an approach to teaching and learning that has its roots deeply planted in the field of cognitive psychology—constructivism.

Psychological Foundations. Constructivism relies on the research of both Swiss psychologist Jean Piaget and Russian psychologist Lev Vygotsky (Slavin, 1997). They maintain that as children develop, their cognitive processes undergo growth and change, in which previously learned material is disrupted by the introduction of new ideas, facts, or skills. Vygotsky in particular emphasizes the social nature of learning as children interact with teachers, parents, and peers while attempting to gain new skills and understand curriculum content. He stresses the need for situated learning that engages children in authentic, real-life tasks and promotes "explorations in the community" (Slavin, 1997, p. 271). Vygotsky argues that the social and cultural milieu in which the child operates will color his/her interpretation of curriculum material (Schcurman, 1998).

Scaffolding and Local Studies. An aspect of constructivist theory that is particularly pertinent to the use of local people, places, and events, both past and present, in the teaching of history/social studies topics and concepts is the idea of scaffolding. As a classroom practice, scaffolding involves having the teacher provide a great deal of structure when children are first introduced to new material and then gradually turn more and more of the responsibility for learning over to the students themselves as they become more competent and confident in the process (Slavin, 1997). In the context of community-based learning, scaffolding can be viewed as the familiar landmarks with which the student comes in contact in his/her daily life—streets, neighborhoods, buildings, parks, monuments. The teacher may introduce an unfamiliar topic, such as industrialization, and connect it to a local factory that students may pass on their walk or bus trip to school. Students then can be given a set of questions to research or speculate on concerning the local factory and the process of manufacturing goods, the roles of owners and workers, environmental impact, and tax revenues for the community. The teacher then may encourage students to develop their own questions about manufacturing and industry, to research in groups, and to make their own connections to material in the text addressing these topics. Such activities can help students master the concepts linked to industrialization that are included in national and state standards documents. They are also consistent with the principles of multiple perspectives (owners and workers) and experiential learning, which are central to multicultural education.

The industrialization exercise described above is consistent with the models of classrooms described by Brooks and Brooks (1993) as they argue the case for learning based on constructivist principles. They emphasize the importance of starting with the big concepts (e.g., industrialization), valuing students' questions, seeking their points of view, and encouraging them to work in groups. The teacher working on industrialization began by creating an atmosphere of inquiry and providing the initial structure for the activities. If he/she followed up by keeping the students on task in their inquiry exercise, providing them with tips concerning resources, and creating guidelines with respect to outcomes and final products, the teacher would be acting in ways consistent with the facilitator model grounded in the principles of constructivism (Scheurman, 1998).

Constructivism and Citizenship. An additional argument for implementing a constructivist approach is that it can foster the development of good citizens, which is the bottom line of all history/social studies education (Jadallah, 2000). Constructivist classrooms invite participation, decision-making, and responsibility, all attributes of a good citizen. They promote the mastery of concepts, rather than the rote memorization of facts. Citizenship in itself is a concept, and embodied in it, as it is viewed in the United States, are related concepts such as democracy, commitment, individual rights, equality, justice, and freedom. Engaging in classroom activities related to these and other social studies concepts by linking them to community history and local issues, problems, conflicts, and celebrations, can help students develop fundamental understandings necessary to reflective, informed, and active citizenship.

RESOURCES FOR MAKING LOCAL HISTORY CONNECTIONS

There are a number of full-length works devoted to explaining various ways that researchers, in this case teachers and students, can "do" local history. It is not within the scope of this book to provide extensive coverage of the many resources, approaches, and tools available to teachers seeking to engage students in local studies. However, a brief overview of some of the most helpful of these will assist those getting started to make choices concerning how to connect local history to mandated learning standards and at the same time integrate multicultural themes.

Institutions as Resources

If a school is located in a community with a local historical society and/or museum, this is usually an excellent starting point for developing lessons and units that highlight outstanding citizens, cultural groups, and the contributions of residents to the major events in U.S. history. Some institutions may already have school programs in place, but for the most part these tend to be geared to elementary classes addressing the concept of community. Teachers of secondary students most likely will have to visit the institution and research the collection in order to identify appropriate topics connected to learning standards at upper levels. However, most historical societies have Web sites that are extremely helpful for generating ideas. They can be located easily by simply typing the name of the community on a major search engine and looking for links to museums, landmarks, things to do, or historical societies. Teachers should be mindful that when they visit such institutions in person there may be some limitations with respect to access. Historical societies, as official keepers of a town's past in the form of precious artifacts, letters, and important documents, are often guarded about sharing them for fear that they may be misplaced, lost, harmed, or destroyed. Officials at such sites may request specific information about how their collections will be used and often will enforce regulations limiting researchers' tools to a pencil and notebook.

Historical societies also tend to be quite traditional with respect to how they interpret a town's past. A teacher in search of documentation relevant to cultural groups and aspects of a community's diverse heritage may have to do his/her own digging to uncover the evidence. The resources may be housed in the collection but not categorized with reference to diversity. It may be up to the teacher and students, when they work with the collections of the historical society or museum, to discover the roles played by Native Americans, women, African Americans, and members of various immigrant and religious groups. These labors carry their own rewards, however, as they help students to become interpreters of their community's heritage, an endeavor in keeping with the pedagogy promoted by multiculturalists.

More explicit with respect to the histories of various cultural groups and their contributions to the local community and the nation's past are heritage societies organized by members of specific ethnic, racial, and religious groups. The Internet is a convenient starting point and provides breakdowns by group organized according to region, state, and, in many cases, individual communities. A quick check recently on my part located the Finnish American Historical Society of the West, the Nipmuc Indian Association of Connecticut, and the Charles H. Wright Museum of African American History in Detroit. Such institutions may highlight a broad range of topics and individuals, but as a rule they are attentive to promoting the local component of the group's history. For students who belong to the group affiliated with the heritage society, studies organized around its collections can be powerful mechanisms for pride and identity. For those outside the target group, such studies can promote understanding and foster an appreciation of the diversity of the community and the nation.

The town or municipal library is another excellent place to begin locating material for local studies. Many have separate rooms or sections displaying collections of primary and secondary sources devoted to the history of the community. Most are free and have flexible hours, trained staffs, and inexpensive photocopy equipment. Some possess artifacts and showcase displays devoted to local history. They almost always maintain a community newspaper archive where students and teachers can find press coverage of local events and notable citizens going back many years. In communities with large numbers of immigrant residents, the public libraries often subscribe to periodicals and purchase books in the native languages of the newer cultural groups. Children who speak the languages of the ethnic collections can explore their own heritage through these resources, and those who do not can begin to build a vocabulary in the target languages and develop a deeper understanding of the culture of their immigrant neighbors.

The Environment as a Resource

In addition to information housed in institutions, local history addressing major topics in the U.S. history curriculum can be found in ordinary places not tagged with historical markers but significant nonetheless for what they can reveal about the past and present. Houses, streets, stores, businesses, and churches in a neighborhood can be as meaningful in promoting mastery of learning standards as official landmarks and historical institutions. Uncovering their stories and making connections to the big picture may take some doing, but the effort can prove particularly rewarding and refreshing because these ordinary resources are free from interpretation imposed by others and thus lend themselves to original analysis provided by students and teachers.

Leone and Silberman (1995) focus on what they call the hidden history of the nation and demonstrate through their examination of aspects of our material culture—maps, artifacts, folk art, buildings—how various dominated groups defined themselves and struggled to resist losing their identities and becoming marginalized by the empowered. Their study of an "invisible America" illustrates how the story of the past can be uncovered and interpreted through resources often neglected by traditional historians. The study is organized chronologically to align with major historical eras, thus providing a framework for teachers seeking to help students at various grade levels master learning standards in U.S. history courses. Leone and Silberman encourage us to look through an inquiring lens at such ordinary/extraordinary sites as churches, barns, factories, railroad stations, department stores, amusement parks, movie theaters, cemeteries, and split-level homes. They pose questions about these and other aspects of material culture that force us to confront the underlying assumptions and values they represent. For a teacher who seeks to make connections between resources that may be situated in the school community and the social history of the United States, such examples can prove to be engaging hooks that can draw students into the complex realm of historical investigation.

Other aspects of the environment that can provide starting points for student learning about the past through the medium of the community are isolated markers and monuments to events and individuals of both local and national significance. These might include street signs, named squares, sidewalk markers, schools, parks, statues, and monuments. Students can investigate the individuals after whom local places were named and do an analysis of who was honored and who was not. If there is a tablet in a local cemetery or a monument in the town square listing the names of those who lost their lives in one of the many wars and conflicts that fill the pages of U.S. history texts, students can try to learn more about the backgrounds of those who died and reach conclusions about which groups are asked to serve and which do the asking. Are schools and parks named after wealthy benefactors who may have endowed them or after local heroes and heroines? Has the community chosen to honor outsiders whose ideals, actions, or sacrifices represent the values of the local residents and their leaders? Investigations of place names can lead students to multifaceted conclusions about their own communities and their connections to the national past. Such endeavors can, at the same time, reinforce the idea that history resides beyond the pages of textbooks and official documents; it lives all around us in places we pass through everyday. It belongs not just to the historians and experts who have been trained to interpret it, but to all of us who take the time to look for it in our own communities.

CONCLUSIONS

Teaching and learning history and the social sciences at the K–12 level is a challenging proposition for all parties engaged in the effort. The challenge has been raised to new heights in recent years by the implementation of rigorous standardized tests based largely on traditional content and basic skills. The color and adventure of social studies courses are in danger of being lost in the maze of core knowledge topics and learning standards that teachers must address in their mission to prepare their classes for the tests. A strategy to meet the testing challenge—one that simultaneously can incorporate necessary content, foster understanding, capture students' interest, recognize diversity, and incorporate multicultural themes—is to interweave the history of the local community into the main fabric of the social studies curriculum. Such an approach is in keeping with the citizenship mission of social studies educators, promotes democratic values, and is consistent with the tenets of constructivist learning theory. In the chapters to follow, we shall see how these themes are brought together in studies, lessons, units, and projects focused on a number of individual communities and groups selected to illustrate the concept of using local history to integrate multicultural themes and promote mastery of learning standards in K–12 classrooms.

Local History from a Multicultural Perspective: A Case Study of Framingham, Massachusetts

IN THE LIBRARIES, historical societies, and municipal buildings of communities throughout the United States, one usually can find a pamphlet, article, or full-length book devoted to telling the story of a town or city's past. Often these publications commemorate the anniversary of the community's founding, and they are celebratory in mission and tone. They may not meet the standards of objective historical research in that their intent is to foster pride and membership in the community rather than to offer a research-based interpretation of its high and low moments and to challenge residents to think critically about the past. They are valuable nonetheless, for their narratives present a timeline of the major events of the community's development and provide a starting point for a teacher who seeks to build a curriculum that links the local to the national and includes a multicultural perspective.

Framingham, Massachusetts, like thousands of other communities across the nation that reflect the narrative of U.S. history, is at the same time both the quintessential American town and a markedly multicultural town. Within its boundaries there are numerous examples of individuals, events, groups, and institutions that are connected to the broader history of the United States and that can be studied through the lens of multicultural education. In so doing, students and teachers in the community can arrive at new insights and a deeper understanding of the town and how its history reflects that of the nation in all its rich diversity. What follows in this chapter are parallel visions of the community where I have lived for the past 30 years, organized around the chronological time periods used in the *National Standards for History* (1996). The discussion of each era begins with a brief summary of the town's history during the targeted time period based on various published sources available in the public library and historical society. Next the multicultural threads are highlighted to substantiate the argument that the town has been diverse from its founding and throughout its history has reflected and played a part in major national events. The purpose is not simply to call attention to the colorful history of my community. A broader goal is, through the retelling of that history, to model how teachers can take what is the conventional story of a city's or town's heritage and inject it with a multicultural perspective, while at the same time identifying people, events, and institutions that can connect it to their curriculum content frameworks and thus help their students meet mandated learning standards. To these ends, the summary of each era in Framingham's history concludes with suggested learning activities built around multicultural themes.

At the conclusion of the chapter are two detailed lesson plans combining the goals of local history, multicultural education, and standards-based learning grounded in the history of Framingham, but that can serve as models for classrooms in other communities. They are aligned with the *National Standards for History* (1996) and the NCSS *Curriculum Guidelines for Multicultural Education* (1991). Suggestions are provided for adapting the plans for use in schools in other locales.

The Focus Questions that open the historical narrative serve two purposes. The first set can help teachers planning local history lessons concentrate on the primary understandings students should gain from participating in a study of their community. The second set illustrates how to shift the emphasis from simply celebrating the history of a community to one that encourages a multicultural perspective.

THE STORY OF FRAMINGHAM

TRADITIONAL FOCUS QUESTIONS

How does my community reflect the historical development of the United States?
What are some unique aspects of the history of my community?

MULTICULTURAL FOCUS QUESTIONS

How might different cultural groups interpret the events in my community's history?
How have different ethnic and cultural groups influenced the development of my community?

Framingham, Massachusetts, is an economically developed suburb with a population of about 65,000 located midway between Boston, the capital city, and Worcester, the geographic center of the state. Incorporated in 1700, the community recently celebrated its tercentennial with a series of historical commemorations and the publication of a new chronicle by the town's historian, Stephen Herring (2000). Its title, *Framingham: An American Town*, clearly presents the author's thesis that, while it maintains a unique and storied identity, the community is the quintessential suburb, incorporating within its past the history of the nation from its earliest roots to the present time.

Three Worlds Meet/Colonization and Settlement (Beginnings to 1763)

The story begins with the Nipmuc (or Nipmuck) Indians, who originally populated the area that would become Framingham but had largely abandoned the region before the arrival of the first British settlers (Herring, 2000; Temple, 1887/1988). Herring (2000) describes the culture of the Nipmuc in the brief "Prologue" to his comprehensive history but notes that their story "properly belongs with the story of the early European settlers with whom they mingled" (p. 6). I suspect that multicultural educators would disagree. Temple devotes a lengthy chapter, which he calls "Indian Occupation," to the lifestyle of the Nipmuc as seen through a 19th-century lens. He sets the tone in the opening paragraphs when he states that "aside from *war* and *games* for the young men—an Indian was averse to everything that required bodily labor. . . . His idea of true dignity and true happiness was, to bask in the sun or over his fire, smoke his pipe, eat to repletion, and doze" (1887/ 1988, p. 33; emphasis in original). Such perceptions underscore the difficulty of accurately presenting the history of the land before the coming of the Europeans.

The Earliest Inhabitants. Using the historical resources available, we can conclude that remains of the Nipmuc, or "fresh water people," a branch of the Algonquin Indians of New England who lived from time to time in the area that would become the town of Framingham, have been identified. These include cooking utensils, arrowheads, and burial grounds that dotted the landscape, with the most prominent sites being in the present-day Saxonville, Cochituate, and South sections of town. Fish were evidently abundant and used by the natives for both food and fertilizer. They cultivated corn, which was dried and stored in granaries; the remains of these are additional indications of native activity in the area. By the time of the first permanent British settlements in Massachusetts, the Nipmuc had largely abandoned the local sites, casualties of both intertribal warfare and contagious diseases, the latter probably introduced by early European explorers and trappers.

The first nonnative resident of the area is thought to have been John Stone, who migrated from nearby Sudbury in search of suitable land on which to build a home for his young family (Callahan, 1974). Property along the

Sudbury River, held by Thomas Danforth, who was originally of Framlingham, England, for which the town was named, eventually would form the major portion of the community's territory. At some point the "l" was dropped, and the first county records use the current spelling (Herring, 2000).

The Eames Family Tragedy. Most accounts of the early history of Framingham highlight an episode in the brutal 1670s conflict, King Philip's War, which involved the Eames family of what is now the Mt. Wayte neighborhood (Callahan, 1974; Herring, 2000; Temple, 1887/1988). Referred to in town accounts as the Eames Massacre, it is a sad story, but one that is subject to different interpretations. It began when British settler Thomas Eames arrived on the scene in 1669 and purchased land around Farm Pond in South Framingham from John Awassamog, an Indian from neighboring Natick and nephew of Wuttawushan, a chieftan who reportedly lived in the territory in the 1620s. According to the town's Web site (*Framingham Historical Narrative*, n.d.), "A great tragedy occurred on February 1, 1676. Thomas Eames had gone to Boston to market. During his absence, a party of Indians attacked his home, killed his wife and five of his children." In *Framingham Historical Reflections*, Callahan (1974) describes the episode as follows: "The attackers burned the barn and the house, killed Mrs. Eames and three children, and carried off five others along with plunder. Mrs. Eames courageously defended her home and family, using hot soap and such weapons as were on hand in the kitchen" (p. 35).

The context of the Eames tragedy, King Philip's War which ravaged the area from June 1675 through August 1676, is one of the bloodiest and most disturbing occurrences in the history of colonial New England (Lepore, 1998; Schultz & Tougias, 1999). With respect to analyzing the Eames tragedy in this war, a question should be raised: Was it a random act of savagery or was there more to the story? Some clues are provided by Callahan (1974), who notes that when some of the attackers were apprehended, they explained that they had returned to the area to look for stored corn in one of their granaries but found none. Desperate for supplies, they decided to raid the nearest farm, which was the Eames property. Mrs. Eames put up such a fight that the Indians retaliated in kind. Two of the Eames boys captured by the natives escaped, and a daughter was later freed for ransom. Perhaps the tragedy resulted from overreaction on both sides and might have been avoided had each understood the other's perspective.

The Salem Witch Connection. Another disturbing episode in New England colonial history, which influenced the development of the community of Framingham, involved the Salem witch trials. In 1692, following a series of unsettling and unexplained occurrences in Salem Village, now Danvers, Massachusetts, a group of young girls began to exhibit alarming physical symptoms that, to the 17th-century Puritan mind, could be explained only as the work of the devil (Davidson & Lytle, 1992; Hansen, 1969). In their desperation to end the tortures of the girls, residents turned on one another, and eventually 20 individuals were executed for the practice of witchcraft. Several Salem Village residents fled the hysteria and settled in the relative wilderness of what would become South Framingham, where they "found a peaceful home" (Temple, 1887/1988, p. 111). One of the town's oldest and most scenic thoroughfares is Salem End Road, where a number of the refugees, including one of the accused, Sarah Clayes, settled.

Along with the Native American and Anglo presence in the territory that would comprise Framingham, another cultural element was introduced during the colonial period, a fact that comes as quite a shock to many residents of all ages today, and that was the involuntary immigration of people of color, delicately listed in the 1760 census as "servants for life" (Temple, 1887/1988, p. 235). At that time, there were seven such residents, but the history of slavery in Framingham can be traced back to the early 1700s, when it was recorded that John Stone held one "Jone, wife of John Jackson" as a slave, and the prominent Colonel Buckminster had a slave girl, Jane, baptized. The Framingham Historical Society possesses a bill of sale for a young child, Phebe, who was purchased by Elizabeth Balch (Herring, 2000), a valuable primary source documenting the practice of slave holding.

Establishment of Institutions During the Colonial Period. In the summer of 1700, the Governor of Massachusetts approved Framingham's petition to be incorporated as a town (Callahan, 1974; Herring, 2000; Temple, 1887/ 1988). The first town meeting was held thereafter, and a slate of town officers elected. One of their most important early decisions was to establish an official church, Puritan in denomination, which was supported financially by all citizens regardless of affiliation. Many early town controversies revolved around the selection of clergymen and their respective interpretation of church doctrine. In addition to the establishment of a town government and church, Framingham saw the creation of its first school system in the early 1700s. Its substandard quality, however, resulted in fines by the Massachusetts General Court. Among the town's first business establishments were grain mills and sawmills, blacksmith shops, tanneries, and taverns. The population of the community reached the 1,000 mark. In these accomplishments, Framingham was not unlike a number of other towns that dotted the New England landscape during the colonial period. The fabric of the town's history was also interwoven, from the very beginning, with distinctly diverse threads, including the story of the original Nipmuc inhabitants, the tragedy of war, the refugees from persecution, and the presence of slavery. Such currents most likely can be found in the history of many other American communities of the same period.

Learning Activities. The Nipmuc presence on the land that would become Framingham might be illustrated in dioramas created by elementary students or through a heritage trail marked out by older students after researching the Native American presence in various neighborhoods. The Eames tragedy could be examined through a "news conference" in which students could assume roles of various participants and present their different points of view. Tracing the role of the Salem End families in the Salem witch episode and their subsequent influence on the development of Framingham could be undertaken by secondary students who might follow up by discussing the role of religion and suspicion in the 17th century and comparing it with the post-September 11 climate of contemporary America. Secondary students also might research the fate of those residents of the town euphemistically called "servants for life."

Revolution and the New Nation (1754–1820s)

As the town grew and transitioned from its colonial to its revolutionary stage, the residents experienced conflicts and debates over the break with England similar to those in communities throughout New England (Callahan, 1974; Herring, 2000; Temple, 1887/1988). Framingham, along with a number of other towns, refused to pay the Stamp Act tax and sent delegates to meetings protesting various British colonial policies. Town leaders supported the Committees of Correspondence organized by Samuel Adams and even created one of their own. They gathered ammunition, organized companies of minutemen, and participated in many of the early battles that are described on the pages of U.S. history texts—Lexington and Concord, Bunker Hill, and Dorchester Heights. Artillery from Fort Ticonderoga passed through town en route to Boston, and residents were recruited to help fill the ranks of the Continental Army.

The Participation of People of Color. One of the most inflammatory events of the period leading up to the conflict with England and the outbreak of the Revolutionary War was the so-called Boston Massacre of 1770. British troops had occupied the city for several months prior to the episode, and tensions between them and Boston's residents had been escalating to the point that when some local ruffians began to throw stones and other objects at the soldiers, the latter fired upon them, leaving five dead and three wounded (Brown & Tager, 2000). As it turns out, one of the Americans, perhaps the ringleader of the crowd, was an escaped slave named Crispus Attucks. Of both Native American and Black ancestry, he had been the property of William Brown of Framingham, who ran a fugitive slave notice in the *Boston Gazette* in 1754 and offered a reward of 10 pounds plus expenses to "whoever shall take up said runaway and convey him to his aforesaid master" (*Historical Narrative*, n.d.). Controversy has long swirled around the character of Attucks, and it has not yet been resolved whether, as the first to die in the Boston Massacre, he was a patriot or a troublemaker who just happened to be at the site of a mob action that has been largely sentimentalized by the writers of the nation's chronicle. Consequently, in March 2000, when the town of Framingham, in a cooperative effort between the local Historical Society, the Historical Commission, and the African-American Heritage Society, dedicated a bridge to Crispus Attucks, the event generated quite a bit of local heat. For many it was a fitting way to honor a long-ago resident who participated in one of the seminal events of the revolutionary period. For others the naming of the bridge was a misplaced effort to honor an individual with a dubious past and an accidental presence on the stage of history (Reuell, 2000).

When the Revolutionary War broke out and soldiers were needed in the fight against the British, African Americans from Framingham were among those who participated. During the Battle of Bunker Hill, the shot that mortally wounded British Major Pitcairn was fired by Peter Salem, a former slave from Framingham. He was given his freedom by his owner, Lawson Buckminster, in order that he might enlist in the company commanded by local resident Simon Edgell (Herring, 2000). Salem was a servant to General George Washington, became a regular member of the Continental Army, and participated in the fight at Stony Point, New York. His grave still stands in the Old Burying Ground Cemetery, and his name is engraved on a marker at the entrance along with those of the other 88 veterans from town who served in the Revolutionary War. Others included emancipated slaves Blaney Grusha and Cato Hart, who served at Lexington and Bunker Hill.

The Theme of Resistance. The American Revolution centers on resistance to the heavy hand of a government that a critical mass of subjects no longer perceived as legitimate. It is worthy of note that during the early revolutionary period in Framingham, rumors spread that slaves in the community were resisting by rising up against their owners (Herring, 2000). In response to the threat, Mehitable Pike Edgell, wife of Simon Edgell who served in one of Framingham's military companies, armed herself with a pitchfork and hid in the barn with her children and 8-year-old slave Phebe (who previously had been the property of Elizabeth Balch). The rumors proved to be unfounded, but the fact that they surfaced is evidence that the same type of unease and guilt usually associated with the South in the pre-Civil War period, was present in an early New England town.

Learning Activities. In their study of the American Revolution, students should be made aware of the fact that a number of those who served were of

African American heritage. Their stories, along with those of other locals who participated in the conflict, can help students see the human side of this formative event in American history as well as recognize the sacrifices made by those who go to war. The journal of Captain Simon Edgell is a primary source housed in the Framingham Historical Society and Museum's collection that could be used by teachers investigating such issues with their students. Similar resources may be preserved in historical societies, local museums, and libraries in other communities dating to the revolutionary period. Students also might reflect and compose essays on how war was used as a vehicle to gain freedom by enslaved African Americans, and could engage in follow-up research on how they fared when the war was over. A detailed lesson plan on the controversy surrounding the naming of the Crispus Attucks Bridge, designed for middle school students (Lesson Plan 2.2), is included at the end of the chapter.

Expansion and Reform (1801–1861)

The early industrial period saw Framingham develop into a convenient stop-over for stagecoaches bound from Boston to Worcester and back. Industry came to town in the form of cotton and woolen mills, which were erected in the Saxonville section where there was an abundant water supply to power the textile machinery. Temple (1887/1988) notes that the Framingham Manufacturing Company got off to a promising start by attracting to the neighborhood a number of families with "children old enough to work in the Mill" (p. 356). Although this particular establishment burned in 1834, Saxonville continued as a textile center due largely to entrepreneurs Michael Simpson and William H. Knight as well as to the labors of the Irish immigrants who moved into the area during the disastrous potato famine in their homeland.

The First Industry. The Framingham Historical Society and Museum houses a modest display paying tribute to the town's "first industry," not textiles, but straw bonnets. The importance of this enterprise to the town's economy is underscored by the 1850 census statistics, which note its value at $140,000, nearly five times that of its nearest competitor, shoes and boots (Statistics of the Town, 1850). The multicultural aspect of this industry is that it was initiated by some clever women in town and largely remained a women's pursuit. According to Temple's (1887/1988) account, the enterprise began around 1800 when Mary Bennett, her daughter Betsey, and their neighbors, Mary Rice and her daughters, began making bonnets from braided straw and selling them at a tidy profit. Rice, whose first-year net earnings amounted to $340, continued in the business for some 50 years, selling her products in the ports of Boston, Salem, and Portland, Maine. Eventually, some men of the community got involved, and the industry continued to grow and turn ever greater profits. Temple describes the business as a family venture in which "the braid was made by the girls and boys at home" (p. 374), and Herring (2000) notes that in later years the work moved from home to factory, where hundreds found employment.

Religious Diversity in the 19th Century. The religious climate of Framingham was diversified by the Irish newcomers who worked in the textile mills, but had begun to change earlier in the century, influenced by the Second Great Awakening, which lasted from about 1800 to 1830 (McLoughlin, 1978). During this period, national leaders seemed bent on establishing an American identity and promoting a sense of unity in the young republic. Religion in part fulfilled these goals, as the image of the United States as a chosen nation took hold. A proliferation of sects, reform groups, and benevolent societies characterized the early 19th century. The community of Framingham exemplified these trends with the founding of "a flock of churches" (Herring, 2000, p. 128). The official Congregational Church was supported by tax funds, but other groups began to gather and build their own houses of worship. The Baptists organized in 1812, and their handsome meeting house in Framingham Centre stands as one of the town's oldest public buildings (Temple, 1887/1988). Today's residents might be surprised to learn that in the attic, a space long since sealed away, rough benches were installed where the congregation's African American members were expected to worship. In order to reach the "slave galleries," individuals had to climb a separate staircase, a strong reminder that segregation was still the rule in this New England town.

During this same period, the Methodists erected a new church in the Saxonville section of town, and the long-entrenched Congregationalists engaged in a conflict with the upstart Unitarians who, by a vote of parishioners who listened to preachers from both denominations, ended up taking over the Congregational Church property. Shortly thereafter, the Congregationalists reorganized and built a new meeting house. In 1832, the town's growing religious diversity deepened with the formation of a Universalist society. A few French Catholics had lived in the community since the 1750s, but they did not have their own church or priest to minister to their religious needs. It would not be until the Irish influx of the 1840s that the first Catholic church, St. George's in Saxonville, was erected.

Learning Activities. For younger students, a field trip to the Framingham Historical Society and Museum, where they could view the straw bonnet exhibit, might be followed by a class activity in which they would attempt to craft their own replicas of the product. Such an exercise would promote an understanding of the skill involved in the endeavor. Older students could research the economic impact of the straw bonnet industry. Another research project for older students related to the town's diversity might involve tracing the development of various religious institutions and analyzing how they exemplified demographic changes and reflected and/or influenced the political and social currents of the era.

Civil War and Reconstruction (1850–1877)

With the 1861 attack on Fort Sumter that sparked the military phase of the long-simmering conflict between South and North, members of Framingham's town meeting voted to support a local militia to send off to the battlefields (Herring, 2000; Temple, 1887/1988). However, when the Massachusetts government voted to support state volunteer regiments, local units such as the one in Framingham were asked to dissolve. Some volunteers ended up serving in the state's regiments, and one of the first to lose his life was Framingham's George W. Stevens. In all, over 500 Framingham men fought in the Civil War, and 52 did not survive.

Protest and Dissent at Harmony Grove. During the tumultuous years leading up to the Civil War, some of the most fervent protest activity in New England regarding the abolition of slavery occurred in Framingham's historic Harmony Grove. This recreational site, developed by Edwin Eames in the 1840s, initially was used for church picnics (Callahan, 1974). A commercial venture on about 4 acres of family land in the Farm Pond section of town, it was fitted with a boathouse, swings, a speakers' platform, and benches with a capacity to seat about 1,000 (Herring, 2000). In addition to its use as a recreational facility, Harmony Grove was a convenient spot for the reformers of the 1840s and 1850s to spread their messages. It was here that Frederick Douglass, William Lloyd Garrison, Wendell Phillips, and Sojourner Truth delivered fiery speeches against the evils of slavery. On an eventful July 4 holiday in 1854, hundreds gathered to hear a number of well-advertised abolitionist speakers. Their platform was conspicuously outfitted for the occasion with an American flag, bordered in black, hanging upside down in protest. As Herring tells it, the first speaker, Garrison, was the most shocking, for after delivering a lengthy tirade against the government's policies on the slavery issue, he proceeded to burn copies of both the Fugitive Slave Act and the U.S. Constitution. The crowd's reaction was mostly negative, but after a break for refreshments, the rest of the prominent speakers made their points, and the "Meeting for True Freedom" concluded.

With the exception of a marker on the corner of two busy streets in a mixed commercial and residential neighborhood of the town, little remains today of the fabled Harmony Grove. In its heyday, however, the gathering place was the scene of a number of spirited protests beyond those calling for an end to slavery. Speakers made use of the natural amphitheater to rail against the evils of alcohol, promote equal rights for women, and chide public officials for dereliction of duty. Ironically, Benjamin Butler, a candidate for governor, delivered there his "great speech against monopolies, including the railroad that provided the train service transporting the multitudinous throngs to Framingham, where freedom of speech prevailed" (Callahan, 1974, p. 59).

African Americans Fight for the Union. The Civil War era saw the participation of residents of Framingham in the storied Massachusetts 54th Regiment, on which the popular film *Glory* is based. The Framingham Public Library's collection includes a pamphlet entitled *Central Massachusetts 'Colored' Veterans of the Civil War* (New England Native American Institute, n.d.). In it Charles Clark, an 18-year-old private from Framingham, is listed as having lost his life in South Carolina. Another soldier, Emery B. Cobb, is noted as having served with the federal troops for "men of color." Cobb died in 1864, the year of his enlistment, at age 24. In all, six Framingham Blacks served in the conflict.

Learning Activities. After researching the protest and reform activities associated with Harmony Grove, students might participate in a role play of some of its historic moments. This activity would be most appropriate for middle school students, who subsequently could identify current issues in need of public attention and formulate ways to highlight and correct them using modern means of communication. Secondary students also might try to learn more about the town residents who served in the Civil War, including their race, social class, military records, and fate. They then might draw conclusions as to who served, who did not, and why.

The Development of the Industrial United States (1870–1900)

In the post-Civil War years, the town assumed many of the characteristics that stamp it with its contemporary identity. The southern section of the community, then as now, was a center of commerce, industry, and transportation. The Boston & Albany Railroad came to town and with it the construction of impressive commercial buildings, the district courthouse, military training grounds, and major businesses.

A Business with Global Connections. One business of the industrial period that foreshadowed future multicultural connections was the Para Rubber Shoe Company, which opened in an industrial complex built by some locals hoping to entice Boston businesses to relocate to Framingham (Herring, 2000). Named after the site in Brazil that was the source of rubber used to fashion a variety of footwear products, the Para Company, a model of successful collaboration among nations in the hemisphere, hosted an 1899 delegation of officials bound for the Pan American Congress in Washington, DC (Evans-Daly & Gordon, 1997). Hundreds of waving local schoolchildren lined the nearby streets marked with the flags of the United States, Spain, and Portugal to welcome them. In recent years, a large influx of immigrants from Brazil has moved to Framingham, underscoring a connection made many years earlier.

An Inventive Resident. Aligned with the industrial expansion of the post-Civil War era came a flood of clever inventions and their marketing to the consumer-oriented American public. A homegrown example of the inventive American was Margaret Knight, one of the first women to be granted patents by the U.S. government. Growing up in the industrial community of Manchester, New Hampshire, Knight was disturbed when she witnessed the injury of a mill operative who was cut by a steel shuttle that had flown out of its slot (Callahan, 1974). Only 12 years old, she designed a part that would prevent such accidents and went on to garner a number of additional patents on inventions ranging from equipment to fold paper bags to an improved silent automobile motor. Considering that she was largely uneducated, and her inventions were highly mechanical, her accomplishments are all the more impressive (James, James, & Boyer, 1971). Knight lived for a number of years in South Framingham, and died there at the age of 76. Her home, now a private residence, still stands, conspicuous only for its marker noting that Knight once lived there.

Learning Activities. There are many possibilities for local lessons on the industrial period. A detailed lesson plan (2.1) for elementary students related to the inventions of Margaret Knight is included at the conclusion of the chapter. Geography lessons for elementary and middle level students based on the five themes—location, place, human environment interaction, movement, and region (National Geographic Society, 2003)—could be centered around the Framingham/Para business connection. Research projects in economics for high school students might be designed around the theme of "Business Then and Now." Students could work in teams organized by neighborhood to compare the businesses that existed in the latter half of the 19th century with those that exist now and discuss their economic significance.

The Emergence of Modern America (1890–1930)

As the 20th century dawned, Framingham, along with much of the rest of the nation, continued to grow more diverse with respect to the variety of ethnic groups moving into the community. The population steadily increased; in fact, Framingham then earned the distinction that it carries to this day of being the largest town in the state (Callahan, 1974). Previously, Irish immigrants had established themselves in the Saxonville section of town, where they worked in the mills and where the first Catholic Church, St. George's, was dedicated in 1847 (Herring, 2000). The census figures for 1850 note that out of a population of slightly over 4,000, 933 were foreign born, with an overwhelming majority of them (713) being from Ireland. Other groups with substantial numbers included residents from England, Scotland, and Nova Scotia. Although the religious diversity of the town was more pronounced with the establishment of the first Catholic parish, the ethnic composition remained largely Anglo-Saxon.

The New Immigrants. By the early 1900s, Framingham's ethnic composition began to change, with large numbers of permanent residents from Italy opening businesses and building homes in town (Herring, 2000). Most of the Italian immigrants were drawn to work in the growing number of large construction enterprises. These included transportation projects, particularly the railroads, as well as the building of reservoirs and companion aqueducts. The Coburnville section of South Framingham evolved into a Little Italy of sorts with the construction of a new Catholic church in the neighborhood, St. Tarcisius, the establishment of the Christopher Columbus Society, and the presence of fruit stands and groceries catering to the tastes of the flourishing Italian population that would become an increasingly powerful political force in the town. A 2004 exhibit of the Framingham Historical Society and Museum, "*Abbondanza!* The Richness of Italian-American Life in Framingham" (Ricciardi, 2004), traces the group's presence through documents and artifacts, many of them lent by local descendants of immigrant families.

It was during this period also that the seeds of what would develop into a prominent Jewish community were sown, and the first synagogue was established in 1908 in South Framingham. A telling primary source, housed in the Framingham Historical Society and Museum, is the constitution of the Female Society of Framingham (1822), which illustrates earlier attitudes toward Jews in America. This group was dedicated not, as students might suspect, to advancing the rights of women, but to the promotion of "Christianity among the Jews," with all funds raised by members to be used for this missionary purpose. Among the names of the charter members are those of a number of Framingham's most prominent families.

Framingham's Suffragists. Multicultural themes can be seen in many other aspects of Framingham's identity as it evolved in the early decades of the 20th century, an era characterized by the reform agenda of the Progressives.

In the drive for Prohibition, child labor laws, consumer protection, voters' rights, and numerous other progressive measures, the women of the United States played a major role, and many living in Framingham at the time were prominently involved in these campaigns. Most striking were those caught up in the final push for women's suffrage. Particularly noteworthy are Josephine Collins and Louise Mayo. The latter was a middle-aged mother of seven who went to Washington in 1917, during the presidency of Woodrow Wilson, and participated in a traffic-snarling Bastille Day celebration near the White House. She and the other 15 protesters were arrested and given the choice of a fine or the workhouse. They chose the workhouse. In a feisty interview with the *Boston Post* ("Family Is Militant," 1917), her daughter declared, "I do hope mother sticks it out with the rest." The article goes on to note that all of Mayo's children were united in support of their mother's civil disobedience. A presidential pardon resulted in Mayo's release after just 2 days of time served. Collins, a single woman from Framingham Centre who demonstrated for the cause of women's suffrage, was arrested in Boston for participating in protests against Wilson's 1919 visit (Herring, 2000). Both Mayo and Collins received pins in the shape of a jailhouse door from the National Woman's Party in commemoration of their dedication to the movement. The Historical Society possesses a number of valuable and informative primary sources related to this slice of American history, including Mayo's pin, her pardon from President Wilson, news clippings from the Boston papers related to her arrest, a letter to Collins from Alice Paul of the National Woman's Party, and an 1895 specimen ballot asking voters to decide on the following question: "Is it expedient that municipal suffrage be granted to women?"

The KKK in Framingham. One of the disturbing aspects of the post-World War I "return to normalcy" was a reaction against foreigners or those whose race, ethnicity, or religion was perceived to be "un-American." The KKK terrorist organization was revived in the 1920s, and a number of individuals in the Framingham area joined its ranks. Reportedly, a 1924 Klan meeting in the central Massachusetts city of Worcester was attended by over 20,000 supporters (Mullen, 1985). The KKK met with tough resistance, however, and a number of riots occurred in eastern Massachusetts between Klan members and those whom they targeted. Two of Framingham's Catholic churches experienced cross burnings, leading to a climate of fear and tension. Serious violence erupted during the summer of 1925 in Sudbury, just over the Framingham line, between Klan and opposing forces, many of them Framingham residents. Klan meetings had been held in the past at the Libbey farm in Sudbury, and, upon hearing news of a gathering there on August 10, a number of mostly men and young people from the surrounding area descended on the spot. Shots were fired, and five men were wounded in the melee that followed. They all survived, but the tension persisted with the arrest of 80 suspected Klan members. A mob, which surrounded the Framingham police headquarters where the suspects were held, was dispersed with some difficulty by officers on horseback. The Klan riot received such widespread press coverage that it might indeed have contributed to the decline of the group in Massachusetts in the years that followed (Herring, 2000).

Learning Activities. Using resources at the historical society or library, students at the upper elementary or secondary levels engaged in studying the new immigrants of the late 19th and early 20th centuries could locate information about the Italian and Jewish newcomers and write essays or present reports addressing why they settled in town, describing any problems they had concerning acculturation/acceptance, and illustrating through drawings or photographs how they changed the environment. In conjunction with their study of the progressive movement, students at the secondary level, using learning packets containing copies of primary sources such as those at the Framingham Historical Society and Museum described earlier, could research the local women involved in demonstrations in support of woman's suffrage. Secondary students learning about nativism in the 1920s could comb old newspapers, available on microfilm in area libraries, to learn details about the 1925 Klan riot and then reflect on why people in their community might join such a group and if the violence could have been avoided.

The Great Depression and World War II (1929–1945)

During the bleak years of the Great Depression, the residents of Framingham shared with the rest of the nation the hardships and heartaches of the period. The early years were the hardest, before some relief came with the introduction of New Deal programs on a local level (Herring, 2000). The town sent young people to the Civilian Conservation Corps and employed adults in a number of public works projects, such as building sidewalks and recreational facilities, which were financed through the Works Progress Administration (WPA).

A Family of Renown. One bright note in this era involved the public recognition of the work of Meta Warrick Fuller, an African American artist whose sculpture studio was described in the local newspaper as "one of the most charming places to visit in Framingham" ("Exhibition," 1933). Fuller received international attention, and her periodic exhibitions were covered regularly by the press. She was a member of the Framingham Women's Club, serving as the chair of its art committee. Throughout her long career, she received a number of awards, including one from the Boston branch of the NAACP for her "rich and continuous contribution to the cause of Civil Rights and Human Freedom, through the art of sculpture" ("Mrs. Meta Warrick Fuller," 1964). The wife of a prominent psychologist, Dr. Solomon C. Fuller, she was commissioned after his death to create a bronze plaque in his memory for the Framingham Union Hospital, where he had been a staff member.

Dr. Fuller was raised in Liberia, the grandson of American slaves, and educated at the Boston University School of Medicine, where he later served on the faculty (Framingham Historical Society, 2001). Selected to study brain degeneration in Germany under the professor for whom Alzheimer's Disease was named, Fuller went on to publish a variety of professional articles and books and to correspond with the giants in the field of psychology, Freud and Jung. In 1974, the Solomon Carter Fuller Mental Health Center at Boston University was named in recognition of his contributions to the field of psychiatric medicine. The Fuller family was suitably honored in 1995 when the renovated middle school on the town's south side, not far from the Fuller home, was named in their honor.

Women in the War Effort. During the war years of the 1940s, Framingham's women contributed to the effort to defeat totalitarianism overseas as did their counterparts in countless communities across the nation. Women's groups in Framingham organized sewing circles, served as nurses and first aid providers, and planted victory gardens to provide for their families and conserve precious resources for the military (Callahan, 1974). About 200 of the town's female residents served in the armed forces, and a former employee of the local bus line, Dorothy McLean, piloted a plane for the Women's Auxiliary Flying Service. Although history textbooks traditionally portray wars as primarily masculine endeavors, they are fought on many fronts, including the one at home. In that realm, as well as increasingly on the battlefronts, women have made significant contributions.

Learning Activities. With their numbers decreasing precipitously with the passing of time, the individuals who remember life during the Great Depression and World War II are a precious resource. Students at all levels can develop a deeper understanding of the time period by interviewing older family members and friends concerning their memories and their participation in the events of the era. Their oral histories could be audio- or videotaped or interviewees could be invited to share their stories in the classroom. This type of cross-generational activity builds personal ties and helps bridge gaps between groups often divided by age and interests. A related project appropriate for the material related to the Great Depression and World War II is the creation of a classroom museum about the era. Students could take photos of the public works projects built under the WPA, create illustrations of the artwork of Meta Fuller, display copies of their oral histories, and collect memorabilia from family members or neighbors who lived in the community during the era and share them with classmates.

Postwar and Contemporary United States (1945–Present)

In the post-World War II era, Framingham experienced a spurt of unprecedented growth due in part to its convenient location midway between the cities of Boston and Worcester and the completion of the Massachusetts Turnpike with two exits within the town's borders. The turnpike access spurred commercial development, which in turn created a great demand for housing. The success of one of the town's major industries, General Motors, which completed construction of its 176-acre plant in 1948, also proved a powerful magnet in drawing new residents and in fostering the creation of support businesses in South Framingham. Along with the increasing population came a proliferation of schools, churches, hospitals, restaurants, recreational facilities, and one of the nation's first shopping malls, Shoppers' World, on heavily traveled Route 9. Large parcels of undeveloped land quickly were transformed with the construction of numerous housing developments, leading to Framingham's designation as the largest town in the Commonwealth of Massachusetts. To this day, its residents have resisted switching from town to city government, despite explosive residential, commercial, and retail development.

During this period of unprecedented growth, another unique event occurred when the community's well-respected medical establishment put the town on the nation's health radar screen with the pioneer Framingham Heart Study, a long-term look at the lifestyles of over 10,000 participants and the identifying characteristics of those who developed heart disease (Framingham Historical Society, 2001). The U.S. Public Health Service selected Framingham due to its participation in a tuberculosis study decades earlier and its demographic profile. Begun in 1948, the heart study early on identified smoking, high cholesterol, diabetes, and obesity as risk factors; we now take this information as a given. Recently, calls have been sounded to add more diversity to the population that is being studied in this ongoing medical project.

It was a sad event that spotlighted the town in 1986 when Christa Corrigan McAuliffe, a graduate of Framingham State College, ended her quest to become the first teacher in space when the Challenger exploded, killing all of its passengers. The community's educational establishment was buoyed more recently, however, when President Clinton signed the American Education Act of 1994 at the newly consolidated Framingham High School, in recognition of both its diversity and its record of achievement.

Class, Prejudice, and Recent Immigrants. As the town became more commercial and industrial, the diversity of its population increased. In the years from 1950 to 1975, the numbers of Hispanic and African American residents increased more dramatically than those of other groups (Herring, 2000). A small but significant number of Asians also moved into the community. With respect to the issue of class in Framingham, some statistics compiled in 1994 by the Mauricio Gaston Institute of the University of Massachusetts at Boston offer food for thought. In a graph of poverty rates comparing percentages for Latinos, Whites, Blacks, and Asians in Framingham in the late 1980s, the highest rates were for Latinos (17%) and Blacks (10.9%), respectively. For Asians the rate of poverty was 3.8%, and for Whites, 5.6%.

One proactive step taken by the town government in response to the changing demographics and disturbing reports from the minority communities concerning unfair treatment and episodes of prejudice and discrimination, was the creation in 1970 of a Human Relations Commission (*Human Relations*, 2002). Appointed by the Board of Selectmen, its 13 volunteer members address civil and human rights violations and issues, and in doing so they oversee the work of the Human Relations Department. The Department looks into reports of acts of discrimination, implements fair housing policies, and in general works to promote harmony and eliminate conflicts among the town's various cultural groups. Acting in conjunction with the Commission is the coalition to build a hate-free community, Stop Hate in Framingham Today (SHIFT).

The Brazilian Revitalization of Downtown. As the town of Framingham moved into the 21st century, its ever present diversity experienced the addition of yet another element—a new and vibrant Brazilian community. Drawn to the abundance of jobs in the service economy of the booming 1990s, the Brazilian immigrants settled in the south side of town, following a pattern established by earlier groups. Their colorful presence is readily apparent in the downtown streets where the green and yellow flag of their homeland is displayed proudly in their many small businesses. The Italian Catholic church, St. Tarcisius, celebrates a mass in Portuguese, and the Framingham public schools offer a bilingual education program in Portuguese as well. Attempts to revive the downtown area, long ago eclipsed by the shopping mall culture of Route 9 with its "Golden Mile" of retail businesses, revolve around the efforts of entrepreneurs of Brazilian heritage. How well they succeed will determine to a great extent the future of this historical section of town.

Learning Activities. For very young learners studying such themes as neighborhood, community helpers, and basic economic concepts, a class walking tour of the area around their schools could be a worthwhile learning activity, especially if teachers were careful to point out landmarks of historical significance and institutions of different cultural groups. As a follow-up, students could create picture books of their town. Older students might brainstorm the town's current problems and needs, and become involved in campaigns to promote reform or volunteer their services to community projects.

CONCLUSIONS

The preceding overview of the history of Framingham, as it parallels that of the United States, presents information from which one can draw answers to the Focus Questions that open the chapter. Framingham reflects the historical development of the United States in that the community began as a wilderness peopled by Native Americans and proceeded through stages that follow the development of the area from a colonial settlement to a densely settled suburban town with a mixed economic base and a diverse population. Its residents over time participated in the national history both at home (during the War for Independence, for example, a train of artillery from Fort Ticonderoga passed through Framingham on its way to Boston, and in 1854 William Lloyd Garrison burned a copy of the U.S. Constitution in Harmony Grove to protest its protection of slavery), and away from home (Louise Mayo was arrested in Washington, DC, when she demonstrated for women's suffrage). At the same time that Framingham is a quintessential American town, and a participant in the great events of various eras, it also is a unique community—the largest town in the state, the home of the inventor Margaret Knight and of many more people and events of distinction, and the site of a pioneering heart study.

The history of the community cannot be fully appreciated without the incorporation of the struggles, contributions, and simple presence of its Native and African Americans, its many religious and ethnic groups, its women, and its varied social classes. Members of these groups might interpret events from a different perspective than mainstream chroniclers. The Eames tragedy during King Philip's War is an early example, while the fact that the Framingham Heart Study may not adequately represent the health patterns of all ethnic and racial groups is a contemporary one. In following these stories as part of the larger narrative of the history of the town and the nation and in engaging in learning activities related to these topics, teachers and students can gain a deeper understanding of both mandated curriculum content and multicultural themes. Every community has such local/multicultural threads that, with some effort and insight, can be woven into the K–12 social studies curriculum.

LESSON PLAN 2.1
A FRAMINGHAM INVENTOR

Grades 2–3

Suggested Length. A 60-minute class

National Standards for History References (for grades K–4)

Topic 1. Living and Working Together in Families and Communities, Now and
Long Ago
Standard 2A. The student understands the history of his or her local community.

K–4. Identify historical figures in the local community and explain their contributions and significance.

NCSS *Curriculum Guidelines for Multicultural Education* Reference

21.0. The multicultural curriculum should make maximum use of experiential learning, especially local community resources.

Prerequisite Knowledge. Students will need to have some understanding of what
an invention is and should be able to give examples.

Materials. Several square-bottom paper bags, markers, scissors, glue, and various craft materials available in the classroom.

Objectives. Students will be able to—

- Name some of the inventions of Margaret Knight
- Explain the importance of one of Knight's inventions
- Work in groups to create their own inventions using square-bottom paper bags
  similar to the ones Knight's machine made and folded

Procedures

Initiation

- Ask students to define the word *invention* and write their ideas on the board.
- Ask students to name some inventions that they use or have in their homes.
- Tell students that they will be learning about an inventor from Framingham,
  Margaret Knight.

Development

- Tell students the story of Margaret Knight (based on the entry in *Notable American Women*, by James, James, & Boyer, 1971), put key words on the board, and refer to a map of New England, where appropriate.
- Show students a square-bottom paper/lunch bag and ask them to suggest some ways to make one with a flat piece of paper.
- Discuss how this process takes a long time if a person is doing the folding by hand.
- Explain to students that Margaret Knight invented a machine to do the job quickly and well.
- Show students a diagram of the invention (available online at http://herstory. freehomepage.com/bios/knight.html/) and discuss why it was important.
- Tell students they will have a chance to become inventors themselves using square-bottom paper bags.
- Divide students into mixed-ability groups.
- Give each group a bag and ask students to come up with some ideas for some-thing new to make from the bag or new uses for the bag.
- Circulate among the groups and write down their ideas.
- Have students decide on one of the ideas from each group to make with the materials on hand or to draw on the paper bags and allow time for them to complete their projects.

Closing

- Review the facts about Margaret Knight and her inventions, referring to the key words on the board.
- List on the board all the ideas the students came up with for new uses for square-bottom paper bags.
- Ask groups to display the inventions they made or drew during class.

Assessment. Students will be assessed on the following criteria: how well they remembered the information about Knight and her inventions, their explanations about why her bag-folding machine was important, and the quality of their paper bag inventions.

Extensions

- Tell or read stories about other important inventions, being sure to include those made by women and members of various ethnic and racial groups.
- Have each group create part of a bulletin board on Margaret Knight using the paper bag inventions and drawings.

Adaptations. This lesson plan can be adapted to young students' study of any local inventor. In identifying an appropriate subject, it is important to search for diverse individuals as well as those whose accomplishments will both interest young learners and connect to required learning standards. The teacher will need to do the initial research, discuss the circumstances that prompted the individual to create the new invention, display pictures or diagrams, and lead a creative activity based on the invention.

LESSON PLAN 2.2
A BRIDGE FOR CRISPUS ATTUCKS?

Grades 5–8

Suggested Length. Two class sessions of 45–60 minutes each

National Standards for History **References**

Era 3. Revolution and the New Nation
Standard 1A. The student understands the causes of the American Revolution.

NCSS *Curriculum Guidelines for Multicultural Education* References

    8.0. The multicultural curriculum should help students understand that a conflict between ideals and realities always exists in human societies.
  11.0. The multicultural curriculum should help students develop their decision-making abilities, social participation skills, and sense of political efficacy as necessary bases for effective citizenship in a pluralistic democratic nation.
  17.0. The multicultural curriculum should help students to view and interpret events, situations, and conflicts from diverse ethnic and cultural perspectives and points of view.

Prerequisite Knowledge. Students previously will have learned about the developing conflict between the American colonists and England and will participate in this lesson in conjunction with their study of the Boston Massacre.

Objectives. Students will be able to

• Work in groups to conduct Internet research on Crispus Attucks, who died at the Boston Massacre
• Describe the significant facts about his life and death
• Debate the issue of whether or not a local bridge should have been dedicated in his honor

Procedures: Day 1

Initiation

• Ask students to name or describe some bridges they have visited or use in their daily lives.
• Discuss the purposes of bridges (e.g., for transportation and to make connections).
• Display photograph of the Crispus Attucks Bridge on Old Connecticut Path in Framingham, MA.

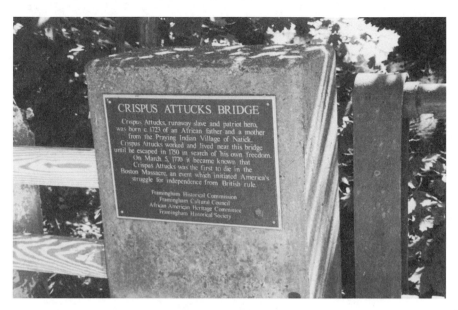

Crispus Attucks Bridge, Framingham, Massachusetts. All photographs by the author.

- Explain to students that this bridge recently was dedicated to Crispus Attucks, and they will be learning more about him and the question of whether or not the bridge should have been named in his honor.

Development

- Review the Boston Massacre and its significance as a cause of the American Revolution.
- Divide class into small groups and direct students to their computer stations where they will locate the Internet site http://www.framingham.com/history/profiles/crispus/index.htm.
- Review the brief historical profile of Attucks.
- Assign each group one of the related links to locate additional information (e.g., Africans in America, and the Murder of Crispus Attucks).
- Students will then take notes on the information about the life and death of Attucks that they found at their respective sites.
- Group members or the teacher will name a spokesperson for each group who will participate in a panel presentation of the information that has been gathered on Attucks.
- The teacher will lead a review session of facts.

Closing

- Ask students to brainstorm the defining characteristics of a hero.
- Explain their homework assignment—write a 3-paragraph essay in answer to the following question: Was Crispus Attucks a hero? Students should incorporate information gathered at the Web site and presented by the panel.

Procedures: Day 2

Initiation

- Ask for a show of hands to determine how many students wrote that Crispus Attucks was a hero.
- Explain to students that when the Crispus Attucks Bridge dedication was planned, some residents of the town objected because they did not believe that he was a hero.

Development

- Divide class into two teams to debate the question: A Bridge for Crispus Attucks, Yes or No?
- Put students who wrote that he was a hero on the negative team and those who wrote that he was not, on the affirmative team, if possible.
- Allow students to compose their debate speeches following a simplified format: opening statements, three or four arguments for the affirmative, three or four arguments for the negative, one rebuttal for each side, and closing arguments.
- After the debate has concluded, poll the class again to see if anyone has changed his/her mind about whether or not Attucks was a hero and deserving of a bridge named in his honor.

Closing

- Refer to the initial question about the purpose of a bridge.
- Ask whether even if Attucks was not a hero, a bridge should have been named in his memory as a way to connect past to present or to connect people of different groups?

Assessment. Students will be assessed on the following criteria: how well they researched and presented information about the life and death of Attucks, the quality of their homework essays, and the effectiveness of their debate.

Extension. Ask students to identify and justify the naming of a bridge or other memorial for a present-day member of their community.

Adaptations. This lesson plan can be adapted to a study of any controversial local individual or event. The key is to encourage multiple perspectives in the lesson, not just through the debate format but also by assigning students to develop arguments for the side that they did not initially choose. High school students could use a more complex debate structure and write formal position papers for assessment.

Exploring Race and Class in Nashville

L OCATED ON the banks of the Cumberland River, Nashville is the state capital and the seat of local government for Davidson County, Tennessee. It is home to over 500,000 residents and can boast of a number of distinguished institutions of higher learning, a busy international airport, a variety of museums, and a sparkling modern entertainment center. Nashville has long been recognized as a center for finance, insurance, and publishing in the mid-South and more recently has earned a reputation as a mecca for the health care and tourism industries (West, 1998). It is also the home of the Grand Ole Opry and the heart of the country music industry. During the civil rights movement of the 1950s and 1960s, Nashville earned its place as one of the key communities where reformers took to the streets to demonstrate how nonviolent resistance could effect lasting change. It is the last two topics, country music and the civil rights movement, that are examined in this chapter, for they shed light on the complex issues of race and social class.

To provide a theoretical foundation for the discussion of Nashville's unique characteristics, the chapter begins with a general overview of the two primary elements of diversity that are the focal points of the narrative on civil rights and country music. The history of the city's African American community, which follows, opens with Focus Questions that are specific to Nashville in that they refer to how the city shaped the civil rights movement and the music industry, yet are general enough to be applied to other sites where teachers may wish to have their students investigate similar themes. The chapter concludes with a lesson plan for younger students related to the civil rights movement and a project plan for secondary students linked to country music and the city's Country Music Hall of Fame and Museum. The project format describes an activity that will take a considerable length of time for students to complete and is not broken down into individual class sessions as the lesson plans are. The topics for the lesson and project provide material for classroom teachers seeking to connect local events to the national picture and at the same time to integrate multicultural themes. Lessons built around Nashville's country music scene and civil rights heritage can, with some imagination, be adapted for use in classrooms throughout the United States.

RACE AND CLASS AS CATEGORIES OF DIVERSITY

Nashville, like most other communities in the United States, provides examples of all the elements under the multicultural umbrella, but the two related to the historical events on which this chapter focuses are race, for its centrality to the civil rights movement, and class, which is fundamental to understanding the nature and purpose of country music. Following are explanations of each based on the work of a number of contemporary multicultural authors.

Defining Race

Although there are those who would argue that race is a biological category based on physical characteristics determined at birth, this traditional interpretation is subject to debate (Rasool & Curtis, 2000). Because so many residents of the United States are of mixed heritage, classifying individuals by race is a somewhat pointless endeavor. Race as a concept was devised by anthropologists studying various cultural groups over a century ago, but in contemporary terms, it may have lost its credibility (Gollnick & Chinn, 2002). While the U.S. Census Bureau may classify residents by race—American Indian, Black, Asian or Pacific Islander, Hispanic, and White—Whites often see themselves as "raceless" or the norm, while all others are viewed as outsiders, on the margins of the mainstream.

Race as a Social Construct. Social scientists and multiculturalists suggest that race is neither biological nor fixed, but is instead a social construct that has been used to separate individuals and maintain the social status of those in the upper ranks of wealth and power. James Banks (1997) underscores the social foundation of race and further reminds us that two individuals with similar biological characteristics can be assigned different racial categories depending on the society in which they reside. He notes that "in the United States, where racial categories are well defined and highly inflexible, an individual with any acknowledged or publicly known African ancestry is considered Black" (p. 18). The individual may indeed look White, but if he or she has any degree of African heritage, the classification is Black. The same individual in Puerto Rico, on the other hand, would be considered White.

Race and History. Such inconsistencies notwithstanding, race has been a powerful force in the history of the United States, and arguably its defining event, the Civil War, was fought at least in part over the inability of residents of the principal regions to arrive at a compromise concerning the issue. Although present in the English colonies almost from the start, as we saw in the history of Framingham, African Americans, due to their original unprotected legal status and condition of servitude, have been fighting since colonial times to be accorded the dignity, respect, and economic opportunities long recognized as fundamental to life in a free society. In the city of Nashville, Tennessee, under consideration here, Blacks were present from the very first settlement and have been integral to the community's identity ever since. In addition, it was the fight waged by the city's Black activists during the civil rights movement that linked them to the larger wave of reform that swept the nation during the 1960s. The history of this southern city illustrates how the presence of racial diversity can be both interwoven into the fabric of its past and present and connected to major events of the nation's history.

Defining Class

Class, more clearly than race, is a category of diversity related to social constructs, yet many would argue that, like physical characteristics, it is inherited at birth. Furthermore, despite the long-standing perception in the United States of earned status and social mobility, class boundaries can be difficult to transcend. Economic well-being is the key, and so-called middle-class values are viewed largely as cornerstones of a democratic society. Yet there are many inconsistencies in these widely held beliefs. The politically revered middle class actually has been shrinking in recent decades, while the gap between rich and poor has been increasing (Rasool & Curtis, 2000). Due to the pervasive belief that the United States has an open society with equality of educational and economic opportunity, the poor often have been viewed as largely responsible for their own misfortune. They are labeled as lazy, lacking in a formal work ethic, and deficient in the strong family values necessary to instill in their offspring proper habits that will lead them out of poverty and into the middle class. Gollnick and Chinn (2002) indicate that although a "blame the victim" mentality exists, there are those who recognize that the principal business, cultural, and educational institutions are controlled by elites who seek to perpetuate the status quo. The opportunity to be successful and enjoy high socioeconomic status is greatest for those whose families have already achieved these goals and who use their wealth to ensure that their children are well prepared through education and other benefits to continue on the same path.

Education and Class. Education is deemed the key to success in the United States, and reformers have long maintained that if every child were given equal educational opportunity, poverty could be eradicated and the under-class eliminated. While no one will deny that progress has been made to-ward providing all children access to schooling at taxpayers' expense, it has been argued convincingly by critics that education for those in the lower socioeconomic strata does not fulfill its promise. Spring (2002) asks his read-ers to consider the proposition that rather than providing the children of the poor with educational opportunities equal to those of the children of the well-to-do, schools simply "reproduce and reinforce social-class differences in-stead" (p. 75). In other words, children of the advantaged have access to higher quality education than do children of the disadvantaged; hence, they are provided with the skills they need to maintain their position in society.

With their heavy reliance on ability grouping and tracking, schools in the United States typically place children from families in low-income brackets in low-ability groups and vocational tracks. Without preparation in rigor-ous academic subjects these children will have a harder time meeting the admission requirements of prestigious 4-year colleges and universities. They tend to drop out of school at higher rates than their more affluent counter-parts, and, if they do enroll in institutions of higher education, their choices are limited to heavily vocational community colleges and less prestigious local universities. Hence, they have a harder time breaking out of their lower so-cioeconomic status, and society continues to be controlled by the powerful and their offspring.

Spring (2002) further argues that the wealth of the community deter-mines the quality of the schools. In affluent communities, residents have the means and the voice to demand excellent schools. Students prepared in such schools generally will reach higher levels of educational attainment and earn higher incomes as adults than those from poor communities. Children reared in communities where there is little wealth attend low-performing schools, have lower levels of educational success, and will, on average, earn less over the course of their lives. It then follows that rather than serving to equalize educational opportunity and reform society, schools in the United States tend to do an excellent job of maintaining the status quo.

Class and Culture. Class also is inextricably linked to culture, with refer-ence to the arts, and often determines one's access to or comfort level with respect to high and low, or popular, culture (Erickson, 1997). Whereas those in the elite upper and upper-middle classes may unself-consciously enjoy art museums, symphony concerts, theater, and ballet, working-class individu-als may not feel comfortable or even welcome at such sites or events. The aspect of Nashville's culture under consideration here, country music, while it has broad popular appeal, tends to be associated with so-called low cul-ture, which is the realm of "ordinary people." It often is dismissed or ridi-culed as "redneck" music unworthy of serious analysis by the intellectual community. It might be argued that the stigma attached to country music may stem more from its humble origins than from any serious analysis of its merits as a form of artistic expression.

As elements of diversity, class and race often go hand in hand, with Whites largely constituting the middle and upper classes, and Blacks and other racial groups linked in the public perception with poverty and low socioeconomic status. Of course, these stereotypes are just that, and, in the history of the city of Nashville, it was poor Whites and educated Blacks who were largely responsible in the 1950s and 1960s for changing and enriching both the local and national culture and setting the standard for righting the wrongs of centuries of injustice.

NASHVILLE'S MULTICULTURAL HISTORY: AN OVERVIEW

FOCUS QUESTIONS

How have people from my community shaped the history
of the United States?
How has my community contributed to the cultural life
of the United States?

Although the story of Nashville often is told in terms of Black and White, it is a city with many prominent cultural groups, and it is growing ever more diverse over time. A recent publication for tourists (Kinnard, 2002) features stories on entertainers and sports figures of color and lists events throughout the calendar year that highlight the community's multicultural flavor. Its summary of the history of Nashville highlights not only the African American community, but also those of its Hispanic Americans, Asian Americans, and Native Americans.

Nashville's Diverse Population

Like so many other states, Tennessee owes its name to Native Americans. The name's origins can be traced to a Cherokee town, Tannassee or Tanasi, which served as one of the group's capitals (Satz, 1979). Today Native Americans represent Nashville's smallest minority group, less than 1% of the population, but in recent years their ranks have been increasing. One of the fastest growing racial groups is Asian Americans, comprising largely immigrants and refugees from countries wracked by the wars of the past century—Cambodia, Laos, and Vietnam. The city's high-profile restaurant scene clearly reflects their presence (Kinnard, 2002). Another rapidly expanding group is made up of Hispanic Americans with roots in Mexico, Puerto Rico, Cuba, and Central and South America. The Hispanic Americans of Nashville currently are concentrating on education and economic initiatives to improve their standard of living and draw attention to their varied and distinctive cultures.

The diversity of contemporary Nashville is highlighted in the Multicultural Sampler section of *The African American Guide to Nashville* (Kinnard, 2002). The significance of this feature is that it calls attention to the fact that while Nashville has long been recognized as a city of Whites and Blacks, it, like so many other communities across the nation, populated by individuals from many racial and ethnic groups. They all share a common home while they take pride in and celebrate their cultural identities.

The African American Presence in Nashville

Despite its growing diversity, by far the most prominent minority group in Nashville continues to be African Americans, who constitute close to 27% of the population of Davidson County. It is members of this cultural group who left an indelible mark on U.S. history through their leadership in the nation's civil rights struggle of the 1950s and 1960s. This was the continuation of a tradition of activism and pride that developed in Nashville in the hopeful years following the Civil War, even in the face of the repression of the Jim Crow laws.

The Early Years. As noted in the brochure for a tour of African American sites of historical interest in the city (Paine & Lovett, 1991), the presence of Blacks in Nashville dates back to the founding of the community in 1748. French fur traders had built an outpost to facilitate commerce with Native Americans of the area, but the first permanent settlement was not established until 1779 when James Robertson and a group of settlers from North Carolina built a stockade that became Fort Nashborough, so named to honor Revolutionary War hero General Francis Nash (Metropolitan Historical Commission, 2002). Among the eight individuals who accompanied Robertson as he staked claim to the land was an African American, and several slave families were included in the 60 or so that made up the Donelson party of new settlers to the area. Although most of the Blacks in early Nashville were slaves, between 15 and 20% were free and could vote in local elections until 1835 (Paine & Lovett, 1991). By then, their growing numbers represented a threat to the institution of slavery, and their rights were greatly restricted (Tennessee State Museum, *Free Blacks*).

Nashville's Black Community in the 19th Century. As free individuals, the Blacks of Nashville retained private property, including a number of service-oriented businesses. One, Robert "Black Bob" Renfro (or Renfroe), oversaw a tavern where Tennessee's future resident of note, Andrew Jackson, was a frequent guest (Paine & Lovett, 1991). Another, Sara Estell, was a caterer who ran an ice cream parlor and provided refreshments for the annual firemen's celebrations in Nashville. Prior to the Civil War, the free Blacks of Nashville were concentrated in the Cedar Street area near Capitol Hill, where they established schools and Black-operated establishments to serve the needs of the residents of the neighborhood. By 1860 there were about 7,000 free Blacks in Tennessee overall. A few were quite prosperous and were themselves slaveholders (Tennessee State Museum, *Free Blacks*).

Despite the presence of a number of free Blacks in Tennessee, among them some notable residents of Nashville, the vast majority of African Americans in the state were not free. On the eve of the Civil War, about one fourth of Tennessee's population, or 275,000 individuals, were slaves, and the state had become a distribution center for the slave trade. Most were agricultural workers who lived on farms and plantations, although some resided in towns. Their culture was derived from West Africa, but there were some Black churches in Nashville that were affiliated with Protestant Christianity, including two Methodist Episcopal congregations (West, 1998). Before the fear and tightening of restrictions with respect to slavery that developed after Nat Turner's insurrection in 1831, there were a number of antislavery societies in Tennessee.

Nashville had evolved into a prosperous community during the first half of the 19th century, and by 1843 was made the permanent capital of Tennessee. However, the Civil War would transform the capital from a thriving city of about 14,000 residents into an area of occupation. Its strategic location on the Cumberland River as well as its recently constructed railroad rendered it valuable to the Union Army, which occupied it from the winter of 1862 until the end of the war (West, 1998). In 1864, the Confederate Army launched there one of its last aggressive campaigns, the Battle of Nashville, but met with defeat. The Union troops fired the opening volleys from Fort Negley, which had been constructed 2 years earlier with the help of a number of African American workers (Metropolitan Historical Commission, 2002; West, 1998). A display in the Tennessee State Museum entitled *The Black Experience in the Civil War: The Black Soldier* emphasizes both the significant contributions of the approximately 200,000 Blacks in the Union Army overall and the segregation of their units. The presentation incorporates primary sources, including volunteer enlistment papers. Those who lost their lives in the battles fought on Tennessee soil were buried in the National Cemetery in Nashville (Paine & Lovett, 1991).

During the Civil War period, the Black population of Nashville tripled, and, after the conflict ended, the city became a center of the postwar civil rights movement in the state (Paine & Lovett, 1991). The city rebounded as business and industry picked up, and education became a primary concern. In 1866, the first private college for the education of Blacks, Fisk University, was opened (West, 1998). The following year, the State Colored Men's Conventions and the local chapter of the Equal Rights League were established to champion the rights of Blacks. African American males were granted the right to vote in 1867, and a Black was elected to the city council the next year. In the period after the Civil War and prior to the institutionalization of Jim Crow laws and policies in the late 1880s, a number of African American men were elected to local and county offices. In 1873, Sampson Keeble of Nashville became the first Black to serve in the Tennessee General Assembly.

The Black population of the city continued to increase, and the number of educational institutions established for the advancement of African Americans grew as well. Central Tennessee College, later renamed Walden University, opened its doors in 1867, and Meharry Medical College was established in 1876 (Paine & Lovett, 1991). Fisk University struggled financially, but the college's Jubilee Singers sprang to its rescue with the launching of a series of tours to raise funds to help keep it going. Their work contributed to Nashville's growing reputation as a center for Black religious music. A number of Black churches in the city were founded during the period, and, as Paine and Lovett (1991) note, they have continued to be a mainstay of the community. James C. Napier, a Black lawyer and city councilor, was appointed to a high position in the U.S. Treasury Department by President William Howard Taft. The number of businesses owned by local Blacks increased, especially along Charlotte Avenue.

Nashville's Blacks in the Early 20th Century. As the 20th century began, a number of key institutions with roots in the African American community in Nashville were established and added to the economic base and cultural richness of the city. Among these were banks, publishing houses, parks, and institutions of higher learning. These reflected both the character of Nashville in general and the fact that, because of the limitations imposed by segregation laws and customs, Blacks had to establish their own such institutions in order to enjoy the services that Whites took for granted. There were a number of notable firsts among these establishments (Paine & Lovett, 1991). The first Black-owned bank in the state, Citizens, which was originally the One Cent Savings Bank, opened its doors in 1904, survived the upheavals of the Great Depression, and is thought to be the oldest such minority-owned financial institution in the country (West, 1998). One of its founders, Reverend Richard Henry Boyd, a former slave, also created the National Baptist Publishing Board to disseminate religious materials for members of the National Baptist Convention. Another Nashville first with ties to its African American community was Hadley Park, a 34-acre parcel of land originally belonging to plantation owner John L. Hadley. After the Civil War,

Hadley worked to help former slaves of the region adapt to their changed status, and, in 1912, the park was opened to provide a recreational site for African Americans. Hadley Park is thought to be the first municipally owned park for African Americans. A few years earlier, a private park for Blacks was opened near Greenwood Cemetery by Preston Taylor, a former slave who had served as a drummer for the Union during the Civil War and later went on to become a successful leader in business and religious circles (Lovett, 1999; West, 1998). The Greenwood Recreational Park for Negroes was the site of the annual State Colored Fair, a popular recreational event for Blacks in the region.

In keeping with Nashville's reputation as an educational center, and perhaps to remedy the fact that Tennessee was the only southern state at the time that did not have a publicly supported university for African Americans, the legislature established the Tennessee Agricultural and Industrial State Normal School in 1912 on a section of the Hadley Plantation (West, 1998). During the 1920s, through the combined fund-raising efforts of Nashville's Black community, business interests, and state legislature, the school was enlarged and enhanced. Tennessee A & I State merged with the University of Tennessee's Nashville campus in 1968 and was renamed Tennessee State University. Among its roster of famous graduates are Olympic athlete Wilma Rudolph and media giant Oprah Winfrey.

Nashville's Black Elites. In his analysis of the African American community in Nashville, Lovett (1999) underscores the significance and complexity of the city's Black elite. Although not large in number, this group was present in the community's antebellum period and persisted well into the 20th century. Consisting at first of free Blacks and a few slaves, the elite Black community sought to distance itself from the masses of ordinary slave laborers and developed an uneasy alliance with upper-class Whites in a system that protected both from violence and caused both some guilt. After the Civil War, it was from the ranks of Nashville's Black elite that many of its community leaders were drawn. In the late 19th century as the Jim Crow system became more rigid, Nashville's upper-class Blacks forged stronger ties with poor African Americans, although largely to ensure that they would support Black elite businesses. The Black elites at the same time kept peace with the White community by adopting the accommodationist policies of Booker T. Washington. According to Lovett (1999): "After Washington's death in 1915 the younger blacks began to resist racism and discrimination by rekindling the 1880s strategies of public protest and confrontation" (p. xv). In the 1920s, cultural pride became more apparent among certain members of Nashville's young African American population, and the city's Black colleges reflected their concerns by offering courses and programs highlighting their history and involvement in the arts. Access to higher education was, according to

Lovett, one of the principal reasons that, by the 1930s, the lines that had separated Blacks into distinct social classes were becoming ever less rigid and discernible.

Nashville's Place in the Civil Rights Movement

It was largely due to Nashville's Black student community, some native Nashvilleans, and others from different regions of the country that the city became such a moving force in the civil rights movement of the 1960s. This is not surprising considering that education had been central to the city's history and that for its African Americans traditionally had represented a means to progress.

Nashville's Early Desegregation Efforts. Shortly after the U.S. Supreme Court issued its landmark *Brown v. Board of Education* decision in 1954, Nashville officials began to consider how to respond concerning the city's segregated school system (Fleming, 1998). As officials deliberated, the process of coming up with a desegregation plan was speeded along by the actions of the city's African American community when Alfred Z. Kelley, father of a Nashville high school student, filed a class action suit seeking to make admission to the community's schools open to all students regardless of race. The court's decision, in favor of Kelley, resulted in the board of education's Nashville Plan for integration. Employing a moderate strategy, the plan called for a grade by grade approach beginning in 1957 with first grade.

Desegregation of the city's public schools got off to a rocky start when, during the first year of implementation, a wing of the recently integrated Hattie Cotton Elementary School was destroyed by a bomb. Residents of Nashville, both Black and White, were shocked that such a violent act could disrupt the city's plan to comply with federal law and integrate its public schools. Critics would charge that the plan itself was inadequate in that it had "become resigned to a mechanical shifting of bodies but not to the much larger task of changing attitudes" (Fleming, 1998, p. 445). Calm was eventually returned to the city, and the much-disputed Nashville Plan became a prototype for other southern cities, despite dissatisfaction on the part of African American community leaders and its only moderate success in achieving the goals of desegregation.

The College Students Take Charge. It would be the influence of Nashville's college students on the city's overall desegregation and the success of their brand of activism that ultimately would spread far beyond the city limits and leave an indelible mark on the national civil rights movement. According to the interpretation of the critically acclaimed PBS television series *Eyes on the Prize*, a prime mover in the nonviolent student movement was James

Lawson, a pacifist divinity student who studied at Vanderbilt University in Nashville in the 1950s and was jailed during the Korean War for his refusal to serve in the armed forces (Williams, 1987). After his parole, he went to India as a missionary, where he learned about Gandhi and his strategy of nonviolent resistance. Lawson met Martin Luther King, Jr., during the Montgomery bus boycott and was urged by King to disseminate Gandhi's methods among the civil rights workers of the South. Lawson began to organize workshops to train civil rights activists in nonviolent resistance in both Nashville and other locales, most significantly at southern Black college campuses.

One of the students who enrolled in a workshop in Nashville was Diane Nash, a Chicago native who was studying at Fisk University. A midwesterner, Nash did not have the same context from which to view segregation that some of her southern classmates did, and she found herself drawn to Lawson's workshops (Williams, 1987). She recalled being engaged in role plays involving fictional scenarios at lunch counters and stores that soon would become realities as the students who were being trained in the mechanisms of nonviolent resistance by Lawson and his followers moved from the classrooms to the streets. Nash joined forces with another student, John Lewis, an Alabaman studying at the American Baptist Theological Seminary in Nashville, and together they would form the nucleus of an organization that came to be known as the Nashville Student Movement.

During the winter of 1960, the students began the first of a number of sit-ins at the city's downtown stores. In one incident, a group of White teenagers attacked the demonstrators, and the Nashville police were called to the scene. When they arrived, they placed the protesters under arrest, but before they had secured them all in the police wagon, a second group of students and then a third took their places at the lunch counter. In April of the same year, Nash was involved in a historic demonstration on the steps of Nashville's city hall during which she defiantly asked the mayor, Ben West, if he thought it wrong for Blacks in the city to be the objects of discrimination at lunch counters and to be refused service at the stores where they shopped. When the mayor agreed that it was wrong, a critical point had been reached in the movement, from which there was no turning back (Fleming, 1998). Now the Nashville merchants, who had been pressing for a settlement, could integrate their lunch counters and blame the mayor for their decision (Williams, 1987). Martin Luther King went to Nashville during the protests not so much to celebrate and provide inspiration for the continued efforts of the students, but, as he said, "to gain inspiration from the great movement that has taken place in this community" (Williams, 1987, p. 140). In May, six of the stores that had been targeted by the demonstrators began to serve Black customers. Galvanized by their victory at the lunch counters, the students went on to protest at other businesses that still refused Blacks services, with a series of sleep-ins, stand-ins, and more sit-ins. Accompanying the student activism was a boycott of downtown businesses by the African American community in Nashville. These combined actions were effective and provided a model for other cities struggling with desegregation in Tennessee and elsewhere.

In an interesting side note, the women of Nashville, both Black and White, have been credited with helping the college students succeed in their crusade to integrate the city's business district because they "protected them during demonstrations, provided transportation, appeared in courtrooms, raised bail for arrested demonstrators, and sent food to the jails" (Perry, 2002). A tradition of working together evidently had been established when women of both races served as volunteers for various church, public service, and charitable organizations, among them the Girl Scouts, a group that had worked for an integrated board in Nashville since the early 1950s.

Learning Activities. The civil rights movement as played out in Nashville provides a number of rich opportunities for teachers in the region seeking to link local history to the national scene as well as for educators in other communities looking for ways to bring the story of the movement alive to their students. Teachers whose schools are located in the Nashville area can provide background knowledge through field trips to such places of historical interest as the Tennessee State Museum, which features a video presentation on African American history and displays highlighting the institution of slavery, the role of Blacks in the development of the state, and their unique contributions during the Civil War. Another field trip possibility linked to the history of African Americans in the Nashville area could involve taking classes on walking tours of the historic sites mentioned earlier, such as Citizens Bank, Fort Negley, Fisk University, and Meharry Medical College. Another stop could be the First Baptist Church, once located on Capitol Hill and presently situated on James Robertson Parkway. This was the site where many of the protesters in the Nashville student movement were trained in the techniques of nonviolent direct action and where they subsequently celebrated their victories (Paine & Lovett, 1991). As an alternative to teacher-planned field trips, professional tours stressing Black history in Nashville are available through the Convention and Visitors Bureau.

In tandem with field trips dedicated to providing students with information concerning the local history of Blacks in Nashville and their part in the civil rights movement of the 1960s, or for those elsewhere teaching about the period, lessons incorporating research, role plays, and simulations can be designed around the significant events of the era. A context can be provided through viewing and discussion of the PBS television series *Eyes on the Prize*, which includes footage in the "Ain't Scared of Your Jails" segment on the workshop training and interviews with key figures in the Nashville demonstrations. Middle and high school students can investigate the lives and contributions of such key figures in the sit-in movement as Diane Nash, James Lawson, and John Lewis, who went on to become a member of the U.S. Congress; present their findings in panel and seminar formats; and reflect on how they might react if they found themselves in similar situations.

For younger students, role plays involving dilemmas such as going to a store, hotel, or movie theater and being refused service, can be useful in achieving objectives in the affective domain if students are encouraged to express their feelings or write about them in journals as debriefing exercises (see Lesson Plan 3.1). The story of the Girl Scouts in Nashville and their struggle to organize and then later integrate should appeal to younger students as well. The Girl Scout Council of Cumberland Valley named one of its camps after Josephine Holloway, a reformer who organized the first African American Girl Scout troop in Nashville, and currently maintains the Josephine Holloway Collection and Gallery in her honor. The Council could be contacted for information and/or guest speakers to help students learn about this chapter in Nashville's social history.

If historical content, critical thinking, and a student-centered approach are the classroom teacher's goals, a mock trial is a worthwhile and challenging activity. A case students could research and recreate related to the civil rights movement in Nashville is *Kelley v. Board of Education*, a 1955 legal milestone that led to the implementation of the controversial Nashville Plan for the gradual desegregation of the city's schools and served as a model for other communities in similar situations. Another topic that lends itself to student-centered activities is the sit-in movement, which trained participants in nonviolent direct action and succeeded in opening up the lunch counters and other services to the Blacks of the region.

Overall, the local history of the African American community in Nashville provides valuable perspectives on a number of important social studies themes, among them culture, conflict, protest, and change. Teachers living in the area as well as those throughout the nation can draw on the history of the city's Blacks to highlight valuable lessons about race and social change in the United States.

Nashville and Country Music: Songs of the People

One of Nashville's handsomest new attractions is the state-of-the-art Country Music Hall of Fame and Museum, which opened its doors in 2001. Located on Fifth Avenue in the center of the downtown district, this 40,000-square-foot complex includes an interactive museum, live entertainment, a restaurant, and an archive. Its eye-catching facade cleverly resembles a piano keyboard, while its well-appointed interior conveys to the museum visitor the impression that little expense was spared in the design, construction, and operation of this world-class institution. It is the successor to a more modest version that

Country Music Hall of Fame and Museum, Nashville, Tennessee.

opened to the public in 1967 in the city's Music Row district to pay homage to the music, entertainers, history, and artifacts of the city's most endearing contribution to popular culture. Ironically, even the less glamorous earlier version of the Country Music Hall of Fame might have seemed a bit off-putting to the original singers of simple songs of the people, the founders of what would become the country music phenomenon.

The Rise of Country Music. Appropriately nicknamed Music City, U.S.A., Nashville owes its rise as the center of the country music industry to radio station WSM and its hugely popular Grand Ole Opry (Country Music Foundation, 1994). Originally called the WSM Barn Dance in the 1920s, by the end of World War II, the Opry had become *the* place for aspiring and established stars of what would become the country music industry to display their talents. Nashville's long-established insurance houses originally provided the capital for the burgeoning music enterprises, which soon were bankrolled by entrepreneurs from outside of the city's local business interests (Doyle, 1985). The so-called "Nashville Sound" emerged in the 1950s and is seen as largely responsible for the success of modern country music (West, 1998). Recording studios, publishing houses, and talent and licensing agents soon congregated on Sixteenth and Seventeenth Avenues, a section of the city dubbed Music Row for its identification with the country music industry.

Thus, country music and its support mechanisms helped shape the contemporary city's physical structure as well as leave an indelible stamp on its local and national image.

Enduring Themes in Country Music. A sometimes overlooked aspect of diversity concerns rural Whites, who, although not a racial minority, have been exploited and neglected by the powerful in ways similar to the manner in which people of color in the United States often have been treated. Song has long been an effective medium through which country people have expressed their identity—their beliefs, concerns, and struggles. Seminal work on the songs, their composers, and singers was conducted by Dorothy Horstman and presented in *Sing Your Heart Out, Country Boy*, originally published in 1969 and revised in 1975. Among the major song categories Horstman identifies with country music are three pertinent to multicultural education. These include songs with a religious focus, those that comment on the contemporary social scene, and those celebrating and lamenting the lives of working people.

With respect to the theme of religion in country music, Horstman (1969/1975) makes the point that "the country gospel repertory predates, and probably will outlive, any other category of country songs" (p. 32). Such music has deep roots in the evangelical Protestantism of the American South. It assumes that its listeners are believers, and it both celebrates the glories of God and inspires the sinner to do better. Most of the performers Horstman interviewed for her book claimed that religious music was central to their upbringing. Many of the individual performers and groups associated with popular gospel songs are now enshrined in the Country Music Hall of Fame and Museum.

Another enduring tradition in country music, with indirect connections to the religious component, involves lyrics that express the sentiments of common people with respect to current events and issues. An immensely popular contemporary example is Alan Jackson's "Where Were You (When the World Stopped Turning)," which summarizes a variety of reactions to the tragedy of 9/11. Horstman (1969/1975) notes that such songs are typically middle of the road, express resistance to change, celebrate White southern solidarity against a hostile outside world, and sum up the reactions of poor people to the events of the day. She argues that they stress the virtues of the honest poor in the face of the shallowness and hypocrisy of modern society. Songs such as "Okie from Muskogee" by Merle Haggard, and Roy Edward Burris and Bill Anderson's "Po' Folks" are typical examples.

Another fertile area for analysis that emerges in the lyrics of country music relates to a major theme of this chapter, social class. While both religious music and the songs of social significance clearly identify with the sentiments of poor people, another specific category of lyrics revolving around the life of the ordinary worker poignantly highlights the issue of class in the United States. Horstman (1969/1975) has collected a number of lyrics in her chapter "The Working Man," which she subtitles "These Hard-Workin' Hands," that deal with trying to eke out a decent living as a farmer, mill worker, laborer, miner, or trucker. She notes that while these songs lament the harshness of life, they are not bitter; and while they appeal to the poor and working class, they are "virtually free from class consciousness" (p. 302). This is a provocative finding that adds dimensions to the portrait of rural Whites that country music paints.

Overall, the centrality of country music to the contemporary image of the city of Nashville and the presence of the Country Music Hall of Fame and Museum within the community offer unique resources for social studies teachers in the area who seek to explore social and economic issues with their students. At the same time, the music itself can be a vehicle to promote a clearer understanding of the perspective of a sometimes overlooked group in the United States—the rural poor. Because the group associated with traditional country music shares many of the characteristics of the mainstream in that its members are largely White Protestants, they are not commonly identified with diversity. Yet they share many of the distinctions held by minority groups, including victimization, discrimination, and social solidarity.

Learning Activities. Lessons and projects involving the songs, their composers, and performers, utilizing the resources of the Nashville community, can help students understand more about class issues and the people from their local region who have celebrated and lamented the lives of otherwise unsung individuals through the medium of music.

A class assignment revolving around the theme of religious diversity could include a field trip to the Country Music Hall of Fame and Museum for students in the Nashville area seeking to conduct research into the lives and religious songs of such artists as A. P. Carter, the Louvin Brothers, Merle Travis, and Hank Williams. They might analyze the lyrics of such classics as "Can the Circle Be Unbroken?," "I Am a Pilgrim," and "I Saw the Light," to determine the values expressed in the songs. A follow-up, teacher-led discussion as to whether this music still reflects the rural southern communities with which it commonly is associated would be an appropriate closing activity for such a project. Teachers in other areas of the South and in various other regions of the nation where country music forms part of the cultural identity could design similar projects using print and Internet resources in place of the field trip. A caveat: Teachers designing lessons and units addressing religious themes must be careful to stress to students, parents, and school authorities that such exercises are intellectual in nature and do not seek to promote or to denigrate any group's religious beliefs. Just as one cannot understand the essence of the Pilgrim and Puritan colonists in New England without examining their religious motives, one cannot appreciate the essence and dimensions of country music without acknowledging its religious origins. Unfortunately, social studies teachers often risk being asked to justify their curriculum choices when they decide to include religious topics, so they must be prepared to defend their decisions.

The topical/current events aspect of country music also lends itself to classroom applications that are particularly appropriate for secondary students. After identifying and analyzing a number of country songs that deal with the social scene, students could compose their own lyrics relating to contemporary events and/or commenting on values and areas in need of reform in their own communities at the present time.

Another interesting challenge for older students would be to examine the lyrics of a number of the songs concerning work and poverty and to speculate as to why they seem so lacking in radical calls for reform. What is it about the individuals who write such songs and the performers who popularize them, as well as the communities from which they hail, that fosters the strength and resignation that seem to characterize much of the country music revolving around the ordinary working person?

An analysis-based activity related to music enjoyed by people all over the United States as well as internationally and that grew from locales in Tennessee could involve a compare and contrast exercise examining the country music of Nashville, which is associated with rural Whites, and the blues of Memphis, which is linked to the Black community. Students could trace the origins of both, identify what they have in common, explain how they differ, and connect them to larger social issues.

The Country Music Hall of Fame and Museum in Nashville is a resource that can help students learn about and understand the history, artists, and themes of the genre. The museum offers a variety of educational programs as an integral component of its mission. While schools and families in the region can take advantage of these offerings via a field trip or family outing, the concept of a hall of fame and museum dedicated to preserving memories and celebrating contributions of notable individuals is one that knows no geographic bounds. It is one that also suggests numerous possibilities for educators, wherever they are located, to build lessons and units and to design projects highlighting local history and at the same time to promote multicultural understandings (see Project Plan 3.1).

CONCLUSIONS

As with Framingham, the first community highlighted in this book, Nashville, is at once an American city and a multicultural community, and it has been so from the start. In addition, Nashville, with its location in the mid-

South; its educational, religious, and cultural institutions, which promoted advances in civil rights; and its links to the country music industry, provides unique opportunities for teachers in the region to promote greater understanding of the multicultural elements of race and social class. African Americans formed the nucleus of the civil rights movement in Nashville and modeled the ways in which those who have been victimized can effect change. Nashville's country music, although now a lucrative component of the entertainment industry, expresses the concerns and longings of rural folk on the lower ends of the socioeconomic scale. Delving into the themes of race and social class through the lens of the local history of Nashville can foster pride in the community and an appreciation of its role as a force in social change and the popular culture of the United States in the second half of the 20th century.

Returning to the Focus Questions that open the chapter, we have seen that through its leadership in civil rights the city of Nashville helped shape the course of a movement that was one of the defining moments in the history of the nation in the 20th century. This reform centered on the question of race in America and was led by African Americans in a community that had a long tradition of Black involvement in important social and educational issues. The second Focus Question asks how the community contributed to the cultural life of the United States. Again we have seen that in the arts, an area often associated with cultural elites, people from Nashville and throughout the South forged new ground in self-expression through music that illustrates concerns and characteristics of a group whose voice often has been muffled in the multicultural dialogue, that of the rural working class. While not every community has had as distinctive an impact on the national identity as Nashville, teachers and students throughout the nation can ask the Focus Questions with respect to their own communities and may be surprised by the answers they uncover.

LESSON PLAN 3.1
DISCRIMINATION AT THE CLASS STORE

Grades 3–4

Suggested Length. Three class sessions of 45–60 minutes

National Standards for History **References (for grades K–4)**

Standard 2A. The student understands the history of his or her local community.

Voluntary National Content Standards in Economics **References**

Content Standard 1. Students will understand that: Productive resources are limited. Therefore, people cannot have all the goods and services they want; as a result, they must choose some things and give up others.

NCSS *Curriculum Guidelines for Multicultural Education* **References**

  8.0. The multicultural curriculum should help students understand that a conflict between ideals and realities always exists in human societies.
 17.0. The multicultural curriculum should help students to view and interpret events, situations, and conflict from diverse ethnic and cultural perspectives and points of view.

Prerequisite Knowledge. Students previously will have learned about some of the heroes of the civil rights movement, such as Rosa Parks and Martin Luther King, Jr.

Objectives. Students will be able to—

• Organize a school store to "sell" desired goods and services to classmates
• Discuss their feelings when refused service at a school store
• Illustrate what happened in Nashville when Blacks decided to protest unfair treatment at local stores and businesses
• Assess the effectiveness of direct action to bring about change
• Explain the vocabulary associated with Nashville's civil rights protests

Procedures: Day 1

Initiation

• Ask students to list some goods and services they want and need in school everyday.
• Tell them they will be setting up a "store" to buy and sell some of these products and services.

Development

- Give each student the same amount of teacher-made currency.
- Set prices of the student-identified goods and services (paper, markers, teacher's directions for activities, textbooks, grades for work completed, etc.).
- Divide students into groups to make signs for the store (one group may decide on a name and make a large sign to post at the classroom door, another may set up the service department at the teacher's desk, and a third may organize the supply corner) and to post prices for the goods and services.

Closing

- Have a representative of each group display and explain the signs students created.
- Inform students that tomorrow during social studies class they will be opening the new store and shopping for goods and services.

Procedures: Day 2

Initiation. Announce to students that today in social studies class goods and services that are necessary for the lesson will be purchased in the classroom store.

Development

- Divide the class into prearranged groups of three or four based on an arbitrary identifier (e.g., first initial of last names).
- Tell the students that they will be working together on projects about their community, and that they will receive grades on their work.
- Announce that all materials and instructions must be "purchased" with the currency they were given in yesterday's class.
- Proceed to have students purchase teacher-prepared handouts about Nashville's landmarks, poster paper, and markers for their projects from students who have been "hired" to staff the supply department of the class store.
- Next tell students that they must purchase the directions for their project from the teacher.
- Call preferred groups to the teacher's desk (e.g., only those whose last names begin with letters from the first half of the alphabet) and quietly provide explicit directions for making a poster of Nashville's landmarks, making sure that groups pay for the service.
- Ignore the other groups, and if they ask for your help refuse to give it to them even if they offer to pay for it.
- Circulate around and facilitate the preferred groups' work, giving suggestions and providing advice.

- After about 20 minutes, collect the work and ask students to write in their journals about how they felt about being denied/provided with a necessary service.

Closing

- Ask students to share their journal entries.
- Explain that tomorrow the class will be learning about a time when the people of Nashville faced just such a situation in their stores and businesses.

Procedures: Day 3

Initiation

- Review the activities of the previous days, including definitions of goods and services.
- Discuss the consequences of some students not being able to purchase necessary services from the teacher.
- Ask students what they might do if the situation had continued and some students were not given instructions or grades (e.g., tell their parents, complain to the principal, request to be transferred out of the class).

Development

- In a story format describe to students the conditions in Nashville's downtown district before lunch counters and other facilities were integrated, drawing comparisons with the class store experiment.
- Ask students what it is like today for people of different races who want to eat at a lunch counter, go to a movie, or use a restroom in the city of Nashville.
- Brainstorm what people who thought the situation in Nashville was unfair before integration might have done to bring about these changes.
- Put ideas on the board or on presentation paper (e.g., refuse to shop at the stores, complain to the mayor, write letters to newspapers).
- Tell students in story format about the efforts of Nashville's African American college students to organize sit-ins and the refusal of Black customers to shop at businesses that denied them equal service.
- Ask students to explain why such actions are effective in bringing about change.

Closing

- Ask students to compare the solutions they suggested with those that were used to integrate Nashville's businesses.
- Remind students of the role played by college students in bringing about change.

Assessment

- Informal assessment could involve observing students as they organize the store, participate in the buying and selling of class goods and services, and discuss the effectiveness of protest to bring about change.
- Student journal entries also will indicate their understanding of the concept of unfair treatment.
- A formal assessment could involve having students create a class mural of the Nashville sit-in movement, with the following sequence: people shopping in downtown Nashville before integration, the student protests and citizen boycotts, and people shopping in downtown Nashville after integration.
- Finish the posters students created of Nashville's landmarks when they were involved in the class store activity, but this time have the teacher review directions with everyone and provide time to make corrections and improvements.
- Another assessment piece could involve checking for student understanding of the vocabulary introduced in the 3-day activity: goods, services, sit-in, boycott, protest, integration, landmarks.

Adaptations. The first two parts of the lesson plan can be used without modification in any community located in a region of the country where a particular group has suffered discrimination(e.g., the Irish in Boston, the Poles in the Midwest, or the Chinese in the West) or when the teacher's objective is to have students understand how it feels to be mistreated for reasons over which people have little or no control (e.g., race, class, religion, gender, ethnicity, or language). The historical follow-up should trace the methods used by a victimized group to fight injustice and to reflect on the current status of its members.

PROJECT PLAN 3.1
NASHVILLE NOTABLES: A MULTICULTURAL HALL OF FAME

Grades 5–12

Description. This project involves the creation of a hall of fame highlighting individuals who have either contributed to the history of the community or lived in the community for a period of time and had an impact on national or world history. There are a number of ways to approach and implement such a project. The one that follows builds on the model of the Country Music Hall of Fame and Museum for inspiration and incorporates some of the elements of diversity highlighted in this chapter.

NCSS *Curriculum Guidelines for Multicultural Education* References

7.0. The curriculum should help students understand the totality of the experiences of ethnic and cultural groups in the United States.
21.0. The multicultural curriculum should make maximum use of experiential learning, especially local community resources.

Steps

• Using the Country Music Hall of Fame and Museum Web site (www.halloffame. org) or after a field trip to the site, students will plan to create a hall of fame in their school dedicated to important individuals from their community.
• They will decide on where to place the hall of fame (in a corner of the classroom, outside in the corridor, in the school library, foyer, or other appropriate space) and on what elements will constitute the display. An alternative presentation could be designed using PowerPoint or other computer-generated programs.
• Using print and Internet resources, students will identify a number of notable individuals from the city of Nashville who might be candidates for the hall of fame.
• The teacher should encourage students to include members of various racial and ethnic groups as well as women, religious leaders, and people from all social classes. The list could include the following individuals highlighted in this chapter or others in *The African-American History of Nashville, Tennessee, 1780– 1930: Elites and Dilemmas* (Lovett, 1999) and various other print and Internet sources: James Robertson, John Donelson, Ann Rodgers Grundy, James K. Polk, Robert Renfro, Andrew Jackson, Sara Estell, Sampson Keeble, James C. Napier, Reverend Richard Henry Boyd, John L. Hadley, Jubilee Singers, Anne Dallas Dudley, Preston Taylor, Joel Owsley Cheek, Edward Emerson Barnard, William Edmondson, James Lawson, Diane Nash, Kelly Miller Smith, Wilma Rudolph, and Oprah Winfrey.

- Students will draw up a set of criteria for election into the hall of fame. They should consider an individual's achievements, length of residency in the city, and any other characteristics they identify as necessary for election to the hall of fame. They also could decide whether a candidate must be accepted by a simple, two-thirds, or three-quarters majority or whether the decision must be unanimous.
- Students then will be assigned, through a random procedure, to conduct in-depth research on the candidates. They will be required to write essays or short research papers on their assigned candidates.
- After students have researched the candidates, they will present their findings in an oral format and vote on whether or not to induct the individuals into the hall of fame, using the guidelines they established earlier.
- Students then will create their displays using traditional artistic and print media or computer-based presentation programs. They might model them on those in the Country Music Hall of Fame and Museum or design their own.
- Students also will decide on an appropriate way to showcase their displays and on how to conduct the induction. They might hold an induction ceremony during which they could take on the roles of the inductees in costume and invite parents, other classes, and/or school administrators. Invitations could be designed and distributed. Local media might be informed of the event.

Assessment. Students can be assessed at various points during the project through grades for their essays involving research on individual candidates for the hall of fame, for their presentations in defense of their assigned notables, for the creativity of their displays, and for the effectiveness of their role-play characterizations.

Adaptations. A project to create a hall of fame to honor diverse individuals who have made a difference or accomplished significant achievements can be adapted to any community, using local and Internet resources. The keys to ensuring that the project is consistent with the goals of multicultural education involve both the selection of diverse inductees and the empowerment of students in the decision-making.

La Survivance: The Struggle to Preserve Ethnic Identity and Language in Woonsocket, Rhode Island

DEFINED BY its location on the Blackstone River, where the American industrial revolution was born, the city of Woonsocket, Rhode Island, presents a poignant example of a community populated in the 19th and early 20th centuries by countless immigrants from a rural agrarian society, in this case Quebec, who struggled on the one hand to find economic security through work in the mills and on the other to preserve their cultural identity—*la survivance*. With their French Canadian heritage firmly rooted in language and religion and with new roles for women and children based on their need to work outside the home, the Quebec habitants of Woonsocket provide insights into a number of aspects of diversity. Theirs is a unique story, yet not completely unlike those of immigrants from other places and other times seeking a better life in the harsh climate of America's industrial cities.

To provide background for interpreting the history of Woonsocket's French Canadian population, the chapter begins with a discussion of ethnicity and language as categories of diversity. The two elements are paired because they are so closely identified with each other, and they are so critical to cultural identity—something the newcomers from Quebec fought so hard to preserve. The Focus Questions that open the section on the history of Woonsocket, which centers largely on the story of the Quebecois habitants, explore the relationship among ethnicity, language, and identity, and ask whether an immigrant group can maintain its culture and at the same time adapt to life in the United States. These questions are targeted at Woonsocket, yet they can be applied to any community with a significant immigrant population. Although the historical narrative underscores ethnicity and language, it also highlights religion and unionism, two themes that will be explored in greater length in later chapters, because no account of the French Canadian settlement in Woonsocket would be complete without addressing these institutions. The lesson plans that conclude the chapter deal with the process of change, both personal, due to movement from one place to another, and community, as neighborhoods evolve over time.

ETHNIC IDENTITY AND LANGUAGE AS CATEGORIES OF DIVERSITY

More than any of the other categories of diversity explored in this book, ethnic identity and language are inextricably linked, at least among newcomers to the United States from nations where the natives do not speak English. Language sets the immigrant apart from both those who do not share the same ethnic heritage and those who do but who have been assimilated into the dominant culture and hence are English speakers. How one communicates verbally is at the heart of one's cultural identity, yet language and ethnicity are obviously not one and the same. An individual may have been born and educated in the United States and be fluent in Standard American English yet still have a strong ethnic identity associated with another nation. Although the story of the French Canadians of Woonsocket and their fight to maintain their cultural identity partly by continuing to speak French and to insist that their children do so as well is one in which language and ethnic identity are clearly interwoven, such is not always the case. Some groups have been able to shed one, their native language, without losing the other, their ethnic identity. Following is a separate look at the two aspects of diversity, ethnic identity and language, that are clearly distinct, but so often linked as they are in Woonsocket, Rhode Island, and in its French Canadian settlers.

The Character of Ethnic Identity

Just as it is difficult to clearly define a number of the other types of diversity examined in this book, the term *ethnic identity* does not lend itself easily to a universally accepted explanation. Since the 1960s when social scientists became more committed to studying and valuing the diverse heritages of those who live in the United States, many professionals have attempted to arrive at a satisfactory definition of ethnic identity (Gollnick & Chinn, 2002). While an ethnic group usually is thought of as those individuals who share a common national origin, ethnic identity may involve having continued loyalty or ties to a nation or place after one has emigrated to another. Some authors include race and religion or even social class and gender as integral aspects of ethnic identity, but in this chapter the narrower concept, emphasizing national origins only, is applied.

Members of ethnic groups in the United States, whether or not they live in close proximity to others of the same group, may have a sense of cohesiveness that draws them together in spirit if not in daily face-to-face contact. They may enjoy strong social networks maintained through family, friends, and recreational and work relationships in the United States, and, among recently arrived immigrants, through frequent contacts with those living in the nation of origin. Such networks may weaken over time as successive generations become acculturated and often lose their strong sense of ethnic identity. Still, when natural disasters or other tragic events strike the country of one's ancestors, he/she may be moved to contribute to relief efforts or to lobby U.S. government officials to provide support (Gollnick & Chinn, 2002). However, it is difficult to generalize about the solidarity of members of various ethnic groups. Those who have arrived recently from another country may have little in common beyond their names and holiday traditions with members of the same national group whose families have been living in the United States for a long time. Nonetheless, there may be cultural threads inextricably tied to one's ways of living and interpreting events, of which a second- or third-generation American may be unaware. Yet they subtly determine how individuals make sense of and react to the world around them.

Common Aspects of Varied Cultures. In her analysis of how culture impacts the classroom, Clayton (2003) describes a number of factors that are common to all groups whatever their size and however different they may be in outward characteristics. She explains that culture is a pervasive template that affects how we act, what we believe, and the ways that we interpret the world around us. Culture is shared and systematically passed along from one generation to another. Yet, Clayton reminds us, despite its generational nature, culture is learned as we are raised by our families and interact with others of the same cultural group. An interesting and sometimes problematic aspect of culture is that it may not even be recognized or discussed among members of the same group. Clayton underscores the point that "our own culture is often unknown to us" (p. 17). She also notes that despite its pervasiveness, culture is not static and thus evolves and takes on new dimensions over time. Her point, that the foundation of our individual identities rests on our culture and as such should not be dismissed or overlooked in our classrooms, is most relevant to the experience of the French Canadian settlers in Woonsocket, Rhode Island. For, as we shall see, these proud and tenacious immigrants and their offspring waged many a battle to ensure that their heritage would not be forgotten in the schools, churches, and social organizations of their new community.

Native Reactions to the Culturally "Different." Over time, the ways that established or mainstream American society has reacted to and its expectations for immigrants from ethnic groups generally perceived to be "different" have varied and represent the political and social climate of different historical eras. Numerous social scientists have developed categories to pigeonhole the various theories related to how immigrants are expected to behave, and those of sociologist Vincent Parrillo (1994) are representative. Parrillo uses a framework with three distinct approaches to how those he calls "ethnically different" (p. 55) people should fit into the larger society. He notes that the different approaches suggest or mandate either assimilation, amalgamation, or accommodation.

The assimilationists argue that the goal for newcomers or those who are "different" should be to "Americanize" as quickly as possible and become similar to the mainstream in their values, lifestyles, and culture. Clearly, the underlying assumption is that the cultural characteristics that the ethnically different should adopt are those of the Anglo American majority—the group that broke away from England and subsequently founded the United States in the late 18th century. Unlike the assimilationists, amalgamationists view the prototypical American not as simply a carbon copy of Anglo ancestors, but as a hybrid comprising the cultural characteristics of the many diverse ethnic groups that have populated the nation over the years. The common metaphor for the amalgamation theory is the melting pot, a concept still held dear by some but that has fallen out of favor among many educators and most multiculturalists. For them, the more acceptable approach to ethnic difference and the one closely aligned with the concept of ethnic identity to be explored in our look at Woonsocket, Rhode Island, is cultural pluralism.

Cultural pluralism begins with the recognition that the population of the United States is and has always been made up of many diverse peoples. Different ethnic and racial groups may and do maintain their cultural characteristics, but this does not mean that they must be oppositional. Parrillo (1994) includes cultural pluralism in his accommodation category. Within this framework, the ethnically different may maintain their defining cultural characteristics but still interact in positive ways with others in the society and be treated fairly and equitably. Sleeter and Grant (1994) point out that despite the tenacity of some ethnic communities in clinging to their distinct cultural identities, there is also an American culture that is to some extent shared by most residents. And some eventually will assimilate into the dominant group. However, in a nation as large as the United States with its immigrant tradition, both voluntary and involuntary, there will always be diversity. Attempts to wipe out all difference and force assimilation will not succeed and often will result in resentment and conflict.

Another universal aspect of ethnic identity, beyond its enduring quality, is the fact that it fosters a belief that one's own culture is at the center of all others and thus inherently superior to them; social scientists call this idea *ethnocentrism*. While this can lead to prejudice and group conflict, it is not necessarily deliberate or even recognized (Parrillo, 1994). Clayton (2003) explains that there are two sides to ethnocentrism. On the positive side is the fact that our very identities are grounded in the security of our belief that our ways are the best. They define who we are, what we value, and how we live. Ethnocentrism's negative side is the fact that it makes us unaware or dismissive of the cultural characteristics of those outside our own ethnic group. If we can come to recognize the fact that all cultural groups view their values as best and routinely pass them on to their offspring as part of the child rearing process, we can reduce some of the negative effects of ethnocentrism. Seeing the world through a cultural lens other than one's own is not easy, but multicultural educators have tried to foster this approach in students by encouraging them to view history, literature, and current events through multiple perspectives. Proud as we may be of our own ethnic identities, we can learn to value and appreciate those of groups outside our own.

Language and Identity

One of the most distinctive and divisive issues related to ethnic identity is the question of language. At the heart of our individual identities is the way that we communicate. Although it can be argued that much of our interaction with others takes place in nonverbal modes through facial expressions, gestures, and bodily postures, and these are often different from culture to culture, it is our verbal communication through language that is most distinctive. Gollnick and Chinn (2002) underscore the importance of language to our sense of ourselves when they assert the following: "Language and dialect serve as a focal point for cultural identity" (p. 242). They go on to explain that language provides a common bond for those with a similar heritage, but it can divide those same individuals from others with different cultures and linguistic traditions.

The Ramifications of Linguistic Diversity. In his analysis of the linguistic diversity of the United States and its relevance to education, Ovando (1997) highlights the significance of language, which he defines as "a system of communication linking sound, written or visual symbols, and meaning," as a means of sharing "knowledge, skills, values, and attitudes within and across cultures" (p. 272). It is our most powerful tool for communicating with others, but it is also a means of socializing children into their respective cultures (Gollnick & Chinn, 2002). The acquisition of language is a complex and highly debated process, but it is one that most children are able to master. The appropriate use of certain words in specific social situations is a nuance of which native speakers are almost instinctively aware, but that can cause embarrassment and unease for those who are learning a second language. Hence the way we use language is determined to a great extent by our culture.

Throughout the history of North America and the portion of the land mass that ultimately would become the United States, there has always been great linguistic diversity. Separate Native American groups had their own distinct languages, and about 175 of those that existed prior to colonization by Europeans have, remarkably, survived (Ovando, 1997). The first European groups to colonize—the Spanish, English, and French—added their means of communication to the mix, as did each successive immigrant group from the Germans of the 19th century to the Southeast Asians of the 20th to the Brazilians of the 21st. In addition, dialects and hybrids, such as pidgin (simplified speech that develops when two groups are in close and frequent contact) and Creole, are common in many locales in the United States. While the diversity of language can be viewed as an affirming aspect of our inherent multiculturalism, it has led to many bitter and ongoing controversies.

Monumental and sustained battles have raged on local, state, and national levels over the issue of bilingual education. Although efforts to establish bilingual programs in public schools are associated with Mexican American and Puerto Rican leaders who wished to preserve Spanish in the schools and lobbied for the passage of the Bilingual Education Act (1968), the issue surfaced much earlier in our history. As far back as the 17th century, there were schools in Philadelphia where German was the language of instruction. However, with the defeat of the French by the British and the presence of the Spanish primarily in the Southwest, English came to be accepted as the language of the thirteen colonies (Timm, 1996). Even so, there was no attempt to formalize the tradition by including a clause in the U.S. Constitution mandating an official language.

With the waves of European immigrants who settled in the cities of the East Coast and the Midwest in the 19th century, and the large numbers of Asians who made their homes in California and elsewhere on the West Coast, came what Timm (1996) describes as "contradictory views of bilingualism" (p. 261). Ethnic communities where English was not the primary language were common, and, where the non-English-speaking groups had some political clout, bilingual education was legal. However, Americanization became the goal of the nation's schools with the efforts of Noah Webster to standardize American English through the vehicle of the dictionary and those of Horace Mann to create a system of common schools with a curriculum that would promote citizenship and belief in the political values of the United States (Spring, 2002). The notorious Indian Boarding Schools, where systematic efforts to eradicate the cultural identity of Native American children were employed, had an English-only mandate. States, such as Illinois and Wisconsin, where there were large enclaves of German immigrants, legislated against bilingual education in order to promote a policy of Americanization (Timm, 1996). Sentiment opposed to German-language instruction accelerated during World War I and the nativist reaction that followed in its wake. Even for English-speaking children, courses promoting the learning of other modern languages became less popular in the nationalistic climate of the 1940s and 1950s.

Bilingual Education Controversies. In the liberal reform spirit of the 1960s, the federal government switched gears and responded to the pleas of Latino activists and others seeking to meet the educational needs of non-English-speaking students with the Bilingual Education Act of 1968, which provided funds for local communities. Another milestone was the 1974 Supreme Court case, *Lau v. Nichols*, which grew from a class action suit on behalf of Chinese-speaking children in San Francisco. Because the city did not provide instruction in Chinese, it was argued that these children were being denied their right to an education, a violation of the equal protection clause of the Fourteenth Amendment (Gollnick & Chinn, 2002). Although the ruling did not specify that bilingual programs be created, it did deem them necessary if schools were to live up to the standard of providing equal educational opportunities to all students regardless of their language.

A number of different types of bilingual and English as a second language programs (ESL) have evolved over the years, and at the same time opposition to them and to their conceptual frameworks has grown. Bilingual education ordinarily seeks to instruct students in content areas in their first language, so that they do not fall behind in their schooling, while at the same time they learn to speak English. Transitional bilingual education programs seek to help students become proficient in English and to move them into regular classes as soon as they can learn effectively in these settings. Maintenance bilingual programs, however, are pluralistic in orientation and attempt to help students function effectively in *both* their first language and English (Gollnick & Chinn, 2002; Timm, 1996). This approach attempts to help preserve the child's identity in his/her native culture. ESL programs, on the other hand, may be taught by individuals proficient in the students' native language, but their goal is definitely to promote teaching and learning in English. Even more focused in this direction are English immersion approaches, where instruction for children is entirely in English, which may be simplified so that students will not be completely lost and can learn some material in core content areas.

The need to address the question of how best to educate students whose native language is not English was accentuated in the 1990s as the number of immigrants moving to the United States increased to record numbers. Simultaneously, bilingual education approaches, always a source of controversy, came under increasingly strong attacks. California led the way in 1998 with the passage of Proposition 227, which resulted in drastic cuts in bilingual programs in the public schools (McCabe, 2004). Consequently, the majority of the state's English language learners were moved into English immersion programs. Studies comparing the academic achievement of students in English immersion programs with that of those who studied in bilingual education classes have not proven conclusive. Despite the lack of definitive research on the effectiveness of English immersion programs, both

Arizona and Massachusetts jumped on the anti-bilingual-education band-wagon and passed legislation similar to that in California. Efforts in Colorado to follow suit, however, were rejected by voters. While it may be common to blame those hostile to the new immigrants for the proliferation of anti-bilingual-education initiatives, many of the most dedicated supporters of such campaigns are immigrants themselves. The fact that a 2003 opinion poll conducted by Public Agenda found that 63% of immigrants were in favor of English immersion approaches underscores the complexity of the issue of how best to educate children attending U.S. public schools who are not proficient in the language of the majority (McCabe, 2004).

The Campaign for "English Only." Efforts to promote the use of English in the United States are not relegated to the field of education, as indicated by the 1980s drive spearheaded by Senator S. I. Hayakawa to introduce an official language amendment to the U.S. Constitution. Such legislation would have made it illegal for states to require the use of languages other than English for laws, orders, programs, and such in order to accommodate the needs of immigrant groups (Gollnick & Chinn, 2002). A number of states passed official language laws or added such amendments to their constitutions, and public opinion polls indicate that the majority of Americans favor legislation making official what has long been a tradition of English as the common language of the nation. Many supporters of an official language for the United States believe that English is not only the means by which political discourse is conducted, but also the key to upward economic and social mobility associated so strongly with the pursuit of the American dream.

The Acculturation Process. The controversy over "English only" and how best to educate children of immigrants will continue, and as it does the children will become acculturated to life in their new environment. How well the process goes depends on a number of factors. As Clayton (2003) points out, educators should be aware of some key issues related specifically to children who are in the process of adapting to life in the United States. In the first place, they probably did not have much to say about finding themselves living in a strange and sometimes frightening new situation. Adults responsible for their care made the decisions that brought them to this country, and the children may have had little time to prepare for the change. The most significant context where young people must learn to adjust to their new life is school. Official policy and how teachers and other students interact with the newcomers can determine to a great extent how well they learn and how comfortable they feel in their new and unfamiliar surroundings. They may adjust, become angry and frustrated, or even withdraw, depending on the circumstances and the support or lack of it they receive from the school, their family, the neighborhood, and other members of their ethnic or cultural group.

Similar to the problem of how best to address the language issue with respect to immigrants, there are a number of opinions as to what the end result of acculturation should be. The traditional goal was viewed by many to be assimilation or "Americanization," whereby the immigrant eventually shed his/her original ethnic identity and adopted the lifestyle, values, and language of the dominant culture. Pluralists, in contrast, suggest that an immigrant can adjust to life in the United States and make adaptations but at the same time not lose his/her cultural identity. Subscribing to newspapers in the home language; worshipping at temples, mosques, and churches where traditional services are conducted; shopping at ethnic groceries; and celebrating familiar holidays are ways that immigrants and their offspring can maintain their cultural identities while at the same time living, working, studying, and playing comfortably in their new homes. Some groups, like the Amish, do not want to make such accommodations and attempt as much as possible to live separated from the dominant culture and all others. Another possibility is that the immigrant loses her/his ties to the home culture but is unable to function comfortably in the new one. Clayton (2003) calls this marginalized state "semi-cultural." As we turn now to the story of the French Canadians of Woonsocket, it would be well to keep in mind these issues and questions concerning acculturation, its goals, and its manifestations.

THE FRENCH CANADIANS OF WOONSOCKET

FOCUS QUESTIONS

How do ethnicity and language shape an individual's
cultural identity?
Can an immigrant group adapt to life in the United States
and at the same time maintain its cultural identity?

The history of Woonsocket, Rhode Island, revolves around the storied Blackstone River and the first stirrings of the industrial revolution in New England (Bellemare, 1974; Rafael, 1997; *Woonsocket*, n.d.). The very first inhabitants, of course, were Native Americans, in this case the Narragansetts, Nipmucs, and Wampanoags of the eastern woodland groups. The earliest European was Richard Arnold, an acquaintance of Rhode Island's founder, Roger Williams. He built a sawmill on the Blackstone River near where Market Square now stands. Early settlers here as elsewhere supported themselves largely through agriculture. With time, however, the energy of the Blackstone was put to work, and those who moved into the area built gristmills, wool-processing mills, and a forge. Woonsocket Falls Village evolved into a significant crossroads for travelers en route to Boston, but little else is known of Woonsocket during the colonial and early national periods beyond the names of some of the first families to settle in the region. Much of the rest of Woonsocket's history revolves around the mills, the operatives who worked in them, and the fortunes of the industries they supported.

Woonsocket: Birth of a Mill City

The opening of the short-lived but colorful Blackstone Canal in the 1820s, an attempt to link inland Worcester, Massachusetts, to Providence and the Atlantic and to rival Boston as a commercial center, marked the beginning of a productive and busy chapter in the story of Woonsocket (Rafael, 1997). Five of the canal's 49 locks were located in Woonsocket, so it was not unusual for lines of barges carrying cargo, as well as boats for passengers, to enliven the landscape as they awaited their turns to pass through the locks. The canal project was responsible for bringing large numbers of immigrant laborers to the area. They were mostly Irish Catholics, whose unfamiliar language and religion may have been a source of concern to established residents. Many stayed on after the canal was completed, finding jobs in the building trades that flourished as the textile industry grew in New England.

The first textile mill in the area was the Social Mill established in 1810 (Bellemare, 1974). Many others soon followed, as Woonsocket's ample water resources provided the power to turn the wheels of industry. Largely due to the Blackstone Canal and later the coming of the Providence & Worcester Railroad, which passed directly through Woonsocket, business and industry expanded. A number of separate mill villages, six in all, sprang up around the various textile mills and gave the area a distinctive identity (*Woonsocket*, n.d.).

The centrally located Woonsocket Falls Village comprised what is today the city's downtown area. In addition to being the location of a number of textile mills, the principal thoroughfare, Main Street, became home to a variety of cultural and commercial institutions such as theaters, churches, banks, and retail establishments. One unusual characteristic of Woonsocket Falls Village's Market Square was the presence of a system of trenches built to trap water from the falls and control the power that kept the mills operating. Photographs of the neighborhood in Bellerose's *Images of America: Woonsocket* (1997) capture the massive stone presence of the mills, the rushing falls, and the more placid waters of the trenches.

One of the most significant of Woonsocket's mill villages was Social Village, which was founded in 1810 when a number of entrepreneurs created the Social Manufacturing Company, an enterprise first housed in an old wooden structure. The company produced cotton thread and soon grew into a major complex that included a large stone mill constructed in 1841 when

Woonsocket Falls, Woonsocket, Rhode Island.

Dexter Ballou, a member of a prominent family of textile mill owners, took control of the business. In need of workers, the new mill recruited laborers from Canada, and thus began the story of the Quebecois of Woonsocket. Housing and shops to accommodate the new residents were constructed as well as additional mills, including the Bailey Wringer Company. Unlike its neighbors, this factory did not produce textiles, but instead turned out mechanical clothes wringers, forerunners of the modern washing machine.

Perhaps the most attractive of the mill villages that eventually would consolidate to form the city of Woonsocket was Bernon Mill Village, whose owners sought to create a model industrial community where both workers and managers would flourish in a pleasant planned work environment. Established in 1827 with the opening of a factory for the Russell Manufacturing Company and originally called Danville, the village prospered when Providence industrialists Crawford Allen and Sullivan Dorr purchased the mill. They gave the village its new name and built the handsome Bernon Mill in Greek Revival style (*Woonsocket*, n.d.). Extremely productive, the Bernon Mill is said to have produced 2 million yards of cotton goods a year, in its heyday in the 1840s, which contributed to the ever-growing demand for immigrant workers (Rafael, 1997).

Three of the villages consolidated in 1867 to officially become the town of Woonsocket, and in 1871 the other three joined to form what are now the boundaries of the community. The boom economic climate of the post-Civil War era contributed to the period of growth that led to this consolidation. New mills were added as European industrialists, enticed by attractive tax incentives, developed and diversified the economic base. One company of note was the Woonsocket Rubber Company, which began by making rollers for clothes wringers and was founded by a local family and an Irish immigrant, Joseph Banigan, of Providence. By 1888 the thriving community was ready to reorganize as a city, and Woonsocket's charter was approved by the Rhode Island legislature.

The Culture of the Quebec Habitants

Although the presence of French culture in the Woonsocket area can be traced back to the late 1700s, when French Huguenot families, the Ballous and the Tourtellots, settled in the region, it was not until the industrial period of the 1840s that the migration of French Canadians began to have an impact. Drawn by the need for mill workers and discouraged by the limitations of agrarian life in Quebec, French-speaking farm families left Canada in large numbers in the mid-19th century and settled throughout New England. The Civil War period saw the greatest influx of French Canadian immigrants (Bellemare, 1974), and nowhere was their influence more significant than in Woonsocket, where by 1900 60% of the population was French Canadian (*Woonsocket*, n.d.).

One might well ask how farm families in rural Quebec learned of the need for workers in Rhode Island. The answer lies in the fact that in addition to word of mouth and family contacts, a major factor in spreading the call for mill workers was active recruitment by the factory owners (Rafael, 1997). Agents were sent to Quebec and advertisements published in Canadian newspapers with promises of steady wages and a higher standard of living in the United States. The harshness of the life that many found when they arrived in mill cities like Woonsocket was barely an improvement over what they had left behind, and some were happy to return to their rural communities after unsuccessful stints in the United States. Perhaps half the 500,000 French Canadians who emigrated south eventually did return, but those who remained in the industrial towns of New England had a tremendous influence on the culture of these communities. It has been said that by the turn of the 20th century, Woonsocket was "the most French city in the United States" (quoted in Rafael, 1997, p. 6).

The World of Work for the French Canadian Immigrants. The Museum of Work & Culture, opened in 1997 in Woonsocket's historic Market Square, illustrates through its *La Survivance* exhibits the daily life of the French Canadian mill workers of the region and the institutions that regulated it.

The tour begins with a typical Quebec farmhouse, which portrays life in rural Canada, where the people grew crops, spun and wove their own cloth, built furniture for their modest homes, and were largely self-sufficient. Never an easy place to farm, Quebec experienced an agricultural crisis in the mid-19th century that paralleled the explosive growth of the textile industry in nearby New England. The combination of a depressed farm economy in Quebec and the need for factory workers in the United States spurred large numbers of rural French Canadians to move to the industrial centers of the Northeast. For a transplanted Quebec farm family, a life built around work in the mills of Woonsocket and other textile towns was nothing less than a traumatic culture shock.

As the Museum of Work & Culture's "Textile Mill Shop Floor" exhibit documents, the new life of the Quebecois revolved around time cards, dangerous equipment, and unsympathetic management, as workers toiled in poorly ventilated, unhealthy factories where long hours, low pay, and women and child laborers were the rule. Interactive exhibits allow visitors to sort bobbins by the clock and experience firsthand the stress of work in the mills. The museum display also points out how the once self-sufficient French Canadians relied on catalogs and shops to supply their material needs and on their employers for housing and even recreation. Despite employers' efforts to regulate closely the lives of the immigrant work force, the settlers from Quebec had a strong affiliation with their home culture, and they clung tenaciously to their familiar customs.

The Spiritual Realm of the Quebec Habitants. One of the most distinguishing and cherished aspects of the French Canadian immigrants' culture was their Catholic faith. The first church founded in Woonsocket to provide for the spiritual needs of the Quebec inhabitants was the Church of the Precious Blood, established in 1874. Destroyed shortly afterward in a windstorm, the building was reconstructed in 1881 on Carrington Avenue. Photographs of this imposing building, which Rafael (1997) calls "a fortress for the defense of French Canadian culture in America" (p. 7), reveal an impressive structure with an interesting belfry, 8-foot gold cross, and stenciled interior (Bellerose, 1997). Monsignor Charles Dauray, who arrived in Woonsocket in 1875, and has been called the patron saint of the community's French Catholics, is credited with creating in the Church of the Precious Blood a model parish complete with a convent, an academy for young boys, a high school for girls, and an orphanage (Thomas, 1976). It has been said that during his tenure, not only the parish but the fortunes of the French Canadian immigrants in general improved significantly (Smyth, 1903). The Church of the Precious Blood was strategically located near the three Woonsocket villages of Hamlet, Globe, and Bernon, where most of the French Canadian residents had settled. Over time, four more Catholic churches established explicitly for French Canadian congregations were built in Woonsocket, an indication of the tremendous growth of their numbers.

The rapid proliferation of French Catholic churches in Woonsocket was directly related to efforts of members of the clergy in the mother country to hold onto their congregations despite the great migration to the United States, which they opposed for obvious reasons (Rafael, 1997). Quebec farm families contemplating a move were warned that they would not be able to maintain their cultural traditions in the inhospitable environment of the United States, which, although founded on the principle of separation of church and state, was distinctly Anglo Protestant in orientation. Although they may have emigrated against the advice of their church leaders, the French Canadians who settled in the mill towns of New England heeded the warnings about having to fight to preserve their faith and ethnicity and were quick to establish parishes with distinctly French identities. In the churches built to serve the immigrants from Quebec, the members of the clergy were French, and the parochial schools they erected to educate the parish children provided instruction in both French and English. Many nuns from Quebec taught in these schools.

Language and La Survivance. The struggle on the part of the French Canadian immigrant families in Woonsocket to preserve their religious and ethnic heritage was known as *la survivance*, the fight for survival. Although the effort was ongoing, the use of the term evidently began to surface in the 1920s in response to what the French Catholics in the city perceived to be unfair treatment at the hands of the bishop of Providence, whose heritage was Irish, not French (Thomas, 1976). Gerstle (1991) describes Woonsocket at this time as "still intensely Quebecois in language and mores: three-quarters of the French-Canadian youngsters still attended French-speaking parochial schools; a majority of second- and third-generation French-Canadians spoke only French at home and married French-Canadian spouses" (p. 145). This effort, which Gerstle argues was an unusually successful formula for ethnic survival, came in direct conflict in the 1920s with civil authorities in what would become known as the Sentinelle Affair.

In 1922, a bill was passed in the Rhode Island General Assembly mandating that major subjects such as mathematics and history be taught in English in all elementary schools, both public and private. Known as the Peck Act, this law generally was perceived by the French Canadians of Woonsocket to be an attempt to eradicate their long-standing policy of *la survivance* (Rafael, 1997). One French language newspaper in the area, *La Sentinelle* [The Guardian], gave voice to their fears by attacking the law as a blatant attempt to Americanize them and to erase their cultural identity. Church leaders, such as Bishop William Hickey of Providence who supported the Peck Act, were vilified. Priests in the French parishes of Woonsocket openly defied the bishop by refusing to contribute to his fund-raising drive to collect money for the construction of new high schools in the diocese (Bouley, 1988). Bishop Hickey then announced that those parishes that did not meet their assessed fund-raising targets would have to make up the difference out of their regular revenues. Encouraged by *La Sentinelle*, some parishes openly resisted. Those who supported acts of defiance against the bishop, the Sentinellistes, sued the parishes that had agreed to his policies. Eventually the courts agreed with the bishop's position.

Bitterness and vitriol characterized the Sentinelle Affair, especially when some of the French Catholic clergy supported the ethnic integration of one of the parochial high schools in Woonsocket. Such acts were seen by the Sentinellistes as attempts to extinguish *la survivance*, and they were driven to even more radical resistance. The Vatican ultimately became embroiled in the controversy and ruled on the side of the moderates who sought to accommodate to the Peck Act. Sixty of the most defiant of the Sentinellistes were excommunicated. This extreme action calmed the conflict in that those who were shut out by the church repented and eventually were reinstated. However, the bitterness and anger over what many of those of French Canadian ancestry perceived to be a calculated threat to their cultural heritage, as embodied in their faith and their language, remained for many years to come.

Learning Activities. Social studies teachers in the Woonsocket area, addressing the curriculum themes of immigration and industrialization, have a rich environment into which they may tap through the familiar learning activities of the field trip and the walking tour. The Museum of Work & Culture is student friendly and provides online curriculum standards references for teachers planning field trips and follow-up lessons based on its displays. The Museum is located in Market Square, a section of the city with a number of historical landmarks related to its mill origins, so a walking tour easily could be included as part of a field trip.

Teachers in any community with an immigrant history such as Woonsocket's can promote both empathy and critical thinking through a number of social studies activities. For younger students, lessons built around the themes of leaving home and coping with an unfamiliar environment can include such activities as letter exchanges and journal keeping (see Lesson Plan 4.1), or packing a trunk and assessing what might be most valuable/useful in a new home. They also can construct "compare and contrast" graphic organizers or create murals illustrating life in the home country and life in the new country. Secondary students can research the experiences of the various immigrant groups who have settled in their community and assess the impact on its social, economic, and political life. They also can delve into the concept of identity and write essays or short stories concerning how one's sense of self is impacted by moving to a new environment where one's language is not that of the native inhabitants and where one's ethnicity and heritage may not be valued.

Woonsocket in Modern Times

Woonsocket, like Framingham and Nashville, underwent striking changes in the 20th century that both added to the diversity of the community and shaped its 21st-century identity. In Woonsocket the French Canadian presence remained, but immigrants from other places began to settle in the area as well, and each added a distinct layer to the character of the city. One important factor that cannot be downplayed in terms of its impact on life in Woonsocket is unionism, which in this community in the 20th century became inextricably woven into the multicultural mix of ethnicity, language, and religion that had been introduced in previous decades.

Mills and Unions: The French Connection. An unusual and distinctive aspect of mill ownership in Woonsocket in the early years of the 20th century concerned the involvement of a number of entrepreneurs from France and Belgium (Gerstle, 1991; Hudson, 1988). Largely due to lobbying on the part of Aram Pothier, who was elected mayor of Woonsocket in 1894 and later served as governor of Rhode Island, a number of European owners, looking to avoid American tariff restrictions, set up shop in town. They were attracted by the large number of French-speaking residents, a potential work force that would be able to understand and thus take directions from the managers and superintendents who would be sent to the United States to run the establishments. In addition to providing jobs for Woonsocket's French Canadian population, the European factories introduced woolen manufacturing to the city in an era when cotton mills were moving to the South. As Gerstle (1991) indicates, the effect was more than economic, for the presence of these factories provided a work environment where the speaking of French rather than English was desirable. Unlike the situation for non–English speakers elsewhere in the United States, in the Woonsocket area a critical aspect of cultural identity was encouraged and valued in the workplace of many residents.

In the troubled decade of the 1930s, the manufacturing establishments in Rhode Island as elsewhere were devastated by the fallout of the Great Depression. Paradoxically, in an era when labor was expendable, the Woonsocket area witnessed the rise of a powerful union, the Independent Textile Union, later called the Industrial Trades Union (ITU), which had a critical European connection. Although officially organized in the 1930s, the origins of the ITU can be traced back to earlier in the century when the French and Belgian mill owners of the region found themselves so short of workers that they had to recruit labor from Europe (Gerstle, 1991). Among those who answered the call were a number of radicals who had been blacklisted on the continent and who were hungry for both employment and new ground on which to plant their socialist doctrines.

Soon these new immigrant workers, who arrived from France and Belgium with a socialist agenda, were protesting conditions in the mills of Woonsocket. Eventually they saw an opportunity to organize fellow workers into an industrial union to rival the waning United Textile Workers (UTW), a branch of the craft-oriented American Federation of Labor. While membership in the UTW experienced a precipitous decline in Woonsocket in the 1920s, labor leaders did not give up on organization, and in the early 1930s the ITU was born. This group differed from the UTW in that as an industrial union it welcomed all mill workers, both skilled and unskilled, and required union officials to continue at their factory jobs (Thomas, 1988). Its most influential president was Joseph Schmetz, a Belgian mule spinner who worked at the Jules Desurmont mill.

Under Schmetz's direction, the ITU organized a number of minor, largely successful strikes during its early years. The growth of the ITU during the mid-1930s was, ironically, the result of violence during the Great Textile Strike of 1934, a national strike called by the rival UTW. Members of the ITU, in solidarity, walked off their jobs in the Woonsocket mills. Most of the mills shut down, but the Woonsocket Rayon Company stayed open to finish a chemical process already underway. When a crowd gathered to demand that the Rayon Company be shut down, the situation deteriorated and a riot resulted. In the following days, vandalism, looting, and unruly behavior continued, causing the intervention of the National Guard. A number of those involved were wounded, including four policemen, and two lost their lives. Property damage was considerable in the Social Village neighborhood, and the Woonsocket Rayon Company was forced to stop production. Throughout the days of unrest, Schmetz and the ITU called for calm, and as a result were viewed by the general public as an acceptable alternative to the UTW.

In the years that immediately followed, the ITU's membership rolls swelled, and the union thrived (Thomas, 1988). Schmetz became full-time president and was ably assisted by secretary Lawrence Spitz, who adhered to the nonviolent philosophy that guided the union. By the 1940s, the ITU had organized over 12,000 textile workers and, in the process, a number of employees in other local businesses and trades not usually unionized, including retail clerks, newspapermen, and cobblers. In addition, the ITU provided a number of social and cultural services for its membership.

In analyzing the success of the ITU, labor historian Gary Gerstle (1991) cites a number of interesting contributing factors. An important point to keep in mind about the French Canadian mill workers of Woonsocket and elsewhere is that they were by nature conservative and unsympathetic to labor radicalism. However, the ITU, originally the creation of European socialists, adopted the language of patriotism and assimilation in the 1930s, perhaps as a survival mechanism. The French Canadians of Woonsocket, although still conscious of their ethnic heritage, seemed comfortable with slogans that equated unionism with Americanism. At the same time, argues Gerstle, they tried to bend the definition of Americanism to include cultural pluralism. They wanted to be accepted as full-fledged members of American society but still cling to their French language and cultural traditions. This accommodation worked for a time with respect to the ITU, but during World War II and the Cold War that followed, newer, narrower definitions of Americanism took hold. As the political climate changed, so did the textile industry in Woonsocket, which was on the decline. The fortunes of the union that had dominated life in the city for a brief moment in its storied history also waned, and a period of stagnation soon followed.

The chapter in Woonsocket's history dealing with the ITU is one with a series of ironic twists and turns. The union was the brainchild of radicals. It thrived in a decade when there was a surplus of labor, and although, like earlier left-leaning groups, it welcomed all workers, skilled and unskilled, its popularity rose when it adopted a moderate stance and tone. It ranks were filled with many workers of French Canadian ancestry, conscious of the fact that their language and culture were being eroded over time, yet they were at home in a union that adopted the trappings of patriotic Americanism. Gerstle (1991) offers the following provocative conclusion concerning the French Canadian workers who supported the ITU in the 1930s: "They sought not to leave their ethnic past behind, but to build that ethnic past into a working-class and American present and future. By becoming American, they sought to change the meaning of what it meant to be American" (p. 148). Their success did not last long, for in the conservative climate of the Cold War, and the geographic shift of textile manufacturing ever more to the South, unionism in Woonsocket declined and the strong ethnic identity of the French Canadian population of the city ebbed as well.

Changes at Mid-Century. The 1950s brought a number of significant changes to the city of Woonsocket. A new city charter and along with it a reform government took charge in 1952, but other upheavals of the decade were not so positive (Crowley, 1988). The flagging textile industry continued to decline, and the unemployment rate in the city climbed to a shocking 25%. The two largest industries were the U.S. Rubber Company and the Taft-Pierce Manufacturing Company, neither of them textile related. Despite the efforts of the Woonsocket Chamber of Commerce and "Operation Jobs," an initiative started by the Industrial Foundation of Greater Woonsocket, employment continued to be elusive. To add to the city's woes, in 1955 a devastating flood triggered by two powerful hurricanes left the business district in shambles and caused millions of dollars in damage. On the positive side, no lives were lost in the flood, and a new, more effective flood control program was launched. The Blackstone River was altered in strategic locations to tame its waters, and a new dam with four floodgates was constructed. New bridges also improved Woonsocket's aging infrastructure.

Two societies established earlier explicitly for the benefit of Woonsocket's French Canadian population continued to exert influence in the middle decades of the 20th century, Club Marquette and L'Union St. Jean-Baptiste d'Amerique (Thomas, 1976). Club Marquette was founded in 1933 by Dr. Auray Fontaine and some friends who sought to revive French culture, which many perceived to be declining as use of the French language was becoming less prevalent in Woonsocket. The group purchased St. Ann's Gym and renovated it to include meeting rooms, bowling alleys, and a banquet hall. It created a scholarship fund, sponsored local baseball and hockey teams, and supported political candidates seen as sensitive to the needs of the residents of French heritage. The Club Marquette Credit Union, which originated in 1944, experienced spectacular growth in the years that followed and eventually built a modern office building on the corner of Social and Pond Streets to house its workers and a number of other businesses.

While Club Marquette was decidedly civic, political, and business minded, L'Union Saint-Jean Baptiste, as its name suggests, was much more religious in orientation. Exclusively Catholic, it was chartered in 1900 as a fraternal and religious organization to bring together a number of independent French societies in the United States for purposes of promoting the social welfare of their members and administering their insurance programs. Like Club Marquette, L'Union had an important economic function, one that eventually defined its identity. French was the official language of L'Union until 1968 when it became bilingual. Until then the group, due to the large number of powerful community leaders who were members, were largely responsible for maintaining Woonsocket's French identity.

A "Lost City" Finds Itself. As Woonsocket modernized in the 1970s and 1980s, its once-overarching French identity waned, but was not entirely eradicated. Spurred by a 1970 article in *The Providence Journal*, which labeled Woonsocket a "lost city" because of its depressed economy and negative self-image, a Neighborhood Development Program was launched to revive the community (Bacon, Crowley, & Mulcahy, 1988). The Social neighborhood, so hard hit by the 1955 flood, was targeted, and saw the construction of a number of new municipal facilities, including the Harris Public Library, a police station, and a post office. The new Marquette Building opened in 1975, keeping alive the French legacy of the community. However, as with many other urban renewal projects, some buildings of historic interest did not survive. Among these were the mill housing complex at Nourse Village, Girard's Diner, and the Gaulin Avenue residential neighborhood. These losses were offset in part by the creation of Woonsocket's first historic district, Cato Hill (which later dropped the designation as too restrictive). Here in the 1880s and 1890s, the city's first Irish American tenement neighborhood had evolved amid the Greek Revival homes. Twentieth-century homeowners in the area took advantage of loans and grants made available due to the historic district designation, and, although not all the rundown housing was restored, enough was accomplished to preserve the character of the neighborhood.

Woonsocket's Continuing Diversity. Although the focus in this chapter has been on the French Canadian community in Woonsocket, many other cultural groups maintained and continue in the present to maintain a strong presence in the city. In the 1820s, long before Woonsocket received its city charter, the building of the Blackstone Canal attracted a number of Irish laborers to the area. Among them was the colorful Michael Reddy, considered to be Woonsocket's first Irish immigrant (Bellerose, 1997; Smyth, 1903; Thomas, 1976). A year after he arrived in the United States, Reddy secured work on on the Rhode Island section of the canal, and soon after settled in Woonsocket with a small number of fellow Irish immigrants. Hungering for an opportunity to practice their religion in an area where anti-Catholicism was blatant, they were successful in persuading a priest who was visiting Providence to come to Woonsocket where a mass was celebrated in the private home of a Quaker family. Thereafter, visiting priests held masses in various locations until a permanent church could be built. Reddy was instrumental in its establishment. He also was able to build a house for himself on Front Street and acquire Logee Hill Farm not far from where he lived. Visiting the aging Reddy in 1878, James Smyth found him to be in good health and able to provide information about his early days in Woonsocket. He died in 1879 around the time that his countrymen were establishing their ethnic enclave in the Cato Hill neighborhood.

While those of Irish heritage can trace their roots in Woonsocket back to the early 19th century, the Southeast Asians of the community are relative newcomers (Lind, 1989). Although they constitute a relatively small percentage of Woonsocket's total population of approximately 43,000, their presence has added a fresh and distinctive element of diversity to the city's already rich ethnic mix. Fleeing war and violence in their homelands, thousands of Cambodians, Hmongs, Laotians, and Vietnamese settled in various locations through the United States, including about 12,000 in Rhode Island. Most moved to the area in the 1980s, each group bringing unique cultural traditions and, as refugees, special sorrows. In addition to the familiar story of hardship and adjustment that these new immigrants share with earlier groups, many Southeast Asians are Catholics, and hence have something in common with those of Irish and French Canadian heritage. Many others, however, follow the Buddhist faith, adding another component to Woonsocket's religious diversity.

One cluster of neighborhoods in Woonsocket that is home to a number of ethnic and racial groups, and thus embodies the diversity of the city, lies close to the Blackstone River and comprises the Constitution Hill, Fairmount, and Veterans Memorial districts (commUNITYTeam, 2000). During the summer of 2000, a number of teens from these neighborhoods were selected by the Woonsocket Neighborhood Development Corporation to engage in a project that entailed interviewing more than 25 residents of all ages, races, and ethnicities to create a community profile. Editor-in-chief of a publication based on their work, Shalisa Williams, one of the young people who conducted the interviews, noted the following: "Often when people think of our neighborhoods, they think of minorities, drugs, fighting, and high school dropouts. With this book, we are giving them 'A Different View'" (commUNITYTeam, 2000, p. 3). Through maps, photographs, and the words of the interviewees, a revealing and insightful portrait of the institutions, cultures, and residents of this ethnically diverse section of the city and how it has changed over time is presented with honesty and a touch of whimsy. The reader learns how African Americans with no job prospects in the South, Cambodians fleeing Communism in Southeast Asia, as well as Cape Verdians, Puerto Ricans, and French Canadians, all searching for a better life, came to Woonsocket and carved out places for themselves with the resources offered by a community with a long history of both welcoming and challenging newcomers.

Woonsocket's Centennial Year and Beyond. In 1988 the city of Woonsocket celebrated the centennial of its incorporation with a spirit of optimism for the future and an interest in preserving the memories of its past (Bacon, 2000). Balls, lectures, parades, a play, and the planting of a time capsule on the grounds of the public library are but a few of the events held to mark the city's first 100 years. A Main Street 2000 Development Corporation was created to oversee a renovation project for the city's key thoroughfare with an eye toward preserving much of Woonsocket's unique history. Grants from the National Endowment for the Humanities and the Blackstone River Valley National Heritage Corridor Commission provided for the creation of the Museum of Work & Culture to be housed in an old mill building in Market Square. Its opening in 1997 was heralded not only in the New England region but also in Canada due to the Museum's interpretation and celebration of the culture of the French Canadian immigrants who helped forge the identity of modern Woonsocket. Additional urban renewal efforts in the years following the centennial celebrations in Woonsocket focused on improving some of the city's most rundown neighborhoods, refurbishing its parks, and repairing roads and bridges.

Despite the optimistic undertakings of the 1980s and 1990s, Woonsocket suffered its share of setbacks, like so many other mill cities that have lost their central economic base to progress, geography, and the uncertainties of boom and bust cycles endemic to market economies. A number of the city's most prominent businesses folded. The once mighty Marquette Credit Union failed and had to be liquidated in 1991. These and other reverses were partly offset by the coming of a number of new retail outlets as well as the expansion of the Woonsocket corporate headquarters of CVS, one of the nation's largest drugstore chains and the only Fortune 100 company located in Rhode Island.

Learning Activities. The 20th-century history of Woonsocket offers a number of topics that link with key social studies themes; one of these is change. The city celebrated its centennial with much fanfare in 1988. Younger students studying local history and community could engage in designing celebrations for future such events or predicting what they think their city will be like when it reaches its 125th, 150th, and subsequent milestones. On another topic, geography lessons could be designed specifically around the culture and origins of Woonsocket's newest immigrant groups.

High school students learning about unionism could investigate the rise and fall of the ITU, explore the ethnic factor, and debate whether the union's approach was in the end beneficial or destructive. The "Philosophical Chairs" technique could be used for this activity (Yell, Scheurman, & Reynolds, 2004). This method has students face one another with desks arranged in a horseshoe formation, identify a controversial question, consider various points of view, seat themselves according to their positions on the question, debate the issue, and change seats if their opinions do. Secondary students who are studying the various decades of the 20th century could research what was happening in their city during the 1920s, 1930s, and beyond, in order to help them connect to the material and to conceptualize such prevailing themes as separation of church and state and economic displacement.

CONCLUSIONS

In this overview of the history of Woonsocket, we have seen a number of mill villages loosely bound by their ties to the Blackstone River evolve into a small city, which, over the years, has endured its share of problems and capitalized on a number of opportunities to ensure a future that includes possibilities for economic health and growth. Woonsocket is a community that is proud of its heritage and has benefited from investment in a museum and renewal projects that emphasize its contributions to the industrial revolution and celebrate its rich diversity.

Woonsocket, like many other cities and towns throughout the United States, has always been home to residents of different backgrounds, but unique to its identity is the fact that it was shaped so distinctively by one ethnic group, the habitants from Quebec. The French Canadian farmers, who moved south to Rhode Island to find work in the mills, came in large numbers and provided their own community through their stubborn insistence on maintaining their language, religion, and culture. They ensured that their heritage would not be lost through *la survivance*, their struggle to preserve their traditions in a sometimes hostile environment and in the face of resistance from within their own ranks, as seen in the Sentinelle Affair. Over time the influence of the Quebecois in Woonsocket has been diluted as other ethnic groups have moved into the old neighborhoods, and the French Canadians themselves have assimilated, to some extent, into the dominant culture.

Their story provides a number of possibilities for classroom teachers in the area and a model for educators elsewhere who seek to connect their students to the past through a study of their local institutions and to help them understand the tensions and triumphs of immigrant groups and their descendants who struggle to adapt while holding onto their identity. These themes are raised in the Focus Questions that open the historical narrative of this chapter and ask how an individual's cultural identity is shaped by ethnicity and language, and whether an immigrant group can adapt to life in the United States and still maintain its cultural identity. No ready answers can be offered, but certainly the story of the French Canadian experience in Woonsocket provides a wealth of material for students to consider concerning the conflicts of immigrant groups and their experiences in the United States.

Following is a lesson plan for younger students that focuses on the theme of change and promotes an appreciation of multiple perspectives through the exchange of letters. For secondary students, the design of a neighborhood study project that involves research based on primary sources and oral histories is provided. Both are based on Woonsocket's history, but can be adapted easily for implementation in schools elsewhere in the nation.

LESSON PLAN 4.1
LETTER EXCHANGE

Grades 3–5

Suggested Length. Three class sessions of 45–60 minutes during the first week and one class session each week for 3 additional weeks

National Standards for History **Reference (for grades K–4)**

Topic 1. Living and Working Together in Families and Communities, Now and Long Ago
Standard 1A. The student understands family life now and in the recent past; family life in various places long ago.
Topic 3. The History of the United States: Democratic Principles and Values and the People from Many Cultures Who Contributed to Its Cultural, Economic, and Political Heritage
Standard 5. The student understands the movements of large groups of people into his or her own and other states in the United States now and long ago.

National Standards for History **Reference**

Era 6. The Development of the Industrial United States
Standard 2A. The student understands the sources and experiences of the new immigrants.

NCSS *Curriculum Guidelines for Multicultural Education* **References**

7.0. The curriculum should help students understand the totality of the experiences of ethnic and cultural groups in the United States.
17.0. The multicultural curriculum should help students to view and interpret events, situations, and conflict from diverse ethnic and cultural perspectives and points of view.

Prerequisite Knowledge. Students previously will have learned about immigration and the reasons that people leave their old communities and make new homes in other countries.

Materials. Wall map of North America, photographs or paintings of farms in 19th-century Quebec (such as those by Edmond J. Massicotte, which are on display at the Museum of Work & Culture and reproduced in *Woonsocket: Highlights of History, 1800–1976* [Thomas, 1976]), photographs or paintings of Woonsocket (such as those in *Images of America: Woonsocket* [Bellerose, 1997]), writing paper (preferably old-fashioned style), pens, index cards, and access to the school library and the Internet.

Objectives. Students will be able to—

- Locate communities and geographic features of both Quebec and Rhode Island on a wall map of North America
- Research Woonsocket and Quebec in the late 19th century
- Work in pairs to compose a series of letters from the perspectives of both an immigrant child and his/her friend back in Quebec
- Compare life in Woonsocket with life in Quebec

Procedures: Day 1

Initiation

- Ask students if they have ever been away from home for a period of time (e.g., visiting relatives, summer camp, etc.) and encourage them to share their feelings about the experience.
- Review with students topics they have been learning concerning immigration and why individuals and families leave their familiar communities and move to unfamiliar ones to make new homes.
- Explain that they will be working in pairs pretending to be children in families that moved from farms in Quebec or children who still live in Quebec whose friends have moved to Woonsocket.

Development

- Ask students what they know about life on a farm today and life on a farm 100 years ago.
- Show students pictures (such as those in *"La Survivance": A Companion to the Exhibit at the Museum of Work & Culture, Woonsocket, Rhode Island* [Rafael, 1997] and *Woonsocket: Highlights of History, 1800–1976* [Thomas, 1976]) that depict the life in Quebec that the French Canadian immigrants to Woonsocket left behind. Discuss the positives and negatives of this life and the motives that prompted so many to move to New England.
- Next describe what Woonsocket was like at the time that large numbers of French Canadians moved into the region. Use resources such as those listed above and *Images of America: Woonsocket* (Bellerose, 1997) to show students pictures of what the city looked like 100 years ago.
- Arrange students in pairs and assign them French names. Following are some examples: André, Francois, Jean, Louis, Pierre, and Victor for boys, and Angelique, Eugenie, Louise, Marie, Victorine, and Yvonne for girls. Note that students of French Canadian heritage may be able to suggest others.
- Use wooden craft sticks or other random selection method to determine who in each pair will be the immigrant child and who will be the child who remained in Quebec.

- Tell each pair of students that they are "best friends" and they are going to be writing to each other for the next few weeks.
- Have a number of students go to the wall map and locate Quebec and its geographic features and do the same for Woonsocket, Rhode Island.
- Tell students they will assume that they have been separated for about a month when they begin their correspondence.

Closing. Brainstorm a number of topics that their letters might include.

Procedures: Day 2

- This class should be devoted to researching the geography and culture of Quebec.
- Students should be instructed to bring their index cards to the school library where they can use encyclopedias, reference books, and the Internet to locate information and take notes on the geography and culture of Quebec. Teachers should prescreen Web sites for those suitable for elementary students. A site for teachers with links to resources on the history of Quebec and French Canadians in the United States is www2.marianopolis.edu. Students in the Woonsocket area could take a field trip to the Museum of Work & Culture for additional background material.
- Students should use their index cards to record factual information to include in their letters.

Procedures: Day 3

- This class will be a letter-writing workshop, where the basics of composing a friendly letter can be reviewed.
- Students working independently then will write the first in their series of letters for the exchange. They should be reminded that if these letters were written in 1900, they would be in French. Their letters will be in English, but the teacher may want to introduce some French vocabulary words for students to incorporate (see Table 4.1 for some appropriate words).
- Students should be instructed that their letters must include both personal sentiments and factual information to show that they are familiar with the geography and culture of Quebec and the life of French Canadian immigrants in Woonsocket. They may wish to add drawings as well.
- Once the first letters have been completed, they may be handed over to the teacher and delivered to the intended recipients.

Procedures: Follow-Up Classes

- Each week following the first letter exchange, students should devote one class to composing return messages and reading their new letters.
- Students should place the letters they receive in folders or boxes for safekeeping.

TABLE 4.1. Vocabulary for Letter Exchange

English	French
the farm	la ferme
the city	la ville
the trip	le voyage
the street	la rue
my house	ma maison
the school	l'école
my family	ma famille
my friend	mon ami (m) mon amie (f)
my brother	mon frère
my sister	ma sœur
my father	mon père
my mother	ma mère
happy	heureux
sad	triste
visit	rendre visite à

- After 3 or 4 weeks, a culminating activity could involve each student selecting a favorite letter to read aloud to the class.
- Students then could complete a chart to summarize what they learned from the activity about life in Quebec and about life in Woonsocket.

Assessment. Students will be assessed on the knowledge of geography and culture of Quebec and of everyday life in Woonsocket that they incorporated in their letters and included on the summary chart.

Adaptations. The format of the letter exchange can be used for any class that is studying a particular immigrant group or immigration in general. The basic steps involve pairing students up, researching the country (or countries) of origin, learning about the local community at a certain point in history, and writing letters back and forth incorporating both personal feelings and content knowledge gained through the research.

PROJECT PLAN 4.1
MY NEIGHBORHOOD THEN AND NOW

Grades 9–12

Description. This project involves the creation of a booklet or a PowerPoint presentation tracing the history of the student's neighborhood since World War II. It should consist of a map; copies of photographs; text describing changes over time with respect to houses, buildings, businesses, and population; and interviews with residents, both old and new.

National Standards for History References

Era 9. Postwar United States
Standard 1. The economic boom and social transformation of postwar United States
Era 10. Contemporary United States
Standard 2. Economic, social, and cultural developments in contemporary United States

NCSS *Curriculum Guidelines for Multicultural Education* References

7.0. The curriculum should help students understand the totality of the experiences of ethnic and cultural groups in the United States.
21.0. The multicultural curriculum should make maximum use of experiential learning, especially local community resources.

Prerequisite Knowledge. Students should be familiar with the social, economic, and cultural history of the United States in the second half of the 20th century.

Rationale. This project will help students to gain different perspectives on historical content by allowing them to see how the concepts covered in their textbooks played out in their own neighborhoods. They will be required to use and create primary sources (photographs and interviews) that will help them to become more familiar with the tools of historians and to appreciate how history is written.

Steps

- Students will first need to define the concept of neighborhood and then each student will need to decide what constitutes the boundaries of his/her own neighborhood. Students who live in the same neighborhood may wish to collaborate on the project.
- Students next will be given the guidelines for the project and will brainstorm ways to fulfill the requirements.

• Students should be given sufficient time to research and put together their projects. They should be required to pass in weekly updates of their progress and drafts of various pieces for the teacher to review.

Guidelines for the Neighborhood Project. The goal is to create a booklet or a PowerPoint presentation tracing the history of your neighborhood over the last half of the 20th century. The project should contain the following elements:

1. A map showing the streets and any geographic elements or other characteristics of note (e.g., river, hill, railroad tracks, or historical landmark).
2. Photographs showing the neighborhood today and any available copies of photographs from the past. The latter may be found in books or at the public library, historical society, or city or town hall.
3. Listing of current and former businesses, stores, or other economic institutions.
4. Listing of any parks, museums, schools, or other cultural institutions.
5. Interviews with a number of residents (4–6), some who are recent arrivals and some who have lived in the neighborhood for many years. Interviews should cover a range of topics, including why the interviewees or their ancestors moved to the neighborhood, what they like/do not like about living there, how the neighborhood has changed over the years, any notable happenings (floods, blizzards, parades) or residents (volunteers, war heroes, famous people), recreation, former businesses, and environmental changes. Students should be encouraged to add topics in which they are interested or that they think are important.
6. An analysis of the interviews, comparing and contrasting the neighborhood of today with that of 50 years ago and commenting on how it reflects the history of the era.
7. A projection concerning the future of the neighborhood.
8. A presentation of the material in booklet or PowerPoint format.

Assessment. Students will be assessed on the appropriateness and thoroughness of each of the required elements, on the originality of their analysis, and on the creativity of their presentation. Teachers may wish to design a rubric for each element or one for the project overall.

Extension. A celebration of the neighborhoods of the community to which some of those interviewed are invited and at which foods associated with the various ethnic groups who have lived in the neighborhoods are served.

Adaptations. The idea for this project grew from the historical narrative on Woonsocket and how its institutions and diversity changed over time. The project plan, however, is generic in design and could be followed in any community where the teacher's goal is to connect the past to the present and to have students investigate how their own neighborhoods reflect the larger national currents of the post-World War II era.

CHAPTER 5

Religious Beliefs and the Role of Women in American Shaker Communities

A S THE YOUNG REPUBLIC of the United States struggled to maintain its independence and at the same time develop a national identity, a wellspring of religious energy with a distinctly American character emerged and left an indelible imprint on the people's beliefs and modes of worship. Dubbed the Second Great Awakening by historians (McLoughlin, 1978), the reform movement was punctuated by countless revivals and sustained a number of fervent religious sects, among them the United Society of Believers, popularly known as the Shakers. Predating the Second Great Awakening by about 20 years, the Shakers were founded in the Northeast by Ann Lee, an unschooled religious dissenter who emigrated from England with her husband in 1774 and went on to gather a number of Shaker communities in the region (Danker, 1986). With their distinctive style of worship, their unorthodox beliefs, their communitarian lifestyle, and their countless contributions to American domestic arts, the Shakers have long been a source of interest and, in recent years, a group largely admired by the mainstream. This was not always the case. One reason the group was suspect in the 19th century concerned its belief system, which described a dual deity, both male and female, insisted on a celibate lifestyle, and provided for equality for women in the organizational structure, if not the power structure, of its communities. Remnants of the latter, about 20 in number, can be found throughout the eastern half of the United States, from Maine to Kentucky, with a few short-lived experiments as far south as Georgia and Florida. Founded by a woman and characterized by unusual beliefs and lifestyles, the Shakers and their legacy contribute to the local history of a number of American towns and offer a rich source of religious and social diversity into which social studies teachers can tap if they are seeking to enliven their study of 19th-century reform movements in ways that promote inquiry and incorporate multicultural education.

RELIGION AND GENDER AS CATEGORIES OF DIVERSITY

Unlike ethnicity and language or even race and social class, aspects of diversity examined earlier, religion and gender do not have a presumed connection in terms of group membership. A Mexican immigrant ordinarily will speak Spanish, and lower socioeconomic status often is associated with people of color in the United States. Most religious groups, however, include both men and women, although the leaders of mainstream religions usually are male. A study of the Shakers offers a rare opportunity to link religion and gender and to focus on *women* because this group was founded by a charismatic female and had a dual hierarchical structure that, while it separated the sexes, accorded power to both in religious and temporal matters.

Issues Related to Religion

Of all the multicultural themes addressed in this book and elsewhere, none is more problematic than religion. It is closely linked to ethnic heritage and yet separate from it, in that while one is born a member of a particular ethnic group and cannot change this affiliation without denying or avoiding one's identity, one ultimately can choose to follow or reject the religious beliefs of one's family and ancestors. In the United States we pride ourselves on protecting an individual's freedom of religion and celebrate the familiar words in the First Amendment, which begins, "Congress shall make no law respecting an establishment of religion, or prohibiting the free exercise thereof." Religious concerns are at the very heart of our origins, first as colonial outposts and later as a unified nation. Indeed the first European explorers from Spain came to the Americas in part to Christianize the indigenous population, and the first settlements in New England were spawned by religious intolerance in England and gathered by Puritan and Separatist sects that continued the tradition of intolerance.

Religious Intolerance in a Land of Religious Freedom. Despite constitutional protections in the United States, there have been countless instances of religious persecution of both groups and individuals. Some of the most shameful episodes in our history have religious mistrust at their roots—the burning of the Catholic convent in Charlestown, Massachusetts, in 1834 (Schultz, 2000), the death of Mormon founder Joseph Smith at the hands of an Illinois mob in 1844 (Marty, 1984), the 1915 lynching of Leo Frank, a Jewish supervisor of a pencil factory in Georgia (Pou, 1999) were among the most notorious. Sadly, in the current post-9/11 climate, the media have reported numerous incidents of harassment, and worse, of Muslims, both immigrant and native born, who have suffered because of the religious affiliation of the suspects in the deaths of thousands of civilians in the terrorist attacks.

Religion in Public Schools. For classroom teachers, religion poses endless challenges and raises many troubling questions. How should the topic of religion be treated in world and U.S. history classes? What should be done about traditional holidays with religious origins? Should schools seek to be inclusive and recognize such events as Christmas, Chanukah, and Ramadan? Or will the commemorations offend those whose holidays and holy days may not be addressed? Will the celebration of the birthdays of members of elementary classes upset those whose religious beliefs do not allow participation in such events? Should the scheduling of tests and due dates for papers and projects consider the religious rituals and holidays of the student body? Should controversial topics with religious overtones, such as abortion rights, gay marriage, or refusal to salute the flag, be discussed openly in civics and current events classes? And finally, how should educators define the word *religion* itself in public schools where the student body comprises members of varied groups whose belief systems may hold differing concepts concerning its meaning?

According to Uphoff (1997), an educator with an extensive background in religious studies, "The word is a common one that seems easy to define but in fact is difficult to explain" (p. 109). The problem, of course, is that while religion is all around us, the concept has various meanings for particular individuals, communities, societies, and nations. Most would agree that religion encompasses a belief system, symbols, and distinctive traditions and/or forms of worship. For the most part, organized religions consist of gatherings of the faithful, who meet in places of worship, are led by trained or chosen individuals, and demonstrate commitment or loyalty to a shared faith. Yet there are well-defined groups, whose members are considered anything but religious by the mainstream, that seem to fit the definitions commonly offered. Hence, when addressing religion as a form of diversity, either as a content item in the social studies curriculum or as a topic for discussion, the classroom teacher must work to establish an acceptable definition.

Another consideration for teachers in the United States to address in seeking ways to incorporate the study of religion, as both a multicultural and historical topic, into their social studies curriculum is the pluralistic nature of religion in this country (Gollnick & Chinn, 2002). Religious diversity has been a characteristic of the United States as far back as its colonial origins and before. Native Americans, who populated the Americas for centuries before the coming of the Europeans, possessed a variety of religious beliefs, less structured than those of the colonists and generally linked to a polytheistic reverence for the natural environment. The early colonists were, for the most part, Christians, and that remains the faith of the majority of residents of the United States to this day. However, within Christianity there are numerous denominations, including

Catholics and mainstream Protestant groups such as Baptists, Episcopalians, Methodists, Presbyterians, and members of the United Church of Christ.

As Gollnick and Chinn (2002) indicate, historically the Protestant groups had strong geographic bases, but, while most still retain their original strongholds, there has been a steady proliferation of influence beyond traditional sites. Those authors provide statistics that indicate that in addition to the Christian denominations, religions with significant numbers in the United States include Judaism, Islam, Hinduism, Buddhism, and Confucianism. In addition, there are a number of smaller sects with a long-standing presence in the United States. Among the most prominent are the Amish, Christian Scientists, Jehovah's Witnesses, Mormons, Seventh-Day Adventists, and members of the Unification Church. Throughout our history, there have been periods of intolerance and discrimination directed toward many of the groups named above, but the fact that we have such widespread religious diversity provides opportunities for schools to promote cultural awareness, understanding of religious differences, and respect for the constitutionally protected right of freedom of religion.

Religion and Gender. The links between religion and gender are both obvious and subtle. Most organized religious groups and their fundamental texts address the role of women. As Gollnick and Chinn (2002) note, "In many of the more conservative religious bodies, the role of women is clearly defined and limited" (p. 219). Despite some calls recently for their inclusion in the priesthood, the Catholic Church does not allow women to be ordained. The Mormon Church, the Southern Baptists, and Islamic groups all have traditions that limit opportunities for women to hold positions of leadership. There are numerous passages in the Bible that may be interpreted as confining women to subordinate roles, leading to the Judeo-Christian paternalistic tradition. Yet, paradoxically, during the Second Great Awakening with which the Shakers were associated, the Evangelical leaders of the movement succeeded in both putting women on a pedestal and "feminization" of Christianity (McLoughlin, 1978, p. 120). In his tenderness and mercy, Christ was characterized in terms usually associated with women. In addition, women in large numbers became fervent members of the new congregations. As women's scholar Cott (1977) observes: "Women's prayer groups, charitable institutions, missionary and education societies, Sabbath School organizations, and moral reform and maternal associations all multiplied phenomenally after 1800, and all of these had religious motives" (p. 132). So although women were not accorded positions of equality in most of the mainstream and newer religious sects emergent in 19th-century America, they enthusiastically supported them and were largely responsible for their success.

Issues Related to the Concept of Gender

The concept of gender as a category of diversity in itself raises a number of issues. Usually thought of as an ascribed characteristic, gender is the basis of cultural stereotyping, inequality, discrimination, and harassment endured by women due to their birth characteristics. Gays and lesbians have suffered similarly due to their sexual orientation. Numerically, women constitute the majority of the population, yet they share the hardships associated with being a member of a minority group. In this chapter, background remarks and observations concerning local history and the Shakers will focus on the role and status of women in the United States and the problems of writing women's history, topics commonly addressed in social studies classrooms.

Women and History. It is not possible or even necessary in the context of this book to trace the history of women in the United States. However, a few remarks concerning their status and treatment within the pages of school texts are relevant to understanding the unique aspects of Shaker women and their place in the religious communities organized by Mother Ann and her followers. As a high school teacher who occasionally taught a course in women's history, I used an initiating activity that involved asking students to review the index of their regular U.S. history text and to simply count the number of male and female name references. As you can imagine, the gap was enormous. The statistics have improved in recent years, but history is still largely a male bastion, with women relegated to token treatments during Women's History Month or covered in little boxes and sidebars added to the regular text materials. Since the 1970s, however, texts entirely devoted to women's history have been available for high school courses such as the one that I taught (Hymowitz & Weissman, 1978; Norton, 1989). These works usually follow standard chronological order and focus on women's contributions or roles in the colonial, revolutionary, industrial, Civil War, progressive, New Deal, and more contemporary eras. They also call attention to problems or themes particular to women, such as witchcraft, the cult of domesticity, lives under slavery and on the frontier, work in the textile mills, sexuality, suffrage, and movements for reform. These works emphasize the fact that women did indeed participate in the great events of the nation's past and at the same time carved out a distinct history all their own.

Essays analyzing the nature of women's history (Berkin, 1989; Lerner, 1989) warn that this undertaking is complex and presents a number of contradictions that lead authors and those trying to make sense of the field to make choices that may not be entirely satisfying. History traditionally has been a male discipline, with such givens as chronological eras and topics worthy of research and study largely defined in terms of events and concepts in which men have assumed the defining roles—war, politics, diplomacy, and power, prominent among them. In a male-dominated society and culture, writing the history of women has led to some awkward and not always satisfying attempts "to fit them into the categories and value systems which consider *man* the measure of significance" (Lerner, 1989, p. 4; emphasis in original).

A further limitation to consideration of women in history is the fact that for the most part, in terms of the male-dominated conceptual framework, women necessarily must be treated either as victims or as subordinate contributors to the events that men consider important. Hence we have school texts examining women's role in the industrial revolution, the Civil War, the progressive movement, and the like, but we are deficient in materials for elementary and secondary students that examine women as a separate culture. Berkin (1989) notes that even this model has problems because "gender is not the only and always defining category for *women themselves*" (p. 16; emphasis in original). Some experiences are exclusive to women's culture, for example, childbearing; others are shared with men, such as reactions to the attacks of 9/11. Berkin sees the major task of women's history to be differentiating those spheres that are shared and recognizing those that intersect. Lerner (1989), on the other hand, calls for a "truly universal history" (p. 9) that gives equal treatment to both men and women and that seeks to eradicate once and for all the male-dominated lens of the field.

The Shaker Perspective. In studying the Shaker communities, which form a unique and interesting segment of the local histories of a number of sites in the eastern United States, teachers and students can explore a number of important questions addressing issues concerning women's history raised by historians as well as those revolving around religious diversity and how a small and private sect can influence the mainstream culture. Unlike most traditional religions, the Shakers were founded by a woman and maintained a separate hierarchy for women in both spiritual and temporal matters in their communities. Hence they may prove an exception to the male-dominated conceptual framework of history so frustrating to historians of women's history. Further, their unusual lifestyle and inventive culture are inherently interesting, and lessons and projects investigating these topics can provide students with insights into difference and enterprise that can be linked to both local history and major currents sweeping the nation when the Shakers were in their heyday.

THE SHAKER WAY OF LIFE

FOCUS QUESTIONS

How do religious groups develop and change?
How have religious groups influenced the culture
of the United States?

The founder of the United Society of Believers, or the American Shakers, was a charismatic woman of humble origins, Ann Lee, born in 1736 in Manchester, England (Danker, 1986). The daughter of a blacksmith, Lee received no formal schooling and was sent to work in the textile mills while still in her early teens. She married Abraham Stanley (or Standerin) and gave birth to four children; none survived beyond infancy. A spiritual person, Lee would come to interpret these losses as God's punishment for her sins of the flesh. She previously had been attracted to the religious teachings of a group of Quaker dissenters led by James and Jane Wardley and had joined their circle. The Wardleys advised Lee to adopt a life of celibacy, which she did despite the objections of her husband. The Wardley group endured harassment and persecution due to their beliefs and their unorthodox and agitated form of worship, which led to the label "Shaking Quakers." During a period of imprisonment, Lee had a vision that she was the female counterpart to Jesus or the Second Coming of Christ (Harlan, 2001). This vision would have a profound effect on the congregation, and she became recognized as the new leader of the group.

The Shakers Come to North America

Tired of their persecution and encouraged by a vision of a holy sanctuary in America described by Mother Ann, as Lee was called, a small group of Shakers emigrated in 1774. Mother Ann's circle included her husband, brother, niece, and five followers. Upon their arrival in New York City, they looked for divine guidance concerning the next step in their mission. Consequently, a number of the Believers set off for Niskeyuna, near Albany, where they acquired some land that they cleared for farming in order to provide themselves with a means of support. Ann remained behind to nurse her ailing husband, who, upon his recovery, left her for a woman of the streets. The marriage was dissolved in 1775, and Ann lived in poverty until the following year, when she was able to join the Believers in Niskeyuna. They gained few converts due to their British roots and commitment to pacifism during the American Revolution (Harlan, 2001).

Mother Ann and the New Light Revival. A turning point in the fortunes of Mother Ann and her followers came amid the fervor of the New Light religious revival that swept the Northeast in the late 1770s and 1780s (Danker, 1986). New converts signed on, and the sect began to grow in numbers. The folly of sins of the flesh, as well as the need for the Believers to withdraw from the secular world and to fashion their own, were themes stressed in the early years that held appeal for many looking for spiritual peace in the still frontier-like environment of the new republic. Mother Ann and some of her trusted assistants, the elders, boldly set off on a mission to New England to gather new converts and to establish model communities. They arrived at

Harvard, Massachusetts, in 1781 and began a campaign to recruit followers, which met with serious opposition from the residents of the town. Mother
Ann persisted in using Harvard as her home base since the site seemed to
replicate an image she had in one of her visions while she was still living in
England. After an exhausting 2-year New England campaign, Mother Ann
died in 1784, and the United Society of Believers entered a new phase of
growth and change.

Success of Early Organizers. Significant in the early years of Shaker success
was Joseph Meacham, Mother Ann's first convert in America. Meacham was
a talented organizer, and, under his leadership, a number of communities
were established, with the one at New Lebanon, New York, serving as the
Parent Ministry. As such, the New Lebanon community directed both the
spiritual and commercial activities of the sect (Danker, 1986; Harlan, 2001).
With respect to the spiritual aspect of the Shakers, they were committed to
their concept of a male/female deity. Each community thus was governed by
two elders and two eldresses, who directed the religious activities and made
decisions concerning matters of faith. In the temporal realm, responsibility
was shared by male and female deacons and deaconesses, respectively. This
dual system of organization was the brainchild of Meacham and not part of
the original doctrine as professed by Mother Ann (Andrews, 1963).

During the so-called "golden period of expansion in the early nineteenth
century" (Campbell, 1978, p. 25), it was a woman, Mother Lucy Wright,
who orchestrated the Shakers' stunning success. Appointed by Meacham to
direct the activities of the women of the sect, Wright later would influence
the entire order for 25 years (Andrews, 1963). She had joined the Shakers
with her husband, Elizur Goodrich, as a young woman and was recognized
early on by Mother Ann as a potential leader. During her tenure as head of
the ministry, Mother Lucy is credited with expanding the *Millennial Laws*
(bylaws organizing the society) as circumstances dictated, invigorating the
Shaker forms of worship through the introduction of hand gestures and marching to step songs, and encouraging attention to the education of the children
in the communities. Under her direction, Shaker settlements were widely expanded beyond the Northeast, and her frequent visits to the various communities helped to ensure uniformity of worship and lifestyle (Horgan, 1987).

Beliefs and Practices

As it evolved in the early years, the Shaker religious code could be summed
up in seven succinct principles (Andrews, 1940). These included service to
God, a celibate lifestyle, separation from the larger society, communal property, pacifism, purity of speech, and service to others. In practical terms, a
convert to Shakerism was required to adopt a communal lifestyle, turn over

all personal property to the church, work without wages for the community, and renounce sexual relations. In addition to belief in a dual deity, Shaker doctrine emphasized the Second Coming, confession of sin, and gender equality (Horgan, 1987). Work was elevated to a form of worship; hence their slogan, based on the teachings of Mother Ann, became "hands to work, hearts to God."

Shakers and the Work Ethic. The Shaker devotion to hard work was one of the principal reasons for the success of their communes. Where other 19th-century utopian experiments failed due to their inability to be self-sustaining, the Shaker communities thrived as productive labor was inextricably linked to the religious doctrine of the society. The *Millennial Laws* that governed the order contained many provisions regarding neatness, order, and the proper maintenance of Shaker villages (Andrews, 1963). The *Laws* attempted both to regulate strictly the everyday life of the membership and to encourage work habits that would promote a comfortable but certainly not lavish standard of living. The Shakers attempted not only to sustain themselves through farming and other agricultural pursuits but also to provide adequate financial resources for their communities through the creation and sale of products to the outside world.

Some of the most successful of the Shaker enterprises included the garden seed industry, the preparation of medicinal herbs, the manufacture of brooms and brushes, the fashioning of oval boxes, and the weaving of poplar and ash baskets (Andrews & Andrews, 1974). The Shakers are credited with a number of inventive adaptations for familiar products, such as the flat broom, far superior in efficiency to the old round models, and the washing machine or mill, which was a gold medal winner at the Philadelphia Centennial Exposition in 1876.

Shaker Care of Children. One aspect of Shaker life that might be of particular interest to elementary and secondary students is their interest in caring for orphans and their belief in providing a quality education for the children of their communities. In the early years of the sect, education was not a priority (Andrews & Andrews, 1974), although designated sisters and brethren routinely were charged with caring for the young girls and boys, respectively, and for training them in the ways of the community. As the *Millennial Laws* were codified, however, the education of the youth of the communities received specific attention. Girls were to be taught in the summer and boys in the winter—never together (Andrews, 1963). The curriculum consisted of the three Rs, farming, architecture, history and geography, manners, and, of course, religion. Bible reading was a must as was the study of the history of the Shakers and the names and various contributions of their leaders. The use of ornate picture books was prohibited, and teachers were cautioned to study only as much as necessary to instruct their students. Higher learning, such as the study of medicine and physics, was reserved for those who received special permission from the elders.

Influential in the evolution of Shaker schools was Seth Y. Wells, a teacher from the Albany area who was appointed superintendent in 1821 (Andrews, 1963). He added music to the course of studies and insisted that the classes be open for public inspection. Shaker schools generally conformed to the regulations of the local districts, earned a reputation for quality, and received some public funding. In some instances, children from outside the communities were enrolled. Despite occasional conflicts with local governments, such as a clash between Horace Mann, when he headed the Board of Education in Massachusetts, and the Harvard Shakers over their refusal to submit to inspection by civil authorities, the schools generally were respected by outsiders (Horgan, 1987). In fact, Shakers Elijah Myrick and John Whitely served on the school committees of the Massachusetts towns where their communities were located.

In addition to attention to education, recreation for the Children's Order, as the youngsters were called, was recognized as appropriate, and various play activities were allowed (Andrews, 1963). Young boys were observed fishing and playing ball, while girls engaged in gymnastics and planted flower gardens for enjoyment. Picnics and sleigh rides with the adult members of the communities were also common. One adult Shaker woman fondly remembered making boats out of bonnets with other children and floating them down the stream for fun (Andrews, 1963). So despite the austerity of the *Millennial Laws* and their attempt to carefully regulate every aspect of daily life, there is evidence that the Shakers did accept the tendency of human nature, particularly with reference to children, to seek out enjoyment and lighthearted pleasures.

The Role of Women

With respect to the role of women, the Shakers were unusual in two respects. Of primary significance is the fact that the order was founded by a woman. Consequently, the Shakers were committed to enforcing gender equality within their communities, and, as previously noted, they maintained a dual hierarchy with respect to both spiritual and temporal organization. However, as Rohrlich (1984) indicates, this commitment to equality did not mean that there was significant deviation from traditional gender roles in terms of the division of tasks related to everyday life.

Women's Work in Shaker Communities. Productive labor was key to the survival of each of the Shaker communities, and the concept was inextricably linked to the spiritual life of the sect as well. Codified within the *Millennial*

Laws are a number of provisions regarding order, neatness, and proper maintenance of Shaker villages (Andrews, 1963). Such specifics as painting all bed-
steads green, staining shop floors yellowish red, laying out fields and gardens
in a square formation, and setting broken window panes before the Sabbath
indicate the extent to which the Shaker leadership attempted to regulate everyday life and to ensure uniformity from community to community.

The brethren routinely were assigned to agricultural duties, carpen-
try, and heavy work, while the sisters cooked, cleaned, sewed, and per-
formed laundry chores. An 1851 sisters' daybook from the community at
Harvard, Massachusetts, includes entries recording the following work
activities: washing sheets, ironing flannels, knitting, making applesauce,
boiling cider, and picking cherries (Danker, 1986). Perhaps the most demand-
ing of all the work assignments for women in Shaker communities was the
preparation of the daily meals. Feeding upwards of 100 residents three times
a day was quite a challenge, but the sisters shared the burden and worked
out a system of rotation to help ease the drudgery. The Shaker tables were
celebrated for their abundance and their well-cooked fare. In addition to the
regular meals, the sisters were expected to prepare special diets for the sick
and the elderly and to pack portable lunches for brethren working in the fields
or embarking on trips to do business with the outside world. The hard work
related to meal preparation was perhaps somewhat mitigated by the fact that
Shaker kitchens were designed for efficiency, and the finest quality cooking
utensils, dishes, and earthenware outfitted the workrooms and pantries. For
women from modest circumstances, the opportunity to work with effective
implements in an attractive environment might have been something of a
novelty, offsetting the heavy labor of the kitchen assignment.

Shaker sisters also cared for all clothing and domestic linens and sewed
all the women's wardrobes. Although there were tailoring shops operated
by the brethren to provide for some of their clothing needs, the sisters fashioned men's articles as well. Shaker women were required to dress simply,
but each was allotted quite an impressive array of clothing articles. An 1840
description of the wardrobe needs of a sister at the Hancock Shaker Village
in Massachusetts listed 130 items, including two cloaks, four worsted gowns,
a riding gown, calfskin shoes, blue cloth shoes, two bonnets, gloves, mittens,
and petticoats (Danker, 1986). Daybooks faithfully record all the labors
involved in the making of the components of the sisters' wardrobes, with
notes on spinning, weaving, sewing, dying, bleaching, and crafting palm leaf
bonnets as well as hats for the brethren. Shaker men and women were not
supposed to exhibit signs of vanity, but dressing neatly and looking proper
for worship on the Sabbath were signs of both respect and the success of the
society in providing for the needs of members.

Although for the most part differentiated and traditional, albeit equally
time-consuming, work roles were assigned to the men and women of the

Shaker communities, there is evidence that some women engaged in unusual or nontraditional endeavors. One sister, Tabitha Babitt, designed a circular saw after observing some brethren waste wood using the more common straight version of the tool (Danker, 1986). Babitt is credited with developing a technique for cutting iron nails and regularly worked as an assistant to Sarah Jewett, who served as a physician for the order.

Shaker women also contributed to the economic life of their communities through their engagement in such revenue-producing endeavors as cultivating and preparing medicinal herbs, putting up preserves, and making applesauce. In addition, they sewed the seed bags for the lucrative Shaker garden seed industry. The sisters of the Harvard community also made sieves, turkey feather fans, and palm leaf hats for sale. For the most part, the food and craft products fashioned by Shaker women were distributed and sold to the outside world by the brethren, who made frequent references to their herb and seed routes and other other business trips in their daily records (Danker, 1986). As Rohrlich (1984) notes: "Shaker women and men led lives that were interdependent but separate; parallel but symbiotic" (p. 57). Both contributed effectively to the everyday functioning and upkeep of the various communities and to the overall economic stability of the order.

Shaker Women in the Spiritual Realm. As interesting and unique as Shaker economy and daily life might be, the most important aspect of the order was, of course, its spiritual side. In this realm, the women of the society made significant and often overlooked contributions. Many came from families with strong religious beliefs and joined after attending a Shaker revival meeting (Campbell, 1978). Seeking salvation, they made a commitment to a life of worship, work, celibacy, and community. With respect to modes of worship, the Shakers were noted for their spirited and emotional services. Spiritual dancing was common, with the men and women grouped separately (Danker, 1986). The goal of the ritual was to shake away sinful desires and doubts that might weaken one's faith. Holding the palms upward toward heaven was a symbolic gesture intended to signify receiving gifts from God, which was followed by inward gestures to indicate the acceptance of such rewards. A ring dance and spiritual marching were added to the Shaker religious services in the 1820s.

Music and song were also essential components of Shaker worship. In 1837, a group of adolescent girls at the Niskeyuna society in New York, while assembled for a routine session of instruction, suddenly burst into song celebrating a heavenly journey. The innovation caught on and became popular with other young girls in the order and eventually was practiced by adults as well. Believers claimed that they received visions or gifts from heaven in the form of spiritual songs, which became incorporated into their services. Two women of the Harvard Shaker community, Eunice Wyeth and her niece

Eunice Bathrick, made noteworthy contributions to the Shaker body of song. Wyeth wrote a number of compositions, including the telling "Wolves Among Sheep," while Bathrick copied and preserved them, adding some of her own to the collection. In his study of the sacred music of the Shakers, Patterson (1979) compiled checklists of the songs attributed to members of various communities and documented the rich musical legacy of the women of the sect.

A rather unorthodox manifestation of Shaker spirituality concerned their belief that certain members could receive communications or spirit messages from Mother Ann and others who had passed away. A Harvard sister who recorded several such communications was a mystical woman named Eunice Wilds (Danker, 1986). Joining the order in its early days in 1791, she remained a member until her death in 1855. During these years, Wilds claimed she received many messages from the Holy Mother, who consoled her on her sufferings as she patiently did God's work on earth, and from one of the angels, who reassured her that she was a faithful follower of Mother Ann. Such revelations on the part of the sisters are evidence of their deep faith and perhaps indications that they might view their many labors, both physical and spiritual, as taxing on body and soul. Shaker sisters such as Wilds spoke of their spirit messages as gifts that they received in such celebratory symbols as crowns, trumpets, gems, and pearls. Sometimes, however, the messages were revealed in such practical, everyday articles as ointments, cakes, puddings, and pies, items that occupied the daily lives of the Shaker sisters as they cared for the sick and prepared meals.

Women's Perspective in Shaker Life. Although their daybooks, diaries, and letters suggest that the women of the Shaker communities were largely contented with their lot (Campbell, 1978), some found that the orderly and strictly regimented lifestyle was not for them. They may have joined in part to relieve themselves of the burdens of childbearing and to provide stability and material comfort in an unpredictable world, but even these attractions and the promise of eternal salvation were not enough for many. Church records are amply sprinkled with the notation "Ap" for apostasy next to the names of women and men alike who joined for a while and then returned to the outside world (Danker, 1986). The so-called "winter Shakers" were infamous for their willingness to sign on as cold weather set in and then to leave with the approaching warmth of the spring sun. Some, however, stayed on for a number of years and then for various reasons decided to rejoin mainstream society. Others, like Roxalana Grosvenor, who had assumed a leadership role as eldress at the Harvard community, and her sister Maria Fidelia, claimed that they were forced out against their will (Horgan, 1987). In the suit they filed against the Shakers, the sisters claimed that they were punished for nonconformity and sought damages. They lost their case, perhaps in part because after leaving the order they embarked on a study of mesmerism (Danker, 1986).

Whatever their fate, the women of the Shaker communities were unique in their adherence to a religious order that was founded by a woman and that developed a communal lifestyle dedicated to principles celebrating celibacy, separatism, and equality for women and men. Both depended on each other's labors to maintain their orderly communities and each participated appropriately, according to the standards of the day, in the economic life of the society. In addition, Shaker women served as spiritual leaders and contributed to the rituals of the order with a body of songs, dances, and spirit messages.

Sister Rebecca Cox Jackson and the Question of Race

Among the many women who joined the Shakers and those who eventually rose to positions of leadership, Rebecca Cox Jackson merits special attention due to her many contributions to the order and the lessons her prominence can teach about the sect's attitude toward both women and African Americans.

When Mother Ann was gathering the order in America in the 1780s, the new nation was in its formative stages, and slavery was legal both in the South and in the Northeast, where she made her headquarters. From the beginning, the Shakers were opposed to the institution and welcomed converts from among Blacks and former slaveholders alike (Andrews, 1963). An 1832 visitor to the Shaker community in New Lebanon, New York, noticed a number of Blacks, both men and women, participating in the service that he observed. However, whether or not Black members were integrated into a Shaker family seemed determined by geography. While visitors to New Lebanon remarked on the presence of Blacks among the worshippers, Kentucky records indicate that a Black family at South Union had its own elder, and in Philadelphia an African American "out-family" conducted its own meetings (Andrews, 1963, p. 214).

Jackson's Early Years. It is the Philadelphia group that is of interest with respect to the leadership of the remarkable Rebecca Cox Jackson. Although information about her early life remains sketchy, it appears that Jackson was born into a free family in 1795 and as a young child was cared for by her grandmother (Humez, 1981). She was taken back by her mother when she was about 6 years old and apparently was then given the responsibility for attending to the needs of her younger stepsiblings. The other children of the family were able to go to school, but Rebecca's child care duties made it difficult for her to receive an education. Rebecca's mother died when she was 13, and little is known about her life for the next several years. She evidently was taken in by an older brother, worked as a seamstress, and married a member of her brother's household, Samuel Jackson (*Brotherly Love*, 2003). During a thunderstorm in the summer of 1830 that terrified Rebecca, she had a religious experience that would profoundly affect the rest of her life.

According to her autobiography, which begins in 1830, the year of her religious conversion, Jackson led a relatively good life in the security of Philadelphia, a city with a strong community of free African Americans who developed their own set of institutions to provide for their religious, social, and economic needs (Humez, 1981). Life became difficult for Jackson when her religious calling inspired her to reject all established churches and to gather her own congregation. Although her followers were mostly women, there were some men among them, and this situation led to criticism of Jackson's independence. Her marriage fell apart, and she became estranged from her brother, whom she faulted for not fulfilling his promise to teach her to read and write. However, after hearing a voice telling her that God would be her teacher, Jackson realized that she could indeed read for herself (*Brotherly Love*, 2003).

Jackson discovered as she began to travel about spreading her religious doctrine, which centered on the message that "self-control brought power" (Humez, 1981, p. 22), that she had much in common with the Shakers, including her belief in leading a celibate life. She spent some time at the Shaker community in Watervliet, New York, but left unhappy with what she saw as a less than enthusiastic effort on the part of the Believers to recruit Blacks (*Brotherly Love*, 2003).

Jackson's Shaker Family. Jackson returned to Philadelphia with a young follower, Rebecca Perot, and eventually they made their peace with the Shaker establishment, which provided them with the resources to help establish an African American family there in the late 1850s. Jackson conducted her first service as a Shaker eldress in Philadelphia in 1859. Although records of the next several years are sketchy, Shaker writings indicate that by the 1870s the Black Philadelphia family consisted of a nucleus of women living in an impressive residence where they supported themselves largely by working as seamstresses and doing laundry (Humez, 1981). The community also included a number of nonresidents in the area who regularly attended services. That the Black Philadelphia branch of the Shakers was considered a full-fledged component of the sect can be supported by the fact that it was visited regularly during the 1870s and 1880s. Although Jackson died in 1871, her protégé, Rebecca Perot, took over, and the community continued for another 40 years.

The story of Rebecca Jackson, an uneducated Black living in the United States during the racially divided 19th century who became a religious visionary and who founded a long-lived religious community, is remarkable in itself. Within the context of the larger story of the Shakers, the success and support of Jackson and Perot offer insight into the beliefs and practices of the United Society of Believers. Although by 21st-century standards the Shakers might not be seen as entirely free from the moral conflict and discrimination that have characterized White America's relationship with African Americans, still they stand apart for their attempts to integrate some of their communities and to provide support for others comprising Blacks.

The Shakers and the Civil War

The Civil War was a defining event for the Shakers, as it was for many individuals and groups living in the United States during the turbulent mid-19th century. Pacifism was central to their belief system, and during the War of 1812 and the Mexican War they refused to serve in the military (Burns, 1993). When converts joined the Shakers, they were required to agree not to engage in violence against others, including participation in war and politics (Neal, 1975). Indeed, early in their history, when they were the targets of angry mobs, the Shakers resisted with prayer and by turning their backs to their tormentors (Melcher, 1968). As they gained in stature and became more widely known, their status as conscientious objectors generally was respected.

With the Civil War and the preservation of the nation at stake, service in the military became a more pressing issue. Laws exempting the Shakers and other pacifist groups from military service were suspended, and in 1862 George Ingals of the North Union, Ohio, Shakers was drafted (Melcher, 1968). Shaker leaders Benjamin Gates and Frederick Evans embarked on a mission to Washington to win a reprieve for Ingals and to plead the case for other young men who might be conscripted (Stein, 1992). Lincoln complied with their request and gave further instructions for a course to be followed by others among them who might be drafted in the future.

For the Shakers at Pleasant Hill and South Union in Kentucky, the Civil War proved particularly stressful. Troops from both sides in the conflict moved through the area, and, due to the reputation of the Shakers for hospitality to outsiders in need, they often were called on to provide meals for the soldiers. Sisters at South Union regularly reported such incidents as one in December 1861 when a southern cavalry unit requested supper for 400 on an hour's notice (Neal, 1977). On some occasions the troops seeking meals from the South Union Shakers numbered over 1,000. The Pleasant Hill Shakers took no compensation, but the more heavily frequented South Union village charged a small fee for services. Food was not the only sought-after commodity, for the troops often combed the settlements in search of horses and wagons, both of which the Shakers were unwilling to surrender. The stress of trying to remain neutral, faithful to pacifist principles, and doing their duty to those in need heavily taxed the Shakers of Kentucky during the war years.

Overall, the Civil War marked a turning point in the history of the Shakers. It would mark the end of the group's growth and expansion and the beginning of a period of retrenchment and decline. American society as a whole was forever changed, as the carnage and destruction helped wipe away the religious fervor and reform spirit of the antebellum era. The secularism and the materialism of the nation at large during the postwar period may have subtly yet irrevocably altered the character of the United Society of Believers. As Burns (1993) notes, "Perhaps partly because of their disillusionment, many Shakers in the second half of the century grew less preoccupied with heaven and hell and more interested in improving earthly life" (p. 151).

Decline of the Shakers

The United Society of Believers grew steadily throughout the first half of the 19th century until membership reached about 6,000 during the 1850s (Andrews, 1963). There were 19 communities scattered throughout the eastern United States from Maine to Kentucky (Horgan, 1987) when the Shakers reached their peak in terms of numbers and vitality. Following the Civil War, the order began a steady decline, despite attempts to establish communities in the deep South. Narcrosse in Florida and White Oak in Georgia, founded in 1896 and 1898, respectively, were short-lived, and, indeed, by the time they were established, the Shakers had diminished in numbers to about 1,000. Today, although there are a number of intact Shaker buildings operating as museums, there are officially only a few members, who live at the Sabbathday Lake Shaker Village in New Gloucester, Maine, where they work and worship much as their predecessors did when the order was in its heyday (Sharp, 2003).

A number of explanations have been offered for the decline of the Shakers, the most obvious being their insistence on a celibate lifestyle. Dependent on converts and the orphans and foundlings whom they raised for the state to fill their ranks, the Shaker membership was always somewhat tenuous. There were other reasons for their decline, some of them rooted in the changing economic and social order of the United States and others stemming from the character of those who sought to join the group in its later stages. With respect to their economic life, the Shakers were renowned for their high-quality crafts and agricultural products, but they could not compete with the mass-produced offerings turned out when the nation industrialized. Andrews (1963) cites mismanagement of assets, overexpansion with respect to land, and increased dependence on outside labor as contributing causes of the Shaker economic decline. Secularism in the larger society, which made membership in the strict religious communes less attractive, and diminished adherence to the sacred principles among those who remained within the

Shaker realm also can be offered as reasons for the group's demise. As the Shakers became more well known in the first half of the 19th century, women, in particular, may have joined to escape from unhappy marriages or to free themselves from the burdens of childbearing when large families were the rule, and the work of maintaining a household among those unable to afford servants was backbreaking. Women who entered the order for these reasons rather than for strictly religious principles perhaps would be less fervent in terms of commitment to the sacred rituals and work ethic necessary for the sect to thrive as a religious entity. Andrews also notes that after the death of the capable Mother Lucy in 1821, the Shakers lacked a single effective leader to hold the group together and to direct both its religious and economic activities. Without such a leader, the Shakers did well to thrive for as long as they did. Although Hancock in Massachusetts, Canterbury in New Hampshire, and Sabbathday Lake in Maine continued on well into the late 20th century, Shakerism as a force had died before World War I.

The Shakers and Local History

Although there are only a handful of Shakers left today, the remains of their villages can be found in Maine, New Hampshire, Massachusetts, Connecticut, New York, Ohio, Indiana, and Kentucky. A number of the villages have been restored and operate as living history museums, while the artifacts and manuscripts of others are housed in libraries and historical societies in various locations. This unique religious society, with its emphasis on work, worship, and equality, is part of the local history of at least 19 communities in eight states and as such is the source of a collection of materials that may be used to help students appreciate American utopianism from a nearby perspective and view it through a multicultural lens.

Learning Activities

Two of the Shaker living history museums, Pleasant Hill in Harrodsburg, Kentucky, and Canterbury in New Hampshire, offer educational programs geared to school groups. At Pleasant Hill, visiting classes can learn about Shaker agricultural activities and crafts through demonstrations and workshops, many of which are hands-on and interactive (*Shaker Village of Pleasant Hill*, 2003a). Aspects of Shaker life and values emphasizing such practical 19th-century activities as sheep shearing, spinning, weaving, gardening, creating herbal remedies, and growing, harvesting, and preparing apple products are stressed, along with museum-imposed themes such as respect for nature and environmentalism. At the Shaker Village in Canterbury, New Hampshire, in addition to guided tours and outreach visits to individual classrooms, the museum integrates age-appropriate curriculum themes to enhance the experience of visiting students (*Canterbury Shaker Village*, 2000). For the youngest students (K–2), the topics include Shaker foods, clothing, schooling, work, and dance. Upper elementary students learn about the Shakers' religious beliefs and how they organized their communities to provide for their material and spiritual needs. Middle school students who visit Canterbury will learn about how the Shakers conceptualized progress and adapted the technology of the day to their lifestyle in order to provide for their material needs. For high school students, the Canterbury tour focuses on the rise and fall of Shaker communities and the impact of the historical forces of the two centuries of their existence on their individual lives and their utopian societies.

Teachers wishing to prepare their students for field trips to Pleasant Hill, Canterbury, or other onsite Shaker museums at Sabbathday Lake in New Gloucester, Maine, Enfield in New Hampshire, Hancock in Pittsfield, Massachusetts, and South Union in Kentucky may seek to have students conduct research beforehand concerning such local history and/or multicultural themes as the influence of the Shakers on the larger community, the attitude of those outside the community toward the Shakers in their midst, the role of women in the village, and the presence of African Americans and their roles in the local Shaker village (see Lesson Plan 5.1). Schoolchildren in areas where the

Round Barn and Garden, Hancock Shaker Village, Pittsfield, Massachusetts.

Shakers once lived but that do not have museums dedicated to preserving the culture may benefit from conducting similar research. After a field trip to a Shaker museum or following research into the group's history and influence on the local community and beyond, teachers may wish to assign a follow-up project or assignments to help connect the local Shakers to such U.S. history topics as the Second Great Awakening, 19th-century reform, the communitarian movement, and the industrial revolution, and to promote greater awareness of the themes of religion and gender (see Project Plan 5.1).

CONCLUSIONS

The Shakers present an example of one of the most successful spiritual utopias in U.S. history, even though their beliefs and practices were dramatically different from those of mainstream religious groups. The facts that they were founded by a woman, practiced gender equality in their villages, and established communities in a number of locations in the eastern portion of the nation make them an interesting and significant group to weave into the social studies curriculum. The Shakers chose a lifestyle that was separate from and in many ways critical of that of most 19th-century Americans, yet they influenced the culture through their industry and inventiveness and anticipated 20th-century reforms with respect to women's rights and integration.

The first Focus Question on the Shaker way of life asks the reader to consider how religious groups develop and change, and certainly the history of the Shakers illustrates how one charismatic person, aided by able loyal followers, can create a religion and how its members both refine the original belief system and attempt to adapt to changing conditions in the larger society. The second Focus Question concerns how religious groups have influenced the culture of the United States. In this realm, the Shakers, with their many inventions and innovations dedicated to the principles of simplicity, workmanship, and practicality, reflect a set of values that resonate with many Americans and offer a characteristic line of crafts and products that are prized by many collectors and ordinary consumers alike. Other religious groups and/or utopian communities, such as the Amana Colonies in Iowa and New Harmony in Indiana, can be analyzed using similar questions and perspectives.

Following are a lesson plan and a project plan that can be used by teachers in districts where the Shakers may have lived or where they may have been neighbors. The plans also may be adapted for use in any community in the nation where religious or utopian groups have settled and spread their influence. Finally, apart from the local aspect, the Shakers have ties to many currents in U.S. history, and a study of their founding, practices, and legacy may be useful to teachers anywhere whose classes are exploring a number of themes related to 19th-century life.

LESSON PLAN 5.1
A FIELD STUDY OF THE SHAKERS

Grades 5–12

Suggested Length. One class session of 60 minutes and a field trip to a Shaker museum with follow-up

National Standards for History References

Era 4. Expansion and Reform
Standard 4B. The student understands how Americans strived to reform society and create a distinct culture.
Standard 4C. The student understands changing gender roles and the ideas and activities of women reformers.

NCSS *Curriculum Guidelines for Multicultural Education* Reference

21.0. The multicultural curriculum should make maximum use of experiential learning, especially local community resources.

Prerequisite Knowledge. Students previously will have learned about some of the reforms of the early 19th century, including abolitionism, the Second Great Awakening, and women's rights.

Objectives. Students will be able to—

- Explain the origins, organization, lifestyle, and influence of the Shakers
- Analyze how the Shakers may have interacted with or influenced the local community

Procedures: Day 1

Initiation

- Display (objects or pictures) the following items: flat broom, packet of garden seeds, oval box, and circular saw.
- Ask if students know what they have in common. They were all invented, designed, or improved by a group known as the Shakers.

Development

- Create a KWL chart (see Table 5.1), and fill in information in the "What do we know about the Shakers?" column.

TABLE 5.1. KWL Chart

What do we KNOW about the Shakers?	What do we WANT to know about the Shakers?	What have we LEARNED about the Shakers?

- Brainstorm questions students would like to research about the Shakers in general and about the Shakers in their local community or state in particular. Add students' questions to the "What do we want to know about the Shakers?" section of the chart.
- Present an interactive lecture about the Shakers (see Figure 5.1), using the information in this chapter and illustrations downloaded from the Web sites cited. Ask questions frequently, both to check on facts and to provide opportunities for discussion.
- Go back and fill in information on the "What have we learned about the Shakers?" section of the chart.

Closing

- Brainstorm topics students would like to investigate further concerning the Shakers in the local area.
- Encourage them to seek information concerning diversity-related themes, such as whether the Shakers were accepted or discriminated against in the local

Figure 5.1. The Shaker Way of Life Lecture

FOCUS QUESTIONS

How did the Shakers develop and change?

How were the Shakers the same and different from other groups in the United States?

TOPICS

Origins of the Shakers

Shaker beliefs and practices

Role of women among the Shakers

African Americans and the Shakers

The Shakers and the Civil War

Decline of the Shakers

The Shaker legacy

LINKS TO CONTENT AND KWL ACTIVITY

Throughout the lecture, pose questions linking the Shakers to the Second Great Awakening, reforms of the pre–Civil War era of the 19th century, and the early industrial revolution. Allow students to generate their own ideas about the legacy of the Shakers.

---

community, the role of women, whether there were African Americans living in the community, and, if so, what role they played.
- Tell students that you will create a composite list of their local topics to bring on the field trip to the Shaker museum.

Procedures: Day 2 (field trip)

Initiation. Distribute the list of local topics for students to explore throughout the field trip.

Development. Encourage students to seek answers to their questions about the local Shakers during the site visit.

Closing. On the trip home or the next day in class, go back to the KWL chart and add to the "What have we learned?" section.

Assessment

- Students can be assessed informally through completion of the "What have we learned" section of the KWL chart.
- Students can be assessed formally by having them write an essay about the local Shaker village, in which they address the themes concerning women, African Americans, and discrimination and/or acceptance of the group by the outside community, or they may complete a full-fledged project on the Shakers (see Project Plan 5.1).

Adaptations. The field study approach can be adapted for classes planning visits to any number of historical sites, whether associated with religious utopias or more secular themes. The key teaching strategies involve providing historical background and clearly linking the trip to learning standards. The KWL chart necessarily involves students in the planning process because it affords them the opportunity to identify what additional information they would like to learn about a particular group or settlement and to debrief the field trip in an organized activity when they finish filling in the "What have we learned?" section of the chart.

PROJECT PLAN 5.1
THE SHAKERS OF MY COMMUNITY

Grades 5–12

Description. This project has been designed to provide students a certain amount of choice based on their individual interests and abilities and to align with a number of the multiple intelligences (MI) described by Howard Gardner (1993). After a field trip to a local Shaker museum or after learning about a Shaker village in the students' local community or home state, the students are asked to complete two assignments from the six lists shown in Figure 5.2. Each list taps a different intelligence, and the students are required to choose the two assignments from two different lists in order to provide practice in two MI categories.

NCSS *Curriculum Guidelines for Multicultural Education* References

15.0. Interdisciplinary and multidisciplinary approaches should be used in designing and implementing the multicultural curriculum.
21.0. The multicultural curriculum should make maximum use of experiential learning, especially local community resources.

Assessment

- Students will be required to share one of their Shaker assignments with the class and will be evaluated on their presentation skills. These may include the following: voice, eye contact, pacing, and ability to maintain interest of the audience.
- Students will submit the second assignment for a formal evaluation based on a rubric that may include the following criteria: research using local resources, historical accuracy, creativity, and style (for writing assignments).

Adaptations. Similar to Lesson Plan 5.1, the Project Plan can be adapted for the study of any local religious, utopian, or secular group with settlements in the region where a school is located. The critical multicultural components involve using an interdisciplinary approach, providing for experiential learning, and encouraging questions related to diversity. Giving students a choice as to which assignments they will complete allows them to "own" the project, and requiring that they choose from two different lists helps them to develop more than one of their multiple intelligences.

Figure 5.2. Directions for the Shakers of My Community Project

You will complete **two** assignments from the lists below. Each assignment must be from a **different** list.

LINGUISTIC

Write a story about a young adult who was cared for by the local Shakers and who must make a decision about whether or not to leave the village.

Write a play about a family living near the local Shaker village. The adults are considering whether or not to join.

LOGICAL/ MATHEMATICAL

Create a graph of the population of the local Shaker community, and based on your knowledge of U.S. history, tell why you think it changed as it did.

Create a timeline of the events of the local Shaker community and underneath include the major events of U.S. history that were going on at the same time.

MUSICAL

Listen to Shaker songs ("Shaker Village of Pleasant Hill: Music and Dance," 2003b) and write one in the same style that has references to the local Shakers.

Analyze the lyrics of three Shaker songs and explain their meanings. If possible, use songs composed by the local Shakers.

SPATIAL

Design a mural of the different historical stages of the local Shaker community showing changes over time.

Make a shoebox diorama of a room in one of the buildings of the local Shakers.

INTERPERSONAL

Working in pairs, develop a dialogue between a Shaker brother or sister and a reporter from the local newspaper doing a feature story on the community.

Interview an elderly member of the community who may remember some stories about the local Shakers.

INTRAPERSONAL

Create a diary from the perspective of a Shaker sister or brother recording everyday life at the community for a 2-week period.

Write a reflective journal from the perspective of a young person who has just joined the Shakers or who has been taken under their care.

Meeting Learning Standards Through Local/Multicultural History

SOME OF THE MORE frequent comments made by social studies teachers concerning their limited use of local history, particularly at the secondary level, focus on the problem of a lack of time to devote to it, due to the pressures of covering mandated curriculum topics and the fact that community studies seem to "belong" to a specified grade at the elementary level. The limited time factor also is cited by those teachers who might like to include more multicultural material but think that they cannot do so because of an already overloaded social studies curriculum or a traditional focus in required state frameworks.

One way to address the lack of time issue is to begin with the content topics in U.S. history that must be studied at a particular grade level and incorporate both local material and a multicultural focus wherever possible. Such a strategy will not necessarily shortchange the study of the mandated topics and may help to heighten students' interest and deepen their understanding of the material. As to the belief that the study of local history belongs only at the lower elementary grades, such a limited view neglects the possibility of addressing the material at the more sophisticated levels that older elementary, middle, and high school students are capable of doing. It also hinders the study of controversial local topics that might not be appropriate for younger students.

This chapter tackles the above issues by using as starting points selected topics from the historical eras identified for study in grades 5–12 by the *National Standards for History* (1996) and linking them to local sites and multicultural themes. A template for organizing required material is provided to help implement a strategy that will incorporate local history and at the same time highlight diversity. Each of the three curriculum topics explored in this chapter is then examined through a historical overview, selected examples of its local connections, a discussion of the multicultural themes associated with the topic, and some suggestions for activities to help students meet learning standards. The chapter concludes with an outline for a curriculum unit highlighting a local event that addresses a number of learning standards and multicultural themes. The curriculum topics selected for inclusion in this chapter come from a variety of chronological eras and illustrate the rich diversity of U.S. history.

A TEMPLATE FOR DEVELOPING CURRICULUM UNITS WITH LOCAL AND MULTICULTURAL CONNECTIONS

FOCUS QUESTIONS

How is my school community connected to historical eras in U.S. history?
What local/multicultural themes can be addressed to help students meet learning standards for historical eras?

Table 6.1 presents one way to begin to organize mandated curriculum units for a U.S. history course at the middle or high school level. The starting point at the left is the standard to be addressed, followed by one or more selected components (abbreviated). The blocks to the right are left blank for individual teachers to insert possible local connections, multicultural themes, and learning activities. The standards are selected from Era 1, Three Worlds Meet (Beginnings to 1620), as framed by the *National Standards for History* (1996) for grades 5–12.

With respect to possible local connections to the standard addressing characteristics of the Three Worlds identified in Era 1 and the patterns of change in indigenous societies that students should understand, teachers might have students investigate Native American groups in their local area to see whether there is evidence concerning development of their lifestyles. Students could conduct archaeological explorations of targeted sites in and around their community or draw upon evidence collected by a local museum, historical society, and/or library to gather data about such topics as providing for material needs, implements and artifacts, family patterns, religious beliefs, and other customs among Native Americans indigenous to the region. When addressing the standard concerning West Africa, students could try to determine whether any customs among African Americans who might have been brought to the region during the age of exploration can be traced back to the land of their origins. Concerning the standard related to how European exploration and colonization resulted in cultural and ecological interactions, teachers could direct students to evidence in their local area that might indicate the nature of such exchanges. These local connections might be in-

TABLE 6.1. Template for Developing Curriculum Units with Local/ Multicultural Connections

Standard	The Student Understands	Possible Local Connections	Possible Multicultural Themes/Issues	Learning Activities
Characteristics of societies in the Americas, Western Europe, and West Africa	Patterns of change in indigenous societies			
	Developments in West African societies during contact with Europeans			
How European exploration and colonization resulted in cultural and ecological interactions	Stages of European exploration and international rivalries			
	Spanish and Portuguese conquest of the Americas			

corporated into large-scale projects, but they also could be simple references within regular lesson plans to help students connect to the material.

Both the standards and all of the selected student understandings (based on components of the standards) provided in the chart for Era 1 include obvious multicultural themes. Some issues teachers may wish to explore from a multicultural point of view involve different perspectives concerning the impact of European exploration and colonization on the land and indigenous people of the students' region, and how the elements of racism, exploitation, and cultural misunderstandings may have influenced events in the students' region when individuals from the Three Worlds had their earliest encounters. The following section provides more detailed treatment of a topic from the next era identified for study in the *National Standards for History* (1996).

KING PHILIP'S WAR

One of the most devastating events to occur in the period of U.S. history designated by the *National Standards for History* as Era 2, Colonization and Settlement (1585–1763), was King Philip's War. As Schultz and Tougias trace in painstaking detail in *King Philip's War: The History and Legacy of America's Forgotten Conflict* (1999), the battles were fought on dozens of sites from eastern Massachusetts, throughout New England, and as far west as the Hudson River. For teachers in the northeast addressing Standard 1B, "The student understands the European struggle for control of North America," local connections abound. The multicultural themes of race, ethnicity, language, religion, and cultural conflict run rife through the content.

Historical Overview

In the 17th century, New England was populated by a number of Algonquin groups including the Wampanoag of southeastern Massachusetts and the Narragansett of what is now Rhode Island. By the time of King Philip's War in 1675, these and other Native American peoples of New England had been weakened greatly by their exposure to European diseases (Calloway, 1997; Lepore, 1998; Schultz & Tougias, 1999). Their traditional lifestyles had been disrupted by the English settlers who encroached on their land and made trade and agriculture difficult. As a survival mechanism, some had adopted English ways—becoming Christians, learning the language, and utilizing English weapons. The majority, however, clung to their familiar way of life, which became ever more difficult as the English settlers increased in number and the struggle for control of the land intensified.

Conflicting Perspectives. A major source of the conflict between the Native Americans and the English settlers concerned their contrasting views of the land. While the latter developed an economy based around permanent settlement, acquisition and ownership of land, and farming, the Wampanoag of Massachusetts and Native Americans throughout the region moved with the seasons, burned the land to promote new growth, and hunted and fished, or, if they were women, planted such crops as beans and corn (Schultz & Tougias, 1999). Unable to understand the Native American concept of wealth and ownership of property, English settlers nevertheless attempted to impose their own views of such matters and to transfer land into their own hands using the Anglo legal system. Population growth among the English increased the pressure for expansion, and new settlements moved further to the west. Skirmishes between the Native Americans and the English on the frontier were common, prompting the colonists to organize a militia system to cope with the violence. In 1643, leaders from the Connecticut, Massachusetts Bay, and Plimoth colonies formed an organization they called the United Colonies, for the purposes of exchanging information and defending themselves from the ever-increasing threat of Native American reprisals.

In 1660, Massasoit, the Wampanoag leader who concluded a peace treaty with Governor Carver of Plimoth and subsequently attended the first Thanksgiving with 90 of his people, died. His son, Metacom, known to the English as King Philip, became chief, or sachem, of the Wampanoag. Unhappy with the treatment of his people at the hands of the English, he believed the Native Americans would be doomed if they did not resist further expansion into their tribal lands. He was unwilling to make treaties with colonial governors, preferring instead to deal directly with the King of England, whom he viewed as his counterpart.

Military Events of the War. The precipitating event of what would become known as King Philip's War occurred in January 1675, when the body of a Christian, or "praying," Indian named John Sassamon, whose neck had been broken, was found in a frozen pond in Middleboro, Massachusetts. Schooled in English customs, Sassamon had attended Harvard College and served as a counselor to King Philip. Rumor had it that he had shared with the governor of Plimoth his suspicion that King Philip and his allies were plotting war against the colonists. After several months, three members of King Philip's tribe were accused of murdering Sassamon, and, within 7 days of the accusation, they were rounded up, charged with the crime, and hanged by English authorities in Plimoth (Pletcher, 1999). The English claimed they had jurisdiction because, as a Christian, Sassamon was considered a British subject. Two weeks later, a band of King Philip's followers, perhaps without his prior knowledge, responded by burning and looting some homes in the village of Swansea (Schultz & Tougias, 1999). King Philip's War had begun.

The fighting spread from southeastern Massachusetts westward to the Connecticut River Valley and northward into Maine. During the first year of the war, several towns in central and western Massachusetts were devastated. All but two homes in Providence, Rhode Island, were destroyed during the fighting in March 1676. During this same period, King Philip and his troops escaped an English siege, and the Narragansett were attacked at the Great Swamp, today South Kingstown, Rhode Island, bringing this powerful tribe into the war. In this bloody battle, perhaps 600 Narragansett died, an event that galvanized the Native American efforts.

The tide turned against the Indians, however, in the spring of 1676. With their itinerant pattern of agriculture totally disrupted by the war, they were in constant need of food. Aware of this weakness, the English were intent on preventing the Native Americans from obtaining food and replenishing supplies (Schultz & Tougias, 1999). The British destroyed food stores wherever they were found and pursued the Native Americans where they were known to fish and hunt. In addition to the problems associated with lack of food, the Indians suffered from a fraying of their leadership due to capture, strategical disagreements, and the desire for peace on the part of some among them.

The war for the most part came to an end with the death of King Philip himself in August 1676, in a Rhode Island swamp. After capturing Philip's wife and 9-year-old son (who later was sold into slavery), Captain Benjamin Church received a tip from one of King Philip's disgruntled followers, Alderman, which led the English forces to his location. Ironically, King Philip's death resulted from a bullet fired by Alderman, who later received one of the sachem's hands as a trophy. King Philip was then decapitated, and his head, a souvenir of one of the bloodiest wars ever fought in North America, was paraded through the streets of Plimoth and left on display for decades (Lepore, 1998).

Consequences of the War. In proportion to the population at the time, King Philip's War was the most devastating ever to occur on North American soil (Pletcher, 1999). The brutal fighting lasted for 15 months during which thousands of lives were lost, sadistic torture and abuse on both sides were common, and 25 colonial towns were destroyed. Countless Wampanoag children were placed in servitude with English families. One in 16 White settlers and nearly 500 British militia lost their lives. The surviving Native American communities were those in southern New England where leaders had not taken part or had assisted the English, or that had been designated as made up of Christian, or "praying," groups. Conventional wisdom declared the Wampanoag culture largely eradicated, although, as we shall see later, this was not the case.

Selected Local Sites and Events

Any number of the many sites where fighting and other events of the war occurred provide fertile ground for study, particularly by secondary students addressing standards related to the colonial era and learning to view historical material from multiple perspectives. In any conflict as complex and as devastating as King Philip's War, a single event can lend itself to a number of interpretations. What to one witness may be a massacre to another may be a desperate fight for survival. The following events from King Philip's War—the Great Swamp Fight, the captivity of Mary Rowlandson, and the burning of Simsbury—are highlighted to provide examples of moments in colonial history tied to specific locales yet inextricably linked to the broader scope of the narrative of the period. Each also lends itself to more than one interpretation concerning what actually may have occurred, why, and the consequences.

The Great Swamp Fight. This defining moment in the war occurred on December 19, 1675, at a site in what is now South Kingstown, Rhode Island. A palisaded fort housing the wigwams of 3,000–4,000 Narragansett, mostly women and children who had sought shelter there, and stores of supplies for the upcoming winter months was attacked by a force of English soldiers organized by the United Colonies (Lepore, 1998; Schultz & Tougias, 1999). Until then, the Narragansett Indians officially had been neutral in the conflict. Canonchet, their leader, was expecting an attack; however, he did not do much to prevent the British from advancing toward the fort. The fight lasted for the better part of a day and is considered one of the bloodiest of the war.

The tactics used by the British forces were particularly ugly. They set fire to the wigwams, and, as the Narragansetts sought to escape, fired mercilessly on them. Then they burned everything in sight, including anything that might have been of value for their own survival. Lepore (1998) points out that, ironically, this attack by the British had all the earmarks of an Indian assault upon the settlers. In fact, the Nipmuc attack on the Massachusetts town of Medfield in February 1676 was nearly identical in nature. What happened at the Great Swamp and at Medfield supports Lepore's thesis that one of the tragedies of the conflict was that in their fight for survival, each side adopted the most vicious tactics of the other. It was not uncommon for the British to scalp their prisoners, while the Indians would draw and quarter theirs.

Other ironies permeate King Philip's War, including the significance of the Great Swamp Fight. The British considered it a great victory. Although the exact number of Narragansett losses can never be determined, some sources have estimated that about 600 were killed (Schultz & Tougias, 1999). Whatever the number of casualties, it was a loss for the Indians. British deaths have been confirmed at fewer than 100. Despite the imbalance in the number of deaths, instead of hastening an end to the overall conflict, the Great Swamp Fight had the effect of drawing the hitherto officially neutral Narragansett into the war and thus prolonging its duration. Furthermore, this battle poked serious holes into the Puritans' argument that they were morally superior to their "heathen" enemy, for the British tactics violated their own rule of war that women and children not be specifically targeted (Lepore, 1998).

The Captivity of Mary Rowlandson. Not long after the Great Swamp Fight came another event in King Philip's War that has been the subject of much speculation as to significance and broader meanings—the captivity of Mary Rowlandson. The saga began on February 10, 1676, when Nipmuc Indians attacked the community of Lancaster, Massachusetts, and took a number of captives, among them Mary Rowlandson, the wife of the town's minister and mother of four (James, James, & Boyer, 1971). She remained a captive for 3 bitter months during which she traveled with her captors south to New Braintree, Massachusetts, and north to Chesterfield, New Hampshire, met King Philip, and carried out domestic chores alongside his family members (Schultz & Tougias, 1999). Rowlandson experienced the emotional heartache of watching her youngest child die from wounds received in the original attack and the physical sufferings of hunger and exhaustion on the long journey. Ransomed and released, she and her husband moved to Wethersfield, Connecticut, where she wrote a remarkable account of her experience, *The Narrative of the Captivity and Restoration of Mrs. Mary Rowlandson.* This primary source provides valuable insights into her personal story as well as an eyewitness description of her Native American captors planning strategy and struggling to survive a brutal war.

Rowlandson was born Mary White in 1635 to an English family who moved to Salem, Massachusetts, in 1639 (James, James, & Boyer, 1971; *Mary Rowlandson*, 2003). She married minister Joseph Rowlandson, and together they had four children. On the day that Mary was taken captive, her husband had gone to Boston to request military assistance from the Massachusetts legislature. The community of Lancaster was attacked at dawn, and several homes were burned. Seeking refuge at the minister's house, which also served as a garrison, were about 3 dozen residents. The Indians surrounded them, killing 12 and taking the rest captive. Mary's youngest daughter, Sarah, who was wounded in the attack, died about a week later.

Rowlandson was a prisoner for nearly 12 weeks during which, according to her account, she and the others who were taken with her as well as their captors endured endless hardships. She was able to negotiate her release for an agreed-upon ransom to be paid by her husband, with whom she was reunited on May 2, 1676. Their two surviving children were freed a few weeks later. The family lived briefly in Boston until Reverend Rowlandson was installed as the pastor of a church in Wethersfield, Connecticut. He died not long after, and Mary remarried. Her new husband, Captain Samuel Talcott, died in 1691, but the hardy Mary lived on until 1710.

Rowlandson's *Narrative* surfaced in Boston in 1682 and received widespread attention, although she at first resisted having this very personal work circulate (Lepore, 1998). Reportedly written for her children, the original manuscript has not survived, but later editions have, and they provide readers with a striking tale of survival and Puritan faith. Excerpts are provided in the Schultz and Tougias (1999) history of King Philip's War. Mary vividly describes the horror of the battle at her home where "we hear mothers and children crying out for themselves and one another" (p. 343). She tells of her nephew William, his leg broken, being then struck on the head and killed. Her sister Elizabeth also was killed, and Mary herself was wounded in the fight. She explains how she had often thought she would choose death rather than captivity but "when it came to trial, my mind changed" (p. 344). Next she describes her first days as a captive trying to nurse her child, who ultimately died and was buried on a hill by the Native Americans. Rowlandson remembers this and other kindnesses as well as acts of wanton cruelty. She recalls a great celebration after the horrific destruction of Medfield, and the brutal tomahawk deaths of a woman and her 2-year-old child for "complaining too much and begging to go home" (p. 346). There are also moments of ordinary activity in this extraordinary journey, including Mary declining to smoke a pipe offered by King Philip himself and thanking God that "He has now given me power over it; surely there are many who may be better employed than to lie sucking a stinking tobacco pipe" (p. 347). Mary describes how Philip asked her to make a shirt for his son, which she willingly did and for which she received a shilling in payment. Mary's skill as a seamstress was one key to her survival, for she was then engaged regularly to make caps and knit stockings for various members of the group. In return Mary was given food and treats that she sometimes hoarded "for fear they would get it from me" (p. 348). As Mary moved from place to place, she took note of the sufferings of the Indians, who themselves were always short of food and often slept in the rain for want of shelter.

Rowlandson's eventual release was arranged by some Christian Indians who appeared at the Wachusett Camp to discuss the possibility of arranging deals for the captors. Schultz and Tougias (1999) note that Mary was shrewd in offering a sum high enough to make it worthwhile for the Native Americans but not so steep that her husband could not afford the transaction. Mary describes how the Indians reacted to her release by at first resisting and then rejoicing in it and "shaking me by the hand, offering me a hood and scarf to ride in, not one moving hand or tongue against it" (p. 354). Thus ended a compelling episode in this complex chapter of colonial history.

The Destruction of Simsbury, Connecticut. One of the most valuable aspects of Mary Rowlandson's story is the personal account she presents of the character of King Philip, the proud warrior who, in the midst of a grave conflict, arranged for a shirt to be fashioned for his son. The story of what happened at Simsbury, although far less personal in nature, resulted in a permanent landmark dedicated to the leader for whom the war was named.

Located in north central Connecticut, Simsbury was settled by the English between 1648 and 1661 through negotiations with the native Massacoe Indians of the Algonquin Nation who inhabited the area (*Brief History of Simsbury*, n.d.). Thought to be named for Symondsbury in Dorset, England, Simsbury was established in a picturesque valley with rich natural resources. When King Philip's War broke out, Simsbury consisted of about 40 homes widely scattered along the Farmington River (Schultz & Tougias, 1999). Due to the nature of the settlement pattern, it was extremely vulnerable to attack.

Recognizing Simsbury's unprotected position, in October 1675, Connecticut officials issued a command for the residents to vacate the area within a week's time. Most followed the order, but came back within a few months when the attack did not materialize. Their return would be a fatal error, for word was received in March that Simsbury was again a target. With little time to organize, the settlers once more were ordered out of the area. On March 26, the Narragansett, who had entered the war in earnest after the Great Swamp Fight, set fire to the town and destroyed most of the homes and other buildings. Legend has it that King Philip himself found shelter in a cave on Talcott Mountain where he could view the destruction firsthand. The spot is called Metacomet Ridge after Philip's Native American name.

Residents did not return to Simsbury until nearly a year after the attack, and many of the original inhabitants never came back. Schultz and Tougias (1999) note that early histories of the war make little mention of Simsbury's demise, going so far as to claim that Connecticut was left largely unscathed. Stories circulated for a while that the residents, when ordered to evacuate a second time, hastily buried their valuables in the swamps and wells. Upon their return, they were unable to retrieve them, so complete was the destruction of the fire. It is more likely that the attackers located the possessions and either looted or destroyed them, as later historians claimed. The Simsbury story adds yet another curious chapter to the saga of the colonial war.

Multicultural Themes

As previously noted, one reason for singling out King Philip's War from among the many topics that might be studied in connection with Era 2 is the fact that the event highlights the importance of viewing history from multiple perspectives and as such underscores the difficulty of both writing objective history and interpreting primary and secondary sources. In the decade following its close, at least 21 accounts of the war were published, some in multiple editions. Lepore (1998) dubs Mary Rowlandson's work a best seller, but others of note include Increase Mather's *A Brief History of the War* and William Hubbard's *A Narrative of the Troubles with the Indians*, both of which were published in the 1670s. Lepore's analysis stresses the concern of these early authors with presenting the truth as they saw it and with discrediting Native American versions of the events of the war.

Conventional wisdom long ago concluded that the Native Americans of New England were so devastated by their loss in the 1675–76 conflict that they nearly disappeared from the landscape, not to resurface as an entity to be reckoned with until the 20th century. A number of contemporary historians, however, have suggested quite the opposite (Calloway, 1997). Still the years after the war were difficult. Native lands gradually were carved up by the colonists, and many Indians were relegated to tightly regulated reservations. Some were forced into slavery or conditions of involuntary servitude, while others were encouraged to shed their cultural identity and adopt Anglo ways. Disease and armed conflict continued to decimate their numbers, but the Native Americans of New England hardly disappeared.

In Rhode Island, the site of the infamous Great Swamp Fight, the Narragansett officially were declared extinct by the state legislature in 1880, and their tribal lands were sold off (Herndon & Sekatau, 1997). While many of the Native Americans of Rhode Island had moved out of the area in the years following the war, some remained. Oral histories tell of their ability to keep their cultural traditions alive while living on reservation land. Still others remained in Rhode Island but moved away from their ancestral lands and lost their cultural identities as they intermarried and forged ties with African American and European groups.

In central Massachusetts, where Mary Rowlandson's capture and odyssey played out, the Indian presence also was nearly wiped out by official interpretations that contradicted the reality of countless Native Americans who enriched the communities where they resided, often in extended families or clans (Doughton, 1997). Doughton argues that, despite the myth of the disappearing Indian, "Native American peoples of central New England . . . were part of the nineteenth-century social landscape, pursuing established patterns of persistence and cultural survival, affirming their Indian identity" (p. 208). In his endnotes, Doughton provides a list of Native Americans of the Nipmuc group who served in the Union army during the Civil War.

Overall, then, King Philip's War and its aftermath provide compelling examples of how history is colored by those who are observing and writing it. The combatants in this war came from strikingly different cultural groups whose worldviews and lifestyles could not be more opposite, with the history of the event recorded largely by those with a written tradition. In the official accounts of the war, presented by those of Anglo background, the Native Americans were portrayed as the aggressors, the defeated, and the obliterated. More recent accounts have tried to take a more balanced approach. For students learning about the colonial era, these sources and the events they portray provide an opportunity to "multiculturalize" a content topic by viewing it through diverse ethnic and cultural perspectives.

Learning Activities

Students engaged in a study of colonial history can find much to investigate concerning the Great Swamp Fight. First there is the question of whether the encounter was a victory for the English, a point that could be the subject of a class debate. For those who live in the area of South Kingstown, Rhode Island, this battle is a significant part of their local history, although the exact location of the fight has never been confirmed. Thus a scenario exists for an inquiry-driven lesson concerning where the fight actually took place. In 1906, based on descriptions in a number of sources, a monument was placed at the spot near the intersection of Route 2 and Route 138 where the Great Swamp Fight is thought to have taken place (Schultz & Tougias, 1999). Annual commemorations are held near the granite marker by descendants of both sets of combatants. However, 20th-century historians dispute the conclusions of their earlier counterparts that the monument accurately marks the spot of this watershed battle. Many of the eyewitness accounts are suspect, and more recent archaeological data fail to confirm the originally designated location of the fort. Some artifacts unearthed in more recent studies point to fields outside the present-day swamp as a more probable site for the Narragansett fort. Secondary students could analyze the various sources and come to their own conclusions as to the true location of one of North America's most significant battles.

Mary Rowlandson is a part of the local history of the many New England communities where she lived and through which she passed during her captivity. Reading and analyzing her *Narrative* is an appropriate assignment for secondary students and should not only provide useful information about Puritan and Native American values and the events of King Philip's War but also raise a number of questions for students to consider. They can reflect on the intended audience and purpose of this primary source and on what can be learned about life at the time it was written. Students also might raise a number of questions they would pose to Mary Rowlandson if they had the opportunity to meet her. If she wrote the *Narrative* for her children, might she have left out some details too personal or too upsetting for them to process? Did she embellish the story of her work ethic to promote a Puritan lesson about leading a useful life whatever the circumstances? Further research might lead students to seek out other accounts that might corroborate Rowlandson's version of events. Did other survivors of Native American captivity share similar experiences? Obviously, such in-depth study of Mary Rowlandson and King Philip's War might be too time-consuming for a survey course with dozens of standards to address in a single year. However, such a project might be one option among many others for a semester or annual research activity. On the other hand, reading and analyzing some excerpts from the *Narrative* would take no longer than one class session and could yield fruitful insights into an era and two cultures that are fundamental to understanding the American experience.

Students in Connecticut might speculate about why the destruction in their state was largely overlooked by contemporary historians of King Philip's War. A cooperative group investigation could be used effectively for this topic. In this activity, students discuss historical material and are encouraged to generate questions to investigate (Yell, Scheurman, & Reynolds, 2004). They then are divided into groups and assigned a specific question or topic that they research individually in order to inform their own group and contribute to a group report that is presented to the entire class. Students similarly could investigate the naming of Metacomet Ridge and decide whether evidence exists to support the story that King Philip used the site to observe the destruction his followers wrought on the area. If not, they could consider why such a legend might have originated.

THE UNDERGROUND RAILROAD

As with King Philip's War in colonial times, the story of the Underground Railroad, which ran its course in the mid-19th century, has been the source of legend and can be interpreted from many perspectives. Spanning Era 4, Expansion and Reform (1801–1861), and Era 5, Civil War and Reconstruction (1850–1877), are curriculum topics that may be studied in response to Standard 2D, "The student understands the rapid growth of 'the peculiar institution' after 1800 and the varied experiences of African Americans under slavery" (*National Standards for History*, 1996), particularly with respect to exploring the ways that Blacks resisted their condition. As a system that operated in a wide geographic area, the Underground Railroad necessarily has numerous local connections, and as one that involved both Blacks and Whites working together, it sheds light on the multicultural theme of race relations.

Historical Overview

Treatment of the Underground Railroad in secondary U.S. history textbooks is relatively skimpy, yet the subject is widely known and inherently interesting to students, perhaps because they are attracted to the stories of individuals taking risks, facing danger, and flaunting an unjust system that are interwoven into the traditional narrative. It is also a subject about which there may be as much myth as reality due to the necessarily secretive nature of the activities and identities of the individuals involved. For multiculturalists the Underground Railroad can be a problematic topic because so many of the accounts about the network and its workings emphasize the courage and cleverness of the White abolitionists who participated in it. The escaping slaves, on the other hand, very often are depicted as frightened victims who could not have succeeded without outside help (Gara, 1998; Hendrick & Hendrick, 2004).

Issues and Myths. Mainstream historians are concerned about the fact that while many of the heroic stories of rescues and escapes on the Underground

Railroad are fascinating, their authenticity cannot be verified. Even the name itself is of disputed origin. One account tells of a frustrated slaveowner complaining that a fugitive slave he was tracking must have disappeared on an "underground road" (Hendrick & Hendrick, 2004, p. 3). Another relates the torture-driven confession of a captured freedom seeker who described being unable to open a trapdoor on a railroad under ground set up by abolitionists. Whatever the origins, the romance of the railroads, which had attracted the public's attention at the time, probably contributed to the popular use of vocabulary such as *passengers*, *conductors*, and *stations* in descriptions of the system and its activities.

Despite the myths and fabrications surrounding the topic, some information about the network that became known as the Underground Railroad can be authenticated and is presented in accounts as factual. A system for helping those seeking freedom from slavery dates back as far as the late 18th century. In fact, George Washington is said to have complained that it was difficult for him to catch up with one of his own fugitive slaves in Pennsylvania because of the number of individuals (in a state with a large Quaker population) who preferred to help the escapee over compliance with the law (Ripley, 1998). A Fugitive Slave Act was passed in 1793, very early in the history of the American Republic. Many stakeholders would complain that it was never strongly enforced. Indeed, perhaps as many as 9,000 so-called fugitives passed through the city of Philadelphia between 1830 and the eve of the Civil War.

The Routes of the Underground Railroad. Rather than a well-defined, continuous network, the Underground Railroad consisted instead of a number of constantly changing routes over which those escaping slavery were helped, usually in the dark of night, until they reached a safe haven (Hendrick & Hendrick, 2004). Activity on the part of antislavery forces was heightened in the reform climate of the 1840s, with 1850 proving to be a watershed year in the history of the Underground Railroad. It was in that year that a tough Fugitive Slave Act broadening federal powers to apprehend escaped slaves was passed as part of the controversial Compromise of 1850. The law was particularly unsettling to antislavery forces in the North because it required all citizens to assist in enforcement, denied jury trials to suspected fugitive slaves, and paid commissioners $10 for each escapee who was returned and only $5 for each suspect who was set free. Contrary to the intent of the supporters of the Fugitive Slave Act, it turned some moderates into lawbreakers, as they defied the legislation and participated in helping escapees seeking freedom (Gara, 1998).

Due to the secretive nature of the undertaking, it is difficult to map precisely the routes of the Underground Railroad, but they roughly followed a logical pattern. Those fleeing from Texas and other western slave states either traveled south into Mexico or north through friendly territory in Illinois, Ohio, and Michigan and often continued on into Canada. In the eastern portion of the country, slave journeys to freedom either crossed through Florida to the Caribbean or followed routes through the border states to cities such as Philadelphia, New York, and Boston. Some fleeing to these northern cities went on to Canada, which did not comply with U.S. government demands that they be returned. All along the way, free Blacks and White abolitionists participated in aiding the freedom seekers.

Aftermath for the Freedom Seekers. When they reached their destinations, the former slaves often had to continue to struggle for autonomy and a decent life. While they found jobs and tried to settle into family life, those who had escaped from slavery and relocated in other parts of the United States faced numerous obstacles in their attempts to lead ordinary lives. According to Ripley (1998): "Blacks struggled against racism, race violence, and an indifferent and hostile political and legal system that in its normal application afforded them little protection and few resources" (p. 67). Despite the obstacles, they founded or became affiliated with Black institutions such as newspapers, schools, and churches that promoted activism and pride.

The operation of the Underground Railroad continued throughout the Civil War, with many northern sites providing assistance to newly freed individuals who sought protection in Union territory after the Emancipation Proclamation was issued by Lincoln in 1863 (Ripley, 1998). Later during Reconstruction, many of those who had participated in Underground Railroad activities became involved in relief efforts to provide funds and necessities to the former slaves, many of whom were left destitute by the upheavals of the war and its aftermath.

Selected Local Sites

Although it is common to associate the Underground Railroad with the abolitionist movement and well-known activists such as Harriet Tubman and Frederick Douglass, many unknown individuals participated, including those who lived in the South, where the flights to freedom originated. Following are descriptions of three sites thought to be part of the Underground Railroad network, one in the South and two in New England.

The Burkle Estate: A Slave Haven? Located in a remote and quiet neighborhood of Memphis, Tennessee, the Slave Haven Underground Railroad Museum (Burkle Estate) presents an intriguing story that is both compelling and shrouded in the mystery that surrounds much of the history of the Underground Railroad. According to the official tour narrative, a German immigrant named Jacob Burkle purchased the property on the outskirts of the city due to its proximity to the Mississippi River. Burkle reportedly was a member of the antislavery movement and offered his home as a safe haven for those escaping via the river to destinations in the North. The dark, damp cellar of the home contains a secret chamber where freedom seekers reportedly were harbored until they could be moved along to the bank of the Mississippi where transportation awaited them. A marker placed by the Tennessee Historical Commission notes that the persistent stories of the Burkle Estate as a stop on the Underground Railroad are part of the "folklore" of the region.

Not much is known about Burkle except that he arrived in the United States in the mid-19th century and probably was trying to avoid being drafted into the German military (Busbee, 1997). The structure that became known as the Burkle Estate was built in 1849 and housed a bakery that the proprietor ran along with a stockyard. Although no documents exist to corroborate the legend that Burkle used his home to give shelter to escaping slaves, there are convincing indicators that this might be the case. Busbee reports that Bill Day, owner of a historical site on Beale Street, was tutored by Burkle's granddaughter, who told him stories about the home's past. Day claims to have seen a letter from a former slave thanking Burkle for his help, but it has not survived. No tunnels were found when archaeological work was done to prepare for the renovations leading to the restoration of the estate and its designation as a Heritage Tours museum in Memphis.

Despite the uncertainty about the role of Jacob Burkle and his home in the history of the Underground Railroad, the museum presents a vivid story complete with hidden passages and a view of the Mississippi. During a 2003 visit to the Burkle Estate, I observed a school group of local 5th graders touring the cramped quarters and listening attentively to the history of slavery and the role of places like the Slave Haven in the system of escape routes that later would be dubbed the Underground Railroad. Students were taken, a few at a time, to the cellar and asked to imagine what it must have been like to be hidden there in the dampness, frightened and in danger, yet determined to take a risk for the sake of freedom. It was a compelling example of experiential learning.

The Underground Railroad in New England. Throughout the Midwest and the Northeast, dozens of sites have been identified as stops along the Underground Railroad. They range from ordinary farmhouses to grand mansions. Some are open to the public, as is the Burkle Estate, and lend their own interpretations to the operation of the Underground Railroad. A number of locations in New England have been designated as landmarks in the system, leading to widespread regional consciousness of the activities of abolitionists and the existence of a network to aid fugitives on their flight to safe havens.

In Newton, Massachusetts, the Jackson Homestead, which is open to the public and offers tours and an educational program for school groups, is a documented stop on the Underground Railroad. Ellen Jackson, daughter of William Jackson, the proprietor, left a written account that supports the claim that the family participated in the network (American Revolution Bicentennial Administration, n.d.; *Newton History Museum*, 2003). Jackson wrote about occasionally hearing pebbles thrown against the window of her home late at night. This was the signal that escapees had arrived to be hidden in between chimney supports until they could be safely sent north. Newton was a safer location than Boston proper because, during the era of the Fugitive Slave Law, slaveowners often traveled to Boston to search for escapees. Jackson also wrote of participating in sewing circles held at her home for the purpose of making much-needed clothing for the freedom seekers who passed through the area. Support for the legitimacy of Jackson's claims that her home was a stop on the Underground Railroad exists in a number of sources, including letters and account books (*Newton History Museum*, 2003).

Another New England site with strong claims to participation in the Underground Railroad is Rokeby, the Rowland T. Robinson home in Ferrisburgh, Vermont (American Revolution Bicentennial Administration, n.d.; Williamson, n.d., 2001). This federal style home overlooking the Champlain Valley was part of a prosperous sheep farm owned by Rowland Robinson, an abolitionist in the William Lloyd Garrison camp. A devout Quaker, Robinson was acquainted with such well-known reformers as Frederick Douglass, Samuel J. May, and Lucretia Mott. He founded both the Ferrisburgh and Vermont Anti-Slavery Societies and, according to his children, frequently harbored freedom-seeking slaves. Unlike other sites that served as temporary secret hiding places, Rokeby often offered employment to the freedom seekers in the relative safety of remote Vermont. This fact belies the myth that all Underground Railroad activities were conducted in secret in the dark of night and carried with them the constant threat of discovery and dire consequences. While such an interpretation might be accurate when applied to the Burkle Estate, it does not fit with Underground Railroad activities in remote northern sites such as Ferrisburgh, Vermont. These contrasts provide provocative material for teachers to analyze with their students when studying the reforms of the 1840s and the Underground Railroad in pre-Civil War America.

Multicultural Themes

Beyond the obvious topics of race relations and reform in the antebellum era, a study of the Underground Railroad provides an opportunity for teachers to meet the multicultural guideline of helping students "understand the totality of the experiences of ethnic and cultural groups in the United States" (NCSS Task Force, 1991, p. 9). Although Blacks and other people of color, as well as the poor and newly arrived immigrants, often are exploited by individuals and institutions in the larger society, they should not be cast as helpless victims. With reference to immigrants, they have taken the bold step of leaving the cultural, if not the economic or political, comforts of the land of their birth in order to seek a better life. With respect to the freedom seekers who embarked on a perilous journey on the Underground Railroad, we again have an example of individuals taking it upon themselves to improve their situations despite the obvious risks. They displayed not only courage but also initiative, ingenuity, knowledge of the environment, and the ability to communicate effectively, skills and qualities necessary for success in their quests for freedom.

Many escaping slaves were aided by White abolitionists, as we have seen in the preceding examples, but so too were many helped by fellow Blacks, some of them members of organized antislavery groups and others private individuals willing to help. The New York Committee of Vigilance is a case in point (Hodges, 2000–2001; Ripley, 1998). Founded in 1835 by Black journalist David Ruggles and a number of other African American activists, this group, among other services, provided material and legal assistance to the freedom seekers. While it received some aid from White abolitionists, the Committee was supported by funds raised and administered largely by Blacks. An analysis of Ruggles and the New York Committee of Vigilance in the context of a larger study of the Underground Railroad can add new dimensions to the topic and belie the stereotype of escaping slaves as victims aided mostly by White reformers.

Learning Activities

While this account of the Underground Railroad has focused primarily on the history of the network, its geographic connections cannot be overlooked. Tracing the routes of the Underground Railroad can make for an interesting geography lesson, especially for students in schools located in regions where stations may have operated. Mapping and discussing the routes address not only the concepts of location and place, but also the important theme of movement with respect to both people and ideas.

From a historical perspective, the Underground Railroad by its very nature is a difficult topic to research. Much of the history has been passed along through oral traditions, not via research-based written documents. However, some primary sources do exist in the form of letters, diaries, and narratives such as those of Levi Coffin, who was known as the president of the Underground Railroad, and William Still, a clerk for the Philadelphia Society for the Abolition of Slavery, who was himself the son of a runaway slave (Hendrick & Hendrick, 2004).

Locating additional primary sources as well as lesson plans has been made easier by the creation of the National Underground Railroad Freedom Center in Cincinnati, Ohio, which welcomes school groups for interactive tours and also maintains a Web site (www.freedomcenter.org/) with a wealth of information for educators. Here teachers can find an inquiry-based "freedom quest" that allows students to submit suggestions for a monument to the Underground Railroad and other creative lesson plans. Located in a community that was a hub of Underground Railroad activity, the Freedom Center oversees the Freedom Stations Program to bring together the resources of a number of institutions in a digital archive that can be used as the basis for further research into the Underground Railroad and related topics.

For teachers who wish to help their students determine local connections to the Underground Railroad, another invaluable resource is the National Underground Railroad Network to Freedom, and its Internet site developed and maintained by the National Park Service (www.cr.nps.gov/ugrr/). Established by legislation adopted in 1998, the National Underground Railroad Network to Freedom program was created in response to Congressional findings that the Underground Railroad bridged sectional and racial differences and was one of the most effective civil rights mechanisms in the history of the United States. These are powerful words and certainly justify carving out some time in the already overloaded social studies curriculum for an in-depth look at this route to freedom, particularly if stops or individuals in the students' own community were involved.

A classroom teacher looking into the possibility of planning a unit of study on the Underground Railroad with links to the region in which her/his school is located can be helped immeasurably by the Network to Freedom. The purpose of the program is to recognize the significance of the Underground Railroad by coordinating federal and local activities related to its historical interpretation, to create and disseminate educational resources, and to establish links with the governments of countries outside the United States, namely, Canada, Mexico, and Caribbean nations, to which the freedom seekers migrated. In order to carry out the mission of the Network to Freedom, the National Park Service has been authorized to coordinate preservation efforts and to aid local historic sites and museums in their efforts to tell the story of the Underground Railroad.

Related to these efforts is the Network to Freedom Database, a logical starting point for teachers and students searching for local or regional sites on the Underground Railroad. A search conducted in 2004 located the Southeast Archeological Center in Tallahassee, Florida, which houses a collection of materials associated with the Underground Railroad during its peak years. This site is run by the National Park Service and open to the public. Currently not open to the public, but informative nonetheless, is another site posted on the Network to Freedom, the Henry and Ann Harvey Farmstead. The Database describes the location as a place where a Quaker family used their log cabin to hide freedom seekers and where their sons and perhaps a grandson were conductors. A working farm now operates where the old cabin was situated. In Wisconsin, another private site, Jonathan Walker's home, is described as up for nomination to become a Network to Freedom member due to the residency there of a sea captain known as "The Man with the Branded Hand," who was marked with an "SS" (for Slave Stealer) and jailed for transporting freedom seekers to the Caribbean. Such stories cannot fail to intrigue students learning about the antebellum era of reform and conflict and to impress on them the sacrifices and risks of those who determined to escape the indignities and horrors of slavery and the many free men and women of good will, both Black and White, who aided them along the way.

THE AMERICAN LABOR MOVEMENT

Another major topic in U.S. history with ties to communities all over the nation and with strong multicultural currents is the American labor movement. So many of the workers who were exploited during the industrial expansion of the United States were immigrants, as were some of their most effective leaders. All of the multicultural themes explored earlier in this book—particularly class, gender, ethnicity, and language—figured prominently in many of the events that defined the historical struggles of workers in the United States to earn a decent living and to have a say in the running of the industries that employed them. Thus students' exploration of the movement's history brings into play a number of the *Curriculum Guidelines for Multicultural Education* (NCSS Task Force, 1991)—addressing the experiences of ethnic and cultural groups in the United States, promoting an understanding that conflict exists between ideals and realities in human societies, and helping students view and interpret events from diverse perspectives.

Because the American labor movement spans more than a century in time, it is linked to a number of eras identified in the *National Standards for History* (1996): Era 6, The Development of the Industrial United States (1870–1900); Era 7, The Emergence of Modern America (1890–1930); Era 8, The Great Depression and World War II (1929–1945); Era 9, Postwar United States (1945 to early 1970s); and Era 10, Contemporary United States (1968 to the present). Several of the learning standards for the various eras relate specifically to the labor movement in the United States and emphasize students' gaining an understanding of such concepts as the factory system, changing conditions in the workplace, child labor, unionization, labor conflict, progressive reform, the decline of unionism, and participation of women and new immigrants in the labor force.

Historical Overview

During the historical eras spanning the late 19th to the early 21st centuries, a significant number of important events related to unionization and the struggles of working people played out in small towns, rural areas, and large cities throughout the United States. It would seem a natural topic to address through a local/multicultural approach. The following historical material emphasizes place, diversity, and the concepts stressed in the *National Standards for History* (1996).

The Early Years. The story of workers joining together to improve their status reaches all the way back to the waning years of the colonial era when tailors in New York went on strike to protest a reduction in their wages (Foner & Garraty, 1991). Most U.S. history texts, however, cite the creation of the National Labor Union just after the end of the Civil War and the formation of the Knights of Labor in 1869 as the beginnings of the rocky ascent of organized labor in the United States. While earlier trade unions organized mainly skilled workers and sought specific redress of their complaints through the mechanism of the strike, those created in the 1860s had broader social goals. The National Labor Union made history in its formative years when it affirmed support for women workers and appealed to them to join the organization (Wertheimer, 1977). The secrecy-oriented Knights of Labor, led in the early years by the morally upright Uriah Stephens, welcomed all workers regardless of race or ethnicity from the start (Freeman et al., 1992), but did not formally invite women to become members until 1881 when its leadership voted to end the policy of clandestine operations (Wertheimer, 1977). Just as it was beginning to make inroads in terms of increased membership and demands for an 8-hour day, the leader of the National Labor Union died, and the short-lived union began to decline. Divisions over whether to focus on the goal of collective bargaining or involvement in politics also contributed to its demise. The Knights of Labor, on the other hand, grew dramatically until a major upheaval brought it to a crashing halt.

Violence and Its Aftermath. The event that led to the precipitous decline of the Knights of Labor was the ill-fated Haymarket bombing. During May 1886, workers across the nation, in a loosely organized protest, were demonstrating in support of the 8-hour day. Particularly active were a number of Chicago area radicals, including German anarchists (Freeman et al., 1992). They distributed some emotional leaflets calling for a protest rally at

Haymarket Square after two unarmed workers were shot in a scuffle at the McCormick Reaper plant where a strike action was in progress. While one of the German radicals was speaking, a bomb was set off, killing a policeman and injuring a number of others, some fatally. When the police retaliated, there were more deaths and injuries. This episode led to a climate of fear and mistrust of radicals, labor unions, and immigrants in general. In the aftermath, hundreds of suspects were rounded up, eight were tried for conspiracy, and four eventually were executed. Although not directly involved in the Haymarket Affair, the Knights of Labor were unfairly blamed for the episode. This backlash, coupled with factionalism within the ranks, led to the decline of the Knights, and an era of labor repression followed.

At the time that the Knights of Labor were fading, a new and different type of union was on the rise. This was the American Federation of Labor (AFL), founded in 1886 when a number of small trade unions banded together. Led by Samuel Gompers, an immigrant and former socialist (Freeman et al., 1992), the AFL eschewed the radicalism that had characterized earlier unions and concentrated instead on building a broad base through a federation of organizations whose members worked largely in the skilled crafts. The AFL did not support the Socialist Party or agitate for social reconstruction of society. In fewer than 20 years after its formal organization, the AFL could boast of 1.7 million members (Foner & Garraty, 1991).

While the relatively conservative AFL was on the rise, a series of tragic strikes occurred in which the workers ultimately were brought to their knees. In 1892 in Homestead, Pennsylvania, the mighty Carnegie Steel Company clashed with the powerful Amalgamated Association of Iron and Steel Workers. After many months and the deaths of both strikers and Pinkerton guards hired by the company to bring order to the plant, the union was humbled, and workers had to accept longer hours and reduced wages at the behest of Carnegie's notorious plant manager Henry Clay Frick. Two years later, in Pullman, Illinois, a company town outside Chicago, the soon to be legendary Eugene V. Debs, president of the American Railway Union, organized a strike against the manufacturer of the nation's railroad sleeping cars. Due to its impact on the delivery of the U.S. mail, President Grover Cleveland ordered in the military, and the strike was broken. Debs ended up in jail for defying a federal injunction and came out a committed socialist who ran for the office of President of the United States many times on the Socialist Party ticket.

A Radical Union. The turn of the 20th century saw the short-lived rise of a radical labor group, the Industrial Workers of the World (IWW), or the Wobblies, who captured the public imagination with their activist approach and their mission to organize those neglected by the AFL—Blacks, unskilled immigrants, and women. Formed by a group of dissident socialists, including Debs, the IWW sought to replace the capitalist economy with one in which the workers would be in control (Freeman et al., 1992). A charismatic leader of the group was westerner William, "Big Bill," Haywood, a veteran of bitter clashes between the Western Federation of Miners and Colorado mining and smelting companies in the early 1900s. Other colorful IWW notables included songwriter Joe Hill, who penned "The Rebel Girl," and the inspiration for the song, the fiery and beautiful Elizabeth Gurley Flynn.

Flynn, along with Haywood and socialists Joseph Ettor and Arturo Giovannitti, helped lead the IWW's most successful action, the Bread and Roses strike of mostly women textile workers in Lawrence, Massachusetts, in 1912. After weeks of strife during which a young woman was killed and the children of the strikers were sent out of the city for both economic and security reasons, the workers won a 5% pay raise. Although celebrated as a great labor victory, it was less than a year before the mill owners were able to rescind most of the concessions won by the workers. IWW strikes were organized against the textile industry in Paterson, New Jersey, and the steel mills in Pennsylvania, but the union began to decline in the anti-immigrant, antiradical climate of World War I. By 1920, it was no longer a powerful union, but the IWW still exists and maintains its headquarters in Chicago and a Web site to disseminate information.

Unions in the Depression Years. During the Great Depression of the 1930s, the character of the labor movement in the United States took another turn with the creation of the Congress of Industrial Organizations (CIO). This group was led by John L. Lewis of the United Mine Workers (UMW), who demanded at the 1934 AFL convention that the AFL work to organize unskilled laborers in mass production industries for collective bargaining. Lewis's proposal did not garner sufficient support, so in 1938 the UMW and a number of other industrial unions formally established the CIO (Foner & Garraty, 1991). Prior to the official founding of the CIO, some member groups were involved in a 6-week strike against the powerful General Motors Corporation. In this dispute, the workers practiced one of their most effective strategies—the sit-down strike. Instead of walking off the job to take action against the company, workers stayed inside the factory and refused to work. Furious at the company speedup policy, hundreds of assembly line workers at plants in Flint, Michigan, and elsewhere seized control of their workplaces and fought for concessions. Until the sit-down strike was declared illegal by the Supreme Court in 1939, perhaps half a million workers participated in this novel type of job action.

In a climate of labor militancy, the federal government, as part of its New Deal policies, enacted legislation that recognized workers' right to unionize and established the National Labor Relations Board to oversee elections in various industries and to encourage companies to bargain in good faith with their employees. Recognizing the national emergency during World

War II and the need for workers to cooperate in turning out the products needed to stave off the threats of fascism, most unions pledged not to strike. There were scattered work stoppages during the war years, but these were relatively minor in comparison to the many walkouts staged in 1946 immediately after the war ended.

Gains and Losses for Unions. Unionism continued to grow during the 1950s, when the two most powerful groups, the AFL and the CIO, merged to form one large unit. Earnings of workers in the heavy industries grew impressively as did social welfare concessions such as pensions and health benefits. Although tainted by charges of corruption and communist infiltration, America's strongest unions joined in the reforms of the 1960s when they supported civil rights legislation. They did not, however, open the ranks of their leadership to women and people of color. Deregulation of heavily unionized industries in the 1970s and the new conservatism of the Reagan era saw union membership fall dramatically. Where one third of the work force was unionized in the early 1950s, the proportion was half that by the end of the 1980s (Foner & Garraty, 1991).

Multicultural Themes

As shown in the preceding historical overview of the labor movement in United States, the participation of individuals from diverse backgrounds was critical. Women, immigrants, and first-generation workers in the mills and factories of industrialized America were the most exploited and often became the most militant supporters and leaders of the union movement. A significant recent chapter in the labor history of the United States centers on the fertile valleys of California. Driven by leaders with Latino origins, and involving some of the nation's most destitute and exploited laborers, migrant farm workers, this chapter of the labor story concerns the creation of the United Farm Workers union. Among the many individuals responsible for organizing this group and for staging some of the most dramatic strikes and boycotts in the history of the labor movement, two individuals stand out for their charismatic leadership, effectiveness, and commitment—Cesar Chavez and Dolores Huerta.

The Rise of Cesar Chavez. Chavez was born in 1927 to a Mexican family living in the Gila Valley of Arizona, not far from the California border (Dalton, 2003; Ferris & Sandoval, 1997). His parents had little material wealth, but Chavez remembered his early childhood as being a happy one despite the bitterness of his schooling. When his parents became migrant workers after the loss of their farm in 1938, his education became difficult, and Chavez is reported to have attended 37 different schools. Feeling that he was an outsider due to language barriers and discrimination, he did not continue his education beyond 8th grade. Later in life, Chavez would speak passionately about the value of an education, and he surrounded himself with great books to help him explore the ideas of the world's best minds.

Fed up with his life as a migrant farm worker, young Chavez joined the Navy in 1944 and served for the next 2 years. Upon his return, he went back to working in the fields, married his longtime sweetheart, and settled into family life. After being displaced by undocumented farm workers from Mexico, Chavez moved his family to San Jose where he found work in a lumberyard and met Fred Ross, a leader in the Community Service Organization (CSO), a group dedicated to fighting for the rights of Hispanics. This event, as well as Chavez's acquaintance with Father Donald McDonnell, whom he accompanied to labor camps to provide assistance to contract workers from Mexico (*braceros*), proved critical to his evolution into a union activist.

Chavez began to work for the CSO as a paid staff member in the Oxnard area, where he documented violations of the law with regard to the *bracero* program. This experience convinced him of the seriousness of the exploitation of migrant workers and of the possibility that they could be organized to improve their condition. When the CSO did not agree to his plans for a union of agricultural farm workers, he resigned and returned to Delano to begin the work in earnest. Here he was joined by relatives and two acquaintances from the CSO, Gil Padilla and Dolores Huerta, who scoured the countryside in search of farm workers to organize.

The Leadership of Dolores Huerta. Dolores Huerta was a native of New Mexico, where her father was a labor activist and member of the state assembly. As a young child in the 1930s, she moved to California with her family after her parents divorced. She grew up in the rough neighborhoods of Stockton, where, as a high school student, she became keenly aware of the discrimination that was directed at people of Mexican heritage (Ferris & Sandoval, 1997). After college, Huerta began a short-lived career in elementary education, but ultimately turned to activism in the CSO as an effective means to make a difference in the lives of poor and victimized people. Huerta became a dynamic organizer in the Stockton area. Her acquaintance with Cesar Chavez was through the CSO, and she wept at the convention in 1962 when he decided to resign after his proposal to organize farm workers into an independent union was turned down. When he and his wife decided to build their organization from a base in Delano in the San Joaquin Valley, Huerta joined the cause.

The United Farm Workers. Chavez and his small group of followers spent the next 3 years trying to build a solid foundation for the National Farm Workers Association (NFWA) (Dalton, 2003). Their first significant action

occurred in 1965 when vineyard workers of the Agricultural Workers Organizing Committee called a strike of grape pickers. Chavez and the NFWA
joined the picket lines, and eventually the two groups merged. In 1972 they
became affiliated with the AFL–CIO, after which they were known as the
United Farm Workers (UFW). Meanwhile, the grape strike took on a life of
its own. Dragging on for 5 years during which Chavez organized a national
consumer boycott of table grapes, it received worldwide attention. Political
forces friendly to agribusiness were angered by Chavez's tactics, but he captured the public imagination and garnered support. In the end, Chavez's group
was victorious and gained the right to collective bargaining. Shortly thereafter, vegetable growers signed contracts with the powerful Teamsters Union,
some suggest in order to avoid having to negotiate with Chavez (Dalton,
2003).

In 1970 the longest vegetable growers strike in U.S. history, *la causa*,
began. Union pitted against union as the Teamsters and the UFW fought for
the right to represent the field workers. In 1975 California passed legislation recognizing the right of farm workers to unionize and bargain collec-
tively for contracts and establishing the Agricultural Labor Relations Board
(ALRB) to oversee organizing and bargaining efforts. Critics would claim,
however, that the ALRB was little more than a tool of agribusiness and did
not operate in the best interests of the farm workers it was charged to protect (Dalton, 2003; Ferris & Sandoval, 1997).

The Legacy of Cesar Chavez. The late 1970s was a period of peak membership for the UFW, which, like other unions across the country, suffered a
decline in the conservative 1980s. The last major strike action for the UFW
during this period was the lettuce strike, which began in the Imperial Valley
of California in 1979 and spread to both the Salinas Valley to the north and
Arizona to the east. As he had during the grape strike of years before, Chavez
tried to organize a consumer boycott of lettuce, but it was not as successful.
Discouraged by the regression of the union movement among farm workers,
Chavez adopted a method he had used twice previously to call attention to
their problems, the fast or hunger strike. His longest fast lasted for 36 days
in 1988, during which he was joined by Reverend Jesse Jackson and a number of entertainers (*The Story of Cesar Chavez*, n.d.). Throughout this period, Chavez turned his attention to the devastating effects of pesticides in
the food industry and used the hunger strike to call attention to the growing
problems associated with their use. No doubt weakened by years of stress
and the effects of fasting, Chavez died quietly in 1993 at the age of 66. He
was mourned by thousands in a public funeral at the site of his first fast in
Delano.

After the death of Chavez, the UFW, although weakened, carried on
under the leadership of his son-in-law, Arturo Rodriguez, who worked to

involve younger workers, and Dolores Huerta, who joined in the efforts to gain recognition for migrant strawberry workers (Ferris & Sandoval, 1997). The UFW today maintains an active Web site with video clips, primary sources, and other educational materials for use in the classroom. In the spring of 2004, the National Chavez Center was opened in California to keep alive the legacy of Cesar Chavez and to provide educational materials for those interested in his work and the history of the labor movement in the fields of the Southwest.

Interface with Local History

The chronicle of workers' struggles for fair wages, an 8-hour day, and decent working conditions parallels the growth of industry, the implementation of the factory system, and the rise of agribusiness. The story is a lengthy one stretching from the middle of the 19th century to the late 20th and beyond. It has been played out by charismatic leaders and ordinary laborers, many of them immigrants or first-generation Americans, in locales from the Northeast, to the Midwest, to the Pacific Coast. Chicago, Homestead, Lawrence, Paterson, Flint, and Delano are but a few of the many sites where workers took a stand and fought to improve their standard of living. But the American labor movement also touched countless other communities throughout the nation whenever and wherever workers fought to unionize or called strikes and job actions to gain better contracts or to improve their working conditions (see Curriculum Unit Outline 6.1). These events are part of the local history of the communities where they took place, and a study of how they came about and their outcomes can help students better make sense of a complicated topic and meet learning standards related to the industrialization and modernization of the nation as well as those related to labor in the Great Depression and the reforms of the 1960s.

Learning Activities

As with most topics of local interest, the resources to get started are usually close at hand—in the library, historical society, or regional museum. However, strikes and labor disputes routinely are covered by the press, so newspaper archives are a rich source for information about such topics. Students can read accounts of the same event in different newspapers in order to detect bias and to consider how the media can influence public opinion on controversial events. Newspapers also may provide details concerning how local and state governments responded to union activities.

Interviews with workers who participated in the events or their children can yield touching insights into the impact of conditions in factories and labor disputes on the lives of participants. Company records and newsletters can provide another perspective and are part of the story as well. Records may be hard for students to obtain, but newsletters sometimes can be found in the local library or historical society, particularly if the company was a major player in the development of the community. Students can use such sources to prepare debates or create first-person narratives and role plays from many perspectives. They can investigate the use of child labor and the role of women and immigrant workers in local businesses. Such activities can help personalize and bring to life a complex and important topic in U.S. history with connections to countless communities and rooted in the experiences of individuals with diverse backgrounds.

CONCLUSIONS

One of the most frequent arguments against increased attention to both local history topics and multicultural education is that teachers do not have enough time to incorporate such material due to the standards movement and increased testing associated with educational reform. Students must become knowledgeable with respect to content associated with the major events and currents in U.S. history, develop sophisticated understandings of related concepts, and practice social science skills, such as interpreting primary sources, to a degree of competency necessary to pass rigorous standardized tests. This chapter addresses the standards mission and answers the arguments concerning lack of time to devote to local and/or multicultural topics by tracing three major events in U.S. history included in the *National Standards for History* (1996) and showing how they are linked to the history of a number of communities in different regions of the country and illustrative of the diversity of the participants.

The points raised in the Focus Questions are explored through the material on King Philip's War, the Underground Railroad, and the American labor movement—all topics with strong links to many individual locales and orchestrated by individuals with diverse backgrounds. Suggested learning activities for the topics presented in this chapter align with the comprehension, analysis, research, and decision-making skills emphasized in standards documents.

Following is the outline of a curriculum unit, "The Hopedale Strike of 1913," which organizes a study of events in a small town in the Blackstone Valley through a set of sequential, interrelated lessons. The unit promotes an understanding of radical labor currents of the early 19th century and multicultural themes of ethnicity and social class. While it is specific to one locale, the unit can be adapted for the study of any controversial local topic with links to U.S. history learning standards.

CURRICULUM UNIT OUTLINE 6.1
THE HOPEDALE STRIKE OF 1913

Grade Level: High School

Suggested Length. Ten class sessions

National Standards for History **References**

Era 6. The Development of the Industrial United States
Standard 2A. The student understands the sources and experiences of the new immigrants.
Standard 3A. The student understands how the "Second Industrial Revolution" changed the nature and conditions of work.
Standard 3B. The student understands the rise of national labor unions and the role of state and federal governments in labor conflicts.
Era 7. The Emergence of Modern America
Standard 1C. The student understands the limitations of progressivism and the alternatives offered by various groups.

NCSS *Curriculum Guidelines for Multicultural Education* References

7.0. The curriculum should help students understand the totality of the experiences of ethnic and cultural groups in the United States.
8.0. The multicultural curriculum should help students understand that a conflict between ideals and realities always exists in human societies.
17.0. The multicultural curriculum should help students to view and interpret events, situations, and conflict from diverse ethnic and cultural perspectives and points of view.
21.0. The multicultural curriculum should make maximum use of experiential learning, especially local community resources.

Historical Background. The town of Hopedale, Massachusetts, was originally a village of the larger community of Milford, established in 1842 as a home for the Practical Christians, a group of utopians led by clergyman Adin Ballou (Danker, 1993, 2003). As such it attracted a number of reformers, who supported the causes of abolitionism, pacifism, and temperance. The little community attracted the attention of a number of well-known activists, including visitors Frederick Douglass, William Lloyd Garrison, and Sojourner Truth. It did not last beyond the mid-1850s, when its assets were bought out by two enterprising members of the group, Ebenezer and George Draper. They established the Draper Company, which one day would boast of being the nation's largest manufacturer of cotton machinery. Hopedale flourished under the direction of the benevolent Draper brothers and their offspring, who turned the village into a model industrial community, showcasing comfortable workers' housing, attractive parks, recreational facilities, and handsome public buildings. In 1886, Hopedale broke away from Milford and was incorporated as a town in its own right.

As the Draper Company grew, so did the need for an inexpensive labor force, and many of the new immigrants from southern and eastern Europe were recruited to work as unskilled operatives. A number of them eventually would be attracted to the radicalism of the Industrial Workers of the World (IWW), and, in the heady aftermath of their dramatic, if short-lived, victory in the Lawrence Bread and Roses strike, the union would help orchestrate a similar walkout in Hopedale. Some would claim the IWW chose this unlikely site for a job action to embarrass Eben Draper, former governor of Massachusetts, who twice had vetoed an 8-hour day bill for public employees. Some of the most celebrated of the Bread and Roses leaders, including Elizabeth Gurley Flynn, came to Hopedale to inspire the pick-eters. Ultimately the action failed, but not before one striker was killed by a bullet in his back, children were dramatically sent out of town, and inflammatory pho-tos of baseball bat–wielding security forces hired by the Draper Company were published on the front page of the local newspapers. It was an ironic turn of events in a community originally founded by a pacifist and developed by entrepreneurs with a mission to promote their realm as a model company town.

Mission. Students will develop an understanding of the employment of immigrant labor and working conditions in American factories during the "Second Industrial Revolution," the goals and strategies of the IWW, the role of government in strikes against major companies, and the perspectives of various participants in such conflicts. They will achieve these understandings through experiential learning, research using primary and secondary sources, and both traditional and perfor-mance assessments.

Unit Activities

Day 1

Students will participate in a walking tour of the center of Hopedale. They will ob-serve the following: street names bearing the utopian heritage of the community, housing for workers, homes of managers and Draper Company executives, public buildings, the Little Red Shop, and the remains of the Draper factory complex.

Day 2

Students will debrief one another on the walking tour and speculate about the everyday life of workers and managers around the turn of the 20th century when the Draper Company was flourishing. They will read the article "A Massachusetts Garden Spot" from *New England Magazine* (Johnson, 1909) and compare the author's conclusions with their own.

The Little Red Shop, Hopedale, Massachusetts.

Days 3–5

Based on readings in their text and supplementary teacher-prepared notes, students will review the following topics: the factory system in the late 19th century, the "new immigration" of the same period, and the rise of unions and the IWW. Students will be quizzed on their knowledge of these content topics.

Days 6 & 7

Working in groups and using newspaper articles available at the Milford and Hopedale libraries, students will prepare a panel/poster presentation on the following topics: Adin Ballou and the Early History of Hopedale, the Draper Family, the Draper Company and Workers, the IWW in the Blackstone Valley, and Hopedale, a Company Town. A whole-group discussion/analysis of the material will follow.

Days 8 & 9

Using a variety of newspaper accounts in the *Boston Daily Globe, Boston Herald, Framingham Evening News, Milford Daily News,* and *New York Times* and the

Draper Company newsletter, *Cotton Chats*, available at the Milford and Hopedale libraries, students will prepare to debate the question of whether the workers and the IWW were justified in calling a strike in 1913.

Day 10

Students will hold the debate and debrief one another on the second week's activities.

Assessment. Students will be assessed on their knowledge of the factory system, the "new immigration," and the labor movement in a traditional quiz that will test both their mastery of the facts and their understanding of the concepts involved. Students will be assessed on their performances in the panel activity and debate using rubrics addressing accuracy and depth of content, logic, and presentation skills.

CHAPTER 7

Securing the Future of Local/
Multicultural History

A S ILLUSTRATED throughout this book, local history has the potential to be an engaging and efficient tool for social studies teachers at all levels to help students develop knowledge, skills, and understandings related to both multicultural education and major U.S. history topics. At the same time, studying local history can instill pride in one's community and thus foster active citizenship. Although there is little danger that local history will disappear from the social studies curriculum, particularly at the elementary level, there is a risk that it will be neglected in the current climate of standards and standardized testing, despite its connections to content topics with which students must become familiar.

In order to ensure that local history is not ignored and that it is incorporated whenever appropriate in all K–12 grades, classroom practitioners must be knowledgeable about content and methods and should be encouraged to learn about the history of the communities in which they teach so that they may help students do the same. There are a number of effective approaches to preparing K–12 teachers to include local history in their classes and to ensuring that it is viewed through a multicultural lens. These include attention to the subjects in preservice curriculum and methods courses, similar staff development projects and graduate courses for teachers, and discussions linking local history to citizenship education.

PREPARING PRESERVICE EDUCATION STUDENTS

For the past several years, I have been teaching social studies curriculum and methods courses for education students preparing to teach at both the elementary and secondary levels. I have always required students in these classes to read articles explaining and promoting both multicultural education and local history and invited guest speakers to share their expertise about museums and resources in the community. Recently I included a more extensive local history requirement, which yielded promising results.

A Local History Assignment

The purpose of the assignment was to help students become more knowledgeable about the history of the community in which they would be doing their student teaching and at the same time to give them practice in lesson planning and presentation skills. After consulting with staff members at the Worcester Historical Museum (WHM) and becoming familiar with the resources of the collection myself, I decided to require that students visit the site to help them come up with ideas and conduct research for a local history assignment. Each student was required to develop an original lesson plan using the resources of the WHM and, if appropriate, to design it for the grade level of the class that he/she was observing at the time.

The Process and Products. Students were prepared for the assignment through readings and discussions of the benefits of local history studies for K–12 classes (Danker, 2001a) and were provided with a set of guidelines for conducting research at the WHM. In addition to preparing the lesson plan to submit for a grade, students were required to present the lesson to our college class either through an overview of the topic, research, and components of the lesson or through teaching a portion of it to peers. Those who were able to teach the lessons to the classes they were observing in the Worcester Public Schools also were encouraged to share with our college class their students' reactions to the lessons. The demonstrations were scheduled far enough into the course so that students had a working knowledge of a variety of social studies methods and assessments and of multicultural themes and approaches before they began to work on the local history project. There was no explicit charge to make the lesson plans multicultural, but it was my hope that the overall focus and content of the course would prompt students to be attentive to the goals of multicultural education. Consequently, a number of the lesson plans *did* highlight diversity issues, particularly with respect to the themes of gender and class. The topics of the preservice teachers' lesson plans fell into the following broad categories: Worcester Firsts and Inventions, Worcester Disasters, Worcester Women's History, and Worcester Participants in National Events.

The most popular topic was Esther Howland and the Valentine. Howland was a Worcester resident who lived from 1828–1904 (*Making Valentines: A Tradition in America*, 2001). As a young woman, she received a valentine from England that, with its paper lace and floral designs, intrigued Howland and her friends. She began to create her own examples and was soon taking orders for the product through the efforts of her brother, a salesman for her father's stationery company. She called upon friends to help her fill the orders, and used the principles of mass production to turn out 10 designs that she had fashioned herself. Howland's business eventually grossed $100,000 annually. Upon her retirement in 1881, she sold her valentine company to another local resident, George C. Whitney, who became the largest producer of the product in the country in the late 19th and early 20th centuries.

The valentine lessons differed in details but most emphasized the entrepreneurship of Howland and promoted critical thinking through comparing and contrasting her product and methods with those used by Whitney. Questions were raised by the preservice students about women's work in the 19th century and why Howland had to depend on her brother to seek out business for her company.

The lesson plans designed to be taught to younger children usually included a valentine-making component, which encouraged creativity and fostered an understanding of mass production techniques. Primary sources in the form of Howland's printed directions for making the valentines and examples of her product also were incorporated. The valentine lesson plans overall promoted pride in the community; mastery of U.S. history and economics standards related to industrialization, supply and demand, and entrepreneurship; and content knowledge related to women's history. The lessons were all designed to be implemented in one class session—underscoring the efficiency of local history and its potential for meeting many goals simultaneously.

Preservice Assignments and State Standards. A number of the students who participated in the local history lesson plan project noted on their course evaluations that this was a valuable experience for them. Future plans for both the elementary and secondary sections of the course include an expansion of the project to include the creation of fully developed curriculum units linking major U.S. history and geography topics to local people, places, and events. Lesson plans will be required to explicitly incorporate NCSS *Curriculum Guidelines for Multicultural Education* (1991). All lesson plans written by students in our state-approved education program must reference appropriate standards from Massachusetts Department of Education Curriculum Framework documents as well. Emphasizing local history in social studies curriculum and methods courses and requiring lesson plans and units to meet state and/or national standards for learning can help ensure that future generations of teachers incorporate into their own classrooms content material related to their school communities. Specific attention to themes and issues related to multicultural education will reinforce the importance of this component as well.

A Transformative Approach for Preservice Teachers

To encourage students in education programs to practice multicultural education in their demonstration lessons, student teaching, and future careers as teachers, it is important that the content they review in conjunction with their methods courses consistently be presented in ways that stimulate them to view the material through multiple perspectives. Teacher educator Andre Branch (2004) provides examples of practicing transformative multicultural education, in keeping with the work of Banks, by constantly asking students provocative questions that enable them to "see curriculum concepts from various racial and cultural perspectives" (p. 33). Such an approach goes beyond just recognizing the contributions of various diverse individuals and groups and instead encourages questions and understandings about the presentation and complexities of school "knowledge" in history/social studies and other subjects.

An example I like to use in my classes relates to the study of what history texts call the westward movement. I begin by referring to the name of the popular 1960s film, *How the West Was Won*, and ask students to respond to the title. I then raise questions about how a film called *How the West Was Lost* might be different in content and perspective. Similarly, Branch (2004) begins a study of the same period by showing students a map of the United States, drawing arrows to the left and asking preservice teachers to tell what they had learned to call the movement of individuals across this expanse. When they respond with such terms as "manifest destiny" or "the westward movement," Branch launches into a discussion of perspective and asks students to think about who is telling the story of what happened on the land in question. Routinely incorporating such strategies and encouraging students to question their own learning of content material will help them to become more sensitive to multicultural issues in their future teaching.

INVOLVING TEACHERS IN LOCAL HISTORY STAFF DEVELOPMENT PROJECTS

Experienced social studies educators as well as preservice teachers can be provided with a rationale, content knowledge, and connections to learning standards related to local history and multicultural guidelines through graduate courses and professional activities. Both venues can be tailored to the needs and interests of teachers in particular districts and can incorporate assignments in which individuals or groups develop curriculum materials for use in their own classes.

Heritage Trails

One particularly exciting type of local history project, involving experienced teachers, which has been gaining in popularity in recent years is the creation of heritage trails marking the sites in a neighborhood or community where events of note occurred. Sometimes the trails are researched and designed by individual teachers, although they are more commonly the work of teams of educators in collaboration with their students. Such efforts are powerful tools for teaching and learning history because they promote a sense of ownership, since the students and their teachers identify and decide what landmarks to include, and craft their own stories of the past rather than reading second- and third-hand accounts. There is a compelling hands-on aspect to the creation of heritage trails—those who are involved in such projects must get out into the community and physically walk the neighborhoods, take photos, research possible sites, and place markers. In some instances, the students act as tour guides for others who wish to learn about the history of their community.

An Example in Framingham. A heritage trail project that has been ongoing in Framingham, Massachusetts, for the past several years is a community service learning initiative funded by a grant from the U.S. Department of Education and administered through Framingham State College. Initially, area teachers enrolled in a graduate course where they learned more about the history of the town and resources for researching its past. In addition they heard lectures about labor history and other multicultural topics and discussed the rationale for emphasizing local history. The major course requirement was to design a local history project, which eventually took the form of the creation of a series of neighborhood heritage trails around the various participating schools in the district. Brochures were written to describe the sites and to provide maps and, in some cases, photos of the designated landmarks. The sites included on the heritage trails, for the most part, fell into the following categories: public buildings, architecturally significant private homes, homes of town notables, parks, businesses, churches, historic streets and roads, and natural features. The heritage trails have connections to the state frameworks and to some degree have been incorporated into the social studies curriculum at the participating schools.

An African American Heritage Trail. Another Massachusetts school heritage trail project involves the island of Martha's Vineyard, which has a distinct multicultural focus (Burdis, 2000). The project began when a teacher and her high school class searched through island primary sources such as wills and obituaries to determine whether and to what extent slavery was present on Martha's Vineyard. After determining that indeed it was common into the 1800s, they expanded the project and added the creation of a heritage trail dedicated to African American history on the island. Sites on the heritage trail include both those associated with slavery, such as cemeteries and pasture lands once the property of slaveowners, and homes of prominent African Americans of later periods. The endeavor grew from a classroom activity into a nonprofit corporation, the African American Heritage Trail History Project, which has published a book and continues to research and add to the trail (*African American Heritage Trail of Martha's Vineyard*, 2002). Students are still involved in the research and maintenance of the trail and act as tour guides for visitors.

The Technology Connection

Another relatively recent development in local history studies is the integration of technology through the creation of Web pages designed by students to showcase their communities. Milson, Lloyd, Estes, and Mayfield (2003) stress the point that most local communities do not make it into the history books, yet they have been affected by the major trends and events that do. It may be challenging for students to locate and analyze local history sources, and, once they do, technology may support and publicize their efforts. Milson and colleagues describe a 5th-grade project in Lorena, Texas, a community with no official Web site, in which the students embarked on an inquiry-based research project on the history of their town and then developed a Web page to highlight their results. They presented their finished product to members of the community, and the project subsequently evolved into an ongoing endeavor. Future school groups in Lorena can add to the Web page as they uncover new information or create new resources through oral histories and photographs. Milson and colleagues note that one possible topic for such research could focus on the Waco Indians. This addition would add a multicultural dimension to the project.

Sometimes it is necessary to provide professional development for teachers in order to help them gain the skills needed to integrate technology into their local history lessons. One such project to enhance the study and appreciation of local history in the Blackstone Valley involved a series of workshops to prepare teachers to use technology more effectively (Danker, 2000). This 1998 grant-funded enterprise, the Learning Network, was launched initially to facilitate the creation of interdisciplinary curriculum units to meet new state learning standards. One branch of the Learning Network resulted in the creation of a virtual museum on the Internet with "displays" designed by teachers and students, who took photographs, wrote essays, and set up the Web pages to showcase the history and the environment of the various communities of the region. Although the museum's developers were not expressly instructed to include multicultural components, some of the museum displays centered on the Nipmuc Indians of the region and the religious origins of the utopian commune in Hopedale.

Courses for Experienced Teachers

Less time-consuming than the creation of heritage trails, Web pages, and virtual museums, but nonetheless effective in fostering interest in local history and mastery of content related to major national events with community connections, are the everyday lessons that teachers can infuse with interesting local information if they are familiar with the material. Graduate courses, summer workshops, and presentations at educators' meetings and conventions can all help teachers become more knowledgeable about state and local history. Armed with the information and resources gained through these and similar efforts, teachers will be prepared to continue the mission to promote multicultural social studies through the study of local history. An important aspect of all such professional development programs, however, is that they promote multiple perspectives in the interpretation of local history and that they routinely are attentive to all cultural groups that participated in the building of communities.

REMEMBERING THE CITIZENSHIP MISSION OF SOCIAL STUDIES

As declared by researchers in the 1970s (Barr, Barth, & Shermis, 1978; Barth & Shermis, 1970) and as described more recently by history and social studies educators (Barton & Levstik, 2004; Evans, 2004), preparing students to be active and effective citizens in a democratic society has been a central purpose of social studies throughout its contentious history as a component of the K–12 curriculum. The NCSS reaffirmed the link between the two in its definition in *Expectations of Excellence: Curriculum Standards for Social Studies* (1994), when the group formally stated: "The primary purpose of social studies is to help young people develop the ability to make informed and reasoned decisions for the public good as citizens of a culturally diverse, democratic society in an interdependent world" (p. vii).

In its rationale for the study of history, the National Center for History in the Schools also stressed citizenship by noting in the *National Standards for History* (1996) that without a knowledge of history and the ability to participate in historical inquiry, "one cannot move to the informed, discriminating citizenship essential to effective participation in the democratic processes of governance and the fulfillment for all our citizens of the nation's democratic ideals" (p. 1). Such statements provide evidence to support the contention that experts in social studies education and in the field of history, which is its major content area, are in general agreement that one cannot be an effective citizen without a knowledge of the past and the ability to ask informed questions and to make thoughtful decisions about public issues.

Effective Citizenship

More than knowledge of the past or even of how the government currently functions, however, is necessary for effective citizenship. Students need to understand that they can influence public policy through activism, and they should be given opportunities to do so while they are still in school. Social studies educators have a long tradition of providing students with such experiences through letter-writing campaigns and other means of contacting legislators and public officials.

Students also should realize that there is still more to citizenship in a democracy than content knowledge and contact with government; they should understand that their participation in the life of what Barton and Levstik (2004) call "civil society" is an important part of the mix. When they work for a charitable institution, church group, or neighborhood improvement society, they are participating in the civil society and learning about democratic practice in ways that may be more meaningful than through more conventional means. Furthermore, these experiences may help them to understand how groups traditionally marginalized by the political process are empowered to change their lives for the better.

Defining Citizenship Through Community. As we have seen, there are many ways to define citizenship beyond the constitutional statement that it comes with birth or naturalization. In 2001, the NCSS Task Force on Revitalizing Citizenship Education developed a list of Characteristics of an Effective Citizen and a companion list of Characteristics of an Effective Citizenship Education Program, both of which refer to knowledge of local history and traditions and involvement in community life as fundamental components. The group's position statement on how to create effective citizens also includes multicultural themes such as giving students opportunities to seek information from different perspectives, participate in conflict resolution, and be involved in school governance.

Community Service and Citizenship. One of the defining characteristics of an effective citizen, according to the NCSS Task Force (2001), is the habit of active involvement in the community, and the group recommends that schools create opportunities for students to participate in community service programs. The rationale is that if young people become involved while still in school, they will continue to do so as adult citizens. As described earlier, the creation of heritage trails is one example of a community service activity that is grounded in local history and that can foster multicultural values.

Although not without controversy, particularly if community service is mandatory (Spring, 2002), such programs have become increasingly popular. Research conducted concerning middle school projects that require a substantial time commitment (Jackson & Davis, 2000), that is, 31 or more hours a year, yielded promising results. Students involved in community service, when compared with others not enrolled in such programs, reported a stronger sense of responsibility toward others and a keener belief that they actually could make a difference—clear attributes of good citizenship. As a preliminary to community service, study of local history and current problems and issues can establish a context and promote a more integrated experience.

History and Citizenship

Among the many qualities of an effective citizen are those promoted throughout this book—a knowledge of one's own community, both as an end in itself and as a vehicle for understanding the main currents of national history, and an appreciation of multicultural values. I would add to this mix, a belief that ordinary individuals make history and that as citizens or residents of a community, the nation, and the world, they have a right to be heard.

Back in the 1980s, as a debate over the content of the social studies curriculum played out, powerful forces in government and education fought for the primacy of history over the social sciences in K–12 classrooms (Evans, 2004). In *Historical Literacy: The Case for History in American Education* (Gagnon & Bradley Commission on History in Schools, 1989), a group of influential historians argued forcefully that all students in American schools be required to study history, with a K–12 social studies curriculum firmly grounded in the subject. Critics of the Bradley Commission claimed that it was one-sided, ignored the fact that history had always been central to the social studies curriculum, and did not recognize that a goal of social studies education was to foster in the "average citizen" a deeper appreciation of history (Evans, 2004, p. 157). One of the members of the Bradley Commission, however, historian Gary Nash, a co-director of the National Center for History in the Schools, which published the *National Standards for History* (1996), argues convincingly for that same goal in his essay "History for a Democratic Society: The Work of All the People" (1989). In so doing he also presents a case, although not explicitly, for local/multicultural social studies.

Nash creates portraits of two ordinary citizens who changed the course of history by acts of courage on a local level that connected them to major national events. One, Rosa Parks, would go on to become a famous heroine of the civil rights movement, and the other, Ebenezer MacIntosh, would remain relatively anonymous despite his role in Stamp Act protests that contributed to the American Revolution. Both were members of groups neglected and marginalized by mainstream history—Parks, as a Black woman, and MacIntosh, as a poor uneducated shoemaker. Both belied the widespread belief that women, the poor, and people of color are history's victims, not its activators. Parks and MacIntosh inspired their neighbors to organize and to bring about changes to societies they saw as unjust. These are acts that define active citizenship at its most effective levels.

CONCLUSIONS

Throughout this book, I have written about individuals who, through their interests and active citizenship, have inspired, engaged in, or changed history through their actions on a local level. Framingham's Margaret Knight and her many inventions were part of the Industrial Revolution. Nashville's college students were integral to ending segregation in the city's businesses and provided models for others seeking to end discrimination elsewhere. Shakers at South Union and Pleasant Hill, Kentucky, gave sustenance to combatants during the Civil War, while trying to remain true to their pacifist ideals. The French Canadian residents of Woonsocket built institutions for worship, education, and recreation that remain to this day in a community with changing diversity that reflects demographic shifts in the nation at large. The Italian immigrants in Hopedale who went on strike against a powerful and well-connected corporation and the migrant workers who joined the United Farm Workers to challenge the forces of agribusiness in California's fertile valleys were significant players in America's checkered labor movement.

Some local residents, unknown at first outside their own neighborhoods, left home to participate in what they saw as reforms or events too important for them to ignore and go on with their daily lives. As such, they provided a personal dimension to history and, perhaps unknowingly, brought it back to their own communities. Louise Mayo left her seven children in Framingham temporarily to go to Washington and demonstrate for women's suffrage. Sister Lucy Wright traveled tirelessly from one Shaker community to another to enforce the *Millennial Laws* of the society, overseeing its expansion during what would become known in history books as the Second Great Awakening. Sometimes, as in the case of the freedom seekers who traveled the Underground Railroad, the history makers were only temporarily a part of the local scene, but their presence, nonetheless, changed both the communities they passed through and the nation's history. Remembering their stories through study and activities in our social studies classrooms can help encourage children to become active citizens and to appreciate that the diversity of the nation has been one of its greatest strengths.

Ensuring that this mission will continue depends on a commitment to prepare future teachers to be well informed about the potential of local history to accomplish many goals of social studies, and to be grounded in a multicultural approach to the curriculum. For those who are already working in the field of social studies, ongoing professional development through hands-on workshops and content-based courses will promote continued attention to the local history connection to multicultural social studies. The overarching theme of preservice preparation and professional development programs to encourage local/multicultural studies must be that they will promote good citizenship in all its many varieties.

References

African American Heritage Trail of Martha's Vineyard. (2002). Retrieved May 22, 2004, from http://www.mvheritagetrail.org/ missioninfo.html

American Revolution Bicentennial Administration. (n.d.). *Underground Railroad in New England* [Booklet].

Andrews, E. D. (1940). *The gift to be simple: Songs, dances, and rituals of the American Shakers.* New York: Dover.

Andrews, E. D. (1963). *The people called Shakers.* New York: Dover.

Andrews, E. D., & Andrews, F. (1974). *Work and worship among the Shakers: Their craftsmanship and economic order.* New York: Dover.

Bacon, R. H. (2000). *Toward the new millennium: Woonsocket, Rhode Island.* Woonsocket, RI: Ayotte.

Bacon, R. H., Crowley, M. P., & Mulcahy, R. C. (1988). The years of resurgence. In Woonsocket Centennial Committee (Eds.), *Woonsocket, Rhode Island: A centennial history, 1888–1988* (pp. 179–203). State College, PA: Jostens.

Banks, J. A. (1993). Multicultural education: Development, dimensions, and challenges. *Phi Delta Kappan, 75*(1), 22–28.

Banks, J. A. (1995). Multicultural education: Historical development, dimensions, and practice. In J. A. Banks & C.A.M. Banks (Eds.), *Handbook of research on multicultural education* (pp. 3–24). New York: Macmillan.

Banks, J. A. (1997). Multicultural education: Characteristics and goals. In J. A. Banks & C. A. M. Banks (Eds.), *Multicultural education: Issues and perspectives* (pp. 3–31). Boston: Allyn & Bacon.

Barr, R. D., Barth, J. L., & Shermis, S. S. (1978). *The nature of the social studies.* Palm Springs, CA: ETC.

Barth, J. L. (1996). NCSS and the nature of social studies. In O. L. Davis, Jr. (Ed.), *NCSS in retrospect: Bulletin 92* (pp. 9–19). Washington, DC: National Council for the Social Studies.

Barth, J. L., & Shermis, S. S. (1970). Defining the social studies: An exploration of three traditions. *Social Education, 34*(8), 743–751.

Barton, K. C., & Levstik, L. S. (2004). *Teaching history for the common good.* Mahwah, NJ: Erlbaum.

Bellemare, M. J. (1974). Social networks in an inner-city neighborhood: Woonsocket, RI (Doctoral dissertation, Catholic University of America, 1974). *Dissertation*

Abstracts International, 36(01), 375A. (University Microfilms No. AAT75-13948)

Bellerose, R. (1997). *Images of America: Woonsocket.* Dover, NH: Arcadia.

Bennett, C. I. (1999). *Comprehensive multicultural education: Theory and practice.* Boston: Allyn & Bacon.

Berkin, C. R. (1989). Clio in search of her daughters/Women in search of their past. In M. B. Norton (Ed.), *Major problems in American women's history* (pp. 10–17). Lexington, MA: Heath.

Bouley, N. D. (1988). The twenties. In Woonsocket Centennial Committee (Eds.), *Woonsocket, Rhode Island: A centennial history, 1888–1988* (pp. 73–93). State College, PA: Jostens.

Branch, A. J. (2004). It didn't feel like manifest destiny to me: Practicing transformative multicultural education—an example from social studies. *Multicultural Perspectives, 6*(3), 33–35.

Brief history of Simsbury. (n.d.). Retrieved March 8, 2004, from http://www.town.simsbury.ct.us/history.html

Brooks, J. G., & Brooks, M. G. (1993). *In search of understanding: The case for constructivist classrooms.* Alexandria, VA: Association for Supervision and Curriculum Development.

Brotherly love. (n.d.). Retrieved December 3, 2003, from http://www.pbs.org/wgbh/aia/part3/3p247.html

Brown, R. D., & Tager, J. (2000). *Massachusetts: A concise history.* Amherst: University of Massachusetts Press.

Burdis, J. (2000, February 27). Digging up a buried past: Students document slavery, create historic trail on Vineyard. *The Boston Sunday Globe,* pp. B1, B7.

Burns, D. E. (1993). *Shaker cities of peace, love, and union: A history of the Hancock Bishopric.* Hanover, NH: University Press of New England.

Busbee, J. (1997). *The persistence of folklore.* Retrieved March 25, 2004, from http://www.memphisflyer.com/backissues/issue419/cvr419.htm

Callahan, R. J. (1974). *Framingham historical reflections* (M. E. Dewar & M. J. Gilbert, Eds.). Washington, DC: McGregor and Werner.

Calloway, C. G. (Ed.). (1997). *After King Philip's War: Presence and persistence in Indian New England.* Hanover, NH: University Press of New England.

Campbell, D. (1978). Women's life in utopia: The Shaker experiment in sexual equality reappraised—1810 to 1860. *New England Quarterly, 51,* 23–38.

Canterbury Shaker Village. (2000). Retrieved December 28, 2003, from http://www.shakers.org/village/index.php?show=ABOUT

Chavez, R. C. (1998). Engaging the multicultural education terrain. In R. C. Chavez & J. O'Donnell (Eds.), *Speaking the unpleasant: The politics of (non) engagement in multicultural education terrain* (pp. 6–15). Albany: State University of New York Press.

Clayton, J. B. (2003). *One classroom, many worlds: Teaching and learning in the cross-cultural classroom.* Portsmouth, NH: Heinemann.

communITYteam. (Eds.). (2000). *A different view: 20th century stories from Fairmount, Veterans Memorial, and Constitution Hill residents, Woonsocket, RI.* Woonsocket, RI: WNDC.

Cott, N. F. (1977). *The bonds of womanhood: "Woman's sphere" in New England, 1780–1835.* New Haven, CT: Yale University Press.

Country Music Foundation. (1994). *Country: The music and the musicians from the beginnings to the '90s.* New York: Abbeville Press.

Crowley, M. P. (1988). The pivotal decade. In Woonsocket Centennial Committee (Eds.), *Woonsocket, Rhode Island: A centennial history, 1888–1988* (pp. 135–159). State College, PA: Jostens.

Dalton, F. J. (2003). *The moral vision of César Chávez.* Maryknoll, NY: Orbis Books.

Danker, A. C. (1986). Women's place in the Harvard Shaker community. *New England Social Studies Bulletin, 44*(3), 15–38.

Danker, A. C. (1993). The Hopedale strike of 1913: The unmaking of an industrial utopia. In D. M. Reynolds & L. Viens (Eds.), *New England's disharmony: The consequences of the Industrial Revolution* (pp. 74–81). Woonsocket: Rhode Island Labor History Society.

Danker, A. C. (2000). Linking technology with social studies learning standards. *The Social Studies, 91*(6), 253–256.

Danker, A. C. (2001a). "All history is local": Using the familiar to teach and learn core knowledge topics. *The New England Journal of History, 57*(2), 84–91.

Danker, A. C. (2001b). Keepers of tradition, agents of change: Social studies teachers and multicultural education. *International Social Studies Forum, 1*(1), 45–62.

Danker, A. C. (2003). Multicultural social studies: The local history connection. *The Social Studies, 94*(2), 111–117.

Davidson, J. W., & Lytle, M. H. (1992). *After the fact: The art of historical detection.* New York: McGraw-Hill.

Dewey, J. (1964). My pedagogic creed. In R. D. Archambault (Ed.), *John Dewey on education: Selected writings* (pp. 427–439). Chicago: University of Chicago Press. (Original work published 1897)

Doughton, T. L. (1997). Unseen neighbors: Native Americans of central Massachusetts, a people who had "vanished." In C. G. Calloway (Ed.), *After King Philip's War: Presence and persistence in Indian New England* (pp. 207–230). Hanover, NH: University Press of New England.

Doyle, D. H. (1985). *Nashville since the 1920s.* Knoxville: University of Tennessee Press.

Erickson, F. (1997). Culture in society and in educational practices. In J. A. Banks & C. A. M. Banks (Eds.), *Multicultural education: Issues and perspectives* (pp. 32–60). Boston: Allyn & Bacon.

Evans, R. W. (2004). *The social studies wars: What should we teach the children?* New York: Teachers College Press.

Evans-Daly, L., & Gordon, D. C. (1997). *Images of America: Framingham.* Dover, NH: Arcadia.

Exhibition of sculpture by Mrs. Fuller. (1933, December 7). *Framingham News.*

Family is militant: Sons and daughters hope suffragist will "stick." (1917, July 18). *The Boston Post.*

Female Society of Framingham. (1822). [Constitution]. Framingham Historical Society and Museum, Framingham, MA.

Ferris, S., & Sandoval, R. (1997). *The fight in the fields: Cesar Chavez and the farmworkers movement.* Orlando, FL: Harcourt Brace.

Field, S. L., & Burlbaw, L. M. (1995). A time for growth, a time for war, a time for leadership. *Social Education, 59*(7), 408–415.

Fleming, C. G. (1998). "We shall overcome": Tennessee and the civil rights movement. In C. V. West (Ed.), *Tennessee history: The land, people, and the culture* (pp. 436–455). Knoxville: University of Tennessee Press.

Foner, E., & Garraty, J. A. (Eds.). (1991). *The reader's companion to American history.* Boston: Houghton Mifflin.

Framingham Historical Society. (2001). *Zeal for healing: A Framingham trait* [Brochure]. Framingham, MA: Author.

Freeman, J., Lichtenstein, N., Brier, S., Bensman, D., Benson, S. P., Brundage, D., et al. (1992). *Who built America? Working people and the nation's economy, politics, culture, and society* (Vol. 2). New York: Pantheon Books.

Freire, P. (1970). *Pedagogy of the oppressed* (M. B. Ramos, Trans.). New York: Continuum.

Gagnon, P., & Bradley Commission on History in Schools (Eds.). (1989). *Historical literacy: The case for history in American education.* New York: Macmillan.

Gara, L. (1998). An epic in United States history: Myth and reality. In United States National Park Service, Division of Publications, *Underground Railroad* (pp. 6–15). Washington, DC: U.S. Department of the Interior.

Gardner, H. (1993). *Frames of mind: The theory of multiple intelligences.* New York: Basic Books.

Garrett, A. (1994). Teaching high school history inside and outside the historical canon. In L. Kramer, D. Reid, & W. L. Barney (Eds.), *Learning history in America: Schools, cultures, and politics* (pp. 71–77). Minneapolis: University of Minnesota Press.

Gerstle, G. (1991). Interpreting Woonsocket history: 1875–1955. In D. M. Reynolds & M. Myers (Eds.), *Working in the Blackstone River Valley: Exploring the heritage of industrialization* (pp. 143–152). Woonsocket, RI: Sheahan.

Gollnick, D. M., & Chinn, P. C. (2002). *Multicultural education in a pluralistic society.* Upper Saddle River, NJ: Merrill Prentice Hall.

Greenawald, D. (1995). Maturation and change: 1947–1968. *Social Education, 59*(7), 416–428.

Hansen, C. (1969). *Witchcraft at Salem.* New York: George Braziller.

Harlan, D. (2001). *The Shakers.* Retrieved May 21, 2003, from http://religious movements.lib.virginia.edu/nrms/Shakers.html

Hendrick, G., & Hendrick, W. (Eds.). (2004). *Fleeing for freedom: Stories of the Underground Railroad as told by Levi Coffin and William Still.* Chicago: Ivan R. Dee.

Herndon, R. W., & Sekatau, E. W. (1997). The right to a name: The Narragansett people and Rhode Island officials in the Revolutionary era. In C. G. Calloway (Ed.), *After King Philip's War: Presence and persistence in Indian New England* (pp. 114–143). Hanover, NH: University Press of New England.

Herring, S. W. (2000). *Framingham: An American town.* Framingham, MA: Framingham Historical Society.

Historical narrative. (n.d.). Retrieved July 20, 2004, from http://www.framingham. com/history/histnarr.htm

Hodges, G. R. (2000–2001). *The hazards of anti-slavery journalism.* Retrieved August 7, 2004, from http://www.hartford-hwp.com/ archives/45a/394.html

hooks, b. (2000). Overcoming white supremacy: A comment. In E. M. Duarte & S. Smith (Eds.), *Foundational perspectives in multicultural education* (pp. 111– 117). New York: Longman.

Horgan, E. R. (1987). *The Shaker holy land: A community portrait.* Harvard, MA: Harvard Common Press.

Horstman, D. (1975). *Sing your heart out, country boy.* Nashville, TN: Country Music Foundation. (Original work published 1969)

Hudson, N. E. (1988). The new century. In Woonsocket Centennial Committee (Eds.), *Woonsocket, Rhode Island: A centennial history, 1888–1988* (pp. 33– 47). State College, PA: Jostens.

Human Relations. (n.d.). Retrieved January 9, 2002, from http://www.framingham. com/townhall/humreldp.htm

Humez, J. M. (Ed.). (1981). *Gifts of power: The writings of Rebecca Jackson, Black visionary, Shaker eldress.* Amherst: University of Massachusetts Press.

Hymowitz, C., & Weissman, M. (1978). *A history of women in America.* New York: Bantam Books.

Jackson, A. W., & Davis, G. A. (2000). *Turning points 2000: Educating adolescents in the 21st century.* New York: Teachers College Press.

Jadallah, E. (2000). Constructivist experiences for social studies education. *The Social Studies, 91*(5), 221–225.

James, E. T., James, J. W., & Boyer, P. S. (Eds.). (1971). *Notable American women: 1607–1950* (Vol. 2). Cambridge, MA: Belknap Press of Harvard University Press.

Jarolimek, J. (1981). The social studies: An overview. In H. D. Mehlinger & O. L. Davis, Jr. (Eds.), *The social studies: Eightieth yearbook of the National Society for the Study of Education, Part II* (pp. 3–18). Chicago: University of Chicago Press.

Johnson, E. S. (1909). A Massachusetts garden spot. *New England Magazine,* pp. 607–613.

Kinnard, R. W. (Ed.). (2002). *The African American guide to Nashville* [Brochure]. Nashville, TN: Kinnard & Associates.

Leone, M. P., & Silberman, N. A. (1995). *Invisible America: Unearthing our hidden history.* New York: Henry Holt.

Lepore, J. (1998). *The name of war: King Philip's War and the origins of American identity.* New York: Vintage Books.

Lerner, G. (1989). Placing women in history. In M. B. Norton (Ed.), *Major problems in American women's history* (pp. 2–91). Lexington, MA: Heath.

Lind, L. (1989). *The Southeast Asians in Rhode Island: The new Americans.* Providence: Rhode Island Heritage Commission & Rhode Island Publications Society.

Lovett, B. L. (1999). *The African-American history of Nashville, Tennessee, 1780– 1930: Elites and dilemmas.* Fayetteville: University of Arkansas Press.

Making Valentines: A tradition in America. (2001). Retrieved May 17, 2004, from http://www.americanantiquarian.org/Exhibitions/Valentines/howland.htm

Martorella, P. H. (1996). *Teaching social studies in middle and secondary schools.* Englewood Cliffs, NJ: Merrill.

Marty, M. E. (1984). *Pilgrims in their own land: 500 years of religion in America.* New York: Penguin.

Mary Rowlandson (c. 1636–1722). (2003). Retrieved March 8, 2004, from http://guweb2.gonzaga.edu/faculty/campbell//en1310/rowland.htm

Mauricio Gaston Institute. (1994). *Latinos in Framingham.* Boston: University of Massachusetts.

McCabe, M. (2004, September 22). English-language learners. *Teacher Magazine.* Retrieved November 29, 2004, from http://www.agentk–12.edweek.org/issues_page.cfm?id=8

McLaren, P. (1997). *Revolutionary multiculturalism: Pedagogy of dissent for the new millennium.* Boulder, CO: Westview Press.

McLoughlin, W. G. (1978). *Revivals, awakenings, and reform.* Chicago: University of Chicago Press.

Melcher, M. F. (1968). *The Shaker adventure.* Cleveland: Press of Case Western Reserve.

Metropolitan Historical Commission. (n.d.). *Nashville Tennessee history and timeline.* Retrieved June 27, 2002, from http://www.nashville.gov/mhc/timeline.htm

Milson, A. J., Lloyd, T. D., Estes, L. K., & Mayfield, C. (2003). Where in the world is Lorena, Texas? Enhancing local history studies with technology. *Social Education, 67*(3), 140–144.

Morrissett, I. (1981). The needs of the future and the constraints of the past. In H. D. Mehlinger & O. L. Davis, Jr. (Eds.), *The social studies: Eightieth yearbook of the National Society for the Study of Education, Part II* (pp. 36–59). Chicago: University of Chicago Press.

Mrs. Meta Warrick Fuller receives NAACP citation. (1964, December 7). *Framingham News.*

Mullen, C. (1985, September 8). KKK, opponents clashed in Sudbury 60 years ago. *The Middlesex News,* p. 3B.

Nash, G. B. (1989). History for a democratic society: The work of all the people. In P. Gagnon & Bradley Commission on History in Schools (Eds.), *Historical literacy: The case for history in American education* (pp. 234–248). New York: Macmillan.

National Center for History in the Schools. (1996). *National standards for history.* Los Angeles: Author.

National Council for the Social Studies. (1994). *Expectations of excellence: Curriculum standards for social studies.* Washington, DC: Author.

National Council for the Social Studies Task Force on Ethnic Studies Curriculum Guidelines (1991). *Curriculum guidelines for multicultural education.* Washington, DC: National Council for the Social Studies.

National Council for the Social Studies Task Force on Revitalizing Citizenship Education. (2001). Creating effective citizens: A position statement of National Council for the Social Studies. *Social Education, 65*(5), 319.

National Council on Economic Education. (1997). *Voluntary national content standards in economics.* New York: Author.

National Geographic Society. (2003). *The five themes of geography.* Retrieved July 18, 2004, from http://www.nationalgeographic. com/resource/ngo/education/themes.html

National standards for history. See National Center for History in the Schools.

Neal, J. (1975). *By their fruits: The story of Shakerism in South Union, Kentucky.* Philadelphia: Porcupine Press.

Neal, J. (1977). *The Kentucky Shakers.* Lexington: University Press of Kentucky.

New England Native American Institute. (n.d.). *Central Massachusetts "Colored" veterans of the Civil War* [Brochure]. Worcester, MA: Author.

Newton History Museum at the Jackson Homestead. (2003). Retrieved March 21, 2004, from http://www.ci.newton.ma.us/Jackson/ news/nurnf.asp

Norton, M. B. (Ed.). (1989). *Major problems in American women's history.* Lexington, MA: Heath.

Ovando, C. J. (1997). Language diversity and education. In J. A. Banks & C. A. M. Banks (Eds.), *Multicultural education: Issues and perspectives* (pp. 272–296). Boston: Allyn & Bacon.

Paine, O., & Lovett, B. (1991). *African American historic sites* [Brochure]. Nashville, TN: Metropolitan Historical Commission.

Parker, W. C. (1997). Democracy and difference. *Theory and Research in Social Education, 25*(2), 220–234.

Parrillo, V. N. (1994). *Strangers to these shores: Race and ethnic relations in the United States.* New York: Macmillan.

Patterson, D. W. (1979). *The Shaker spiritual.* Princeton, NJ: Princeton University Press.

Perry, E. I. (2002). The very best influence: Josephine Holloway and Girl Scouting in Nashville's African American community. In C. V. West (Ed.), *Trial and triumph: Essays in Tennessee's African American history* (pp. 313–333). Knoxville: University of Tennessee Press.

Pletcher, L. B. (1999). *It happened in Massachusetts.* Helena, MT: TWODOT.

Pou, C. (1999). *The Leo Frank case.* Retrieved December 20, 2003, from www.cviog. uga.edu/Projects/gainfo/leofrank.htm

Rafael, A. (1997). *"La Survivance": A companion to the exhibit at the Museum of Work & Culture, Woonsocket, Rhode Island.* Providence: Rhode Island Historical Society.

Rasool, J. A., & Curtis, A. C. (2000). *Multicultural education in middle and secondary classrooms: Meeting the challenge of diversity and change.* Belmont, CA: Wadsworth Thompson Learning.

Ravitch, D. (1995). Multiculturalism: E pluribus plures. In K. Ryan & J. M. Cooper (Eds.), *Kaleidoscope: Readings in Education* (pp. 458–464). Boston: Houghton Mifflin.

Reuell, P. (2000, March 3). Bridge dedicated to Crispus Attucks. *Metrowest Daily News,* pp. C1–C2.

Ricciardi, D. D. (2004). *Abbondanza!* The richness of Italian-American life in Framingham. *Framingham History, 1*(2), 3–5.

Ripley, C. P. (1998). The Underground Railroad. In U.S. National Park Service, Division of Publications, *Underground Railroad* (pp. 45–75). Washington, DC: U.S. Department of the Interior.

Rohrlich, R. (1984). The Shakers: Gender equality in hierarchy. In R. Rohrlich & E. H. Baruch (Eds.), *Women in search of utopia: Mavericks and myth makers* (pp. 54–61). New York: Schocken Books.

Satz, R. N. (1979). *Tennessee's Indian peoples: From White contact to removal, 1540–1840.* Knoxville: University of Tennessee Press.

Scheurman, G. (1998). From behaviorist to constructivist teaching [Electronic version]. *Social Education, 62*(1), 1–6.

Schlesinger, A. M., Jr. (1992). *The disuniting of America: Reflections on a multicultural society.* New York: Norton.

Schultz, E. B., & Tougias, M. J. (1999). *King Philip's War: The history and legacy of America's forgotten conflict.* Woodstock, VT: Countryman Press.

Schultz, N. L. (2000). *Fire and roses: The burning of the Charlestown convent, 1834.* New York: Free Press.

Shaker Village of Pleasant Hill. (2003a). Retrieved December 28, 2003, from http://www.shakervillageky.org/

Shaker Village of Pleasant Hill: Music and dance. (2003b). Retrieved August 5, 2004, from http://www.shakervillageky.org/vill/villexp2musico.asp

Sharp, D. (2003, July 20). Last 4 Shakers find plenty of "friends." *The Daily News,* p. F6.

Slavin, R. G. (1997). *Educational psychology: Theory and practice.* Boston: Allyn & Bacon.

Sleeter, C. E., & Grant, C. A. (1994). *Making choices for multicultural education: Five approaches to race, class, and gender.* New York: Merrill.

Smyth, J. W. (1903). *History of the Catholic Church in Woonsocket and vicinity, from the celebration of the first mass in 1828, to the present time.* Woonsocket, RI: Charles E. Cook.

Spring, J. (2002). *American education.* New York: McGraw-Hill.

[Statistics of the town of Framingham taken by the assessors]. (1850). Unpublished raw data.

Stein, S. J. (1992). *The Shaker experience in America: A history of the United Society of Believers.* New Haven, CT: Yale University Press.

The Story of Cesar Chavez. (n.d.). Retrieved January 11, 2004, from http://www.ufw.org/cecstory.htm

Temple, J. (1988). *History of Framingham, Massachusetts 1640–1885.* Somersworth, NH: New England History Press. (Original work published 1887)

Tennessee State Museum. *The black experience in the Civil War: The Black Soldier.* [Permanent display]. Nashville.

Tennessee State Museum. *Free blacks.* [Permanent display]. Nashville.

Thomas, A. P. (1976). *Woonsocket: Highlights of history, 1800–1976.* East Providence, RI: Globe.

Thomas, P. H. (1988). The Great Depression. In Woonsocket Centennial Committee (Eds.), *Woonsocket, Rhode Island: A centennial history, 1888–1988* (pp. 95–113). State College, PA: Jostens.

Thornton, S. J. (1996). NCSS: The early years. In O. L. Davis, Jr. (Ed.), *NCSS in retrospect: Bulletin 92* (pp. 1–7). Washington, DC: National Council for the Social Studies.

Timm, J. T. (1996). *Four perspectives in multicultural education.* Belmont, CA: Wadsworth.

Titus, C. (1992). *Social studies teachers and multicultural education: A pilot study of attitudes, practices, and constraints* (Report No. S0-023-202). Washington, DC: U.S. Department of Education. (ERIC Document Reproduction Service No. ED366516)

Uphoff, J. K. (1997). Religious diversity and education. In J. A. Banks & C. A. M. Banks (Eds.), *Multicultural education: Issues and perspectives* (pp. 108–126). Boston: Allyn & Bacon.

Wertheimer, B. M. (1977). *We were there: The story of working women in America.* New York: Pantheon Books.

West, C. V. (Ed.). (1998). *The Tennessee encyclopedia of history and culture.* Nashville: Rutledge Hill Press.

Williams, J. (1987). *Eyes on the prize: America's civil rights years, 1954–1965.* New York: Viking.

Williamson, J. (n.d.). *A private museum confronts the Underground Railroad.* Retrieved March 25, 2004, from crm.cr.nps.gov/ archive/20–20/20_2–8.pdf

Williamson, J. (2001). *Rowland T. Robinson, Rokeby, and the Underground Railroad in Vermont.* Retrieved March 21, 2004, from www.vermonthistory.org/ journal/69/vt69_so3.pdf

Woonsocket: My hometown on the web. (n.d.). Retrieved January 19, 2004, from http://www.woonsocket.org/industrial.html

Yell, M. M., Scheurman, G., & Reynolds, K. (2004). *A link to the past: Engaging students in the study of history* (NCSS Bulletin 102). Silver Spring, MD: National Council for the Social Studies.

Zimmerman, J. (2002). *Whose America? Culture wars in the public schools.* Cambridge, MA: Harvard University Press.

Index